EVERYTHING YOU NEVER KNEW YOU WANTED TO KNOW ABOUT SEX

■ Cold showers boost the production of sex hormones in men and women.

■ If you suffer from Peyronie's disease, your penis is shaped like a boomerang.

■ A Los Angeles man was arrested in 1981 for sneaking under the tables at the university library and painting women's toenails.

■ A Frenchman left his monster 9¾-inch penis to a friend in his will.

■ Chickens can reverse their sex from female to male, but not the other way around.

■ In Tibet there's a courting custom called *t'lao mao hui*. A man steals the hat of a woman he fancies, and if she likes him, she visits him to get it back.

SEX:

* A User's Guide

Stephen Arnott

Delta Trade Paperbacks

SEX: A USER'S GUIDE
A Delta Book

PUBLISHING HISTORY
Ebury Press edition published 2002
Delta trade paperback edition / July 2003

Published by
Bantam Dell
A Division of Random House, Inc.
New York, New York

Cataloging in Publication Data is on file with the publisher.

ISBN 0-385-33706-X

Manufactured in the United States of America
Published simultaneously in Canada

ROS   10 9 8 7 6 5 4 3 2 1

I'd like to thank Cathy Rundle, Andrew Goodfellow, Matthew Parker, and Claire Tilbury for their help in preparing this manuscript.

CONTENTS

CONTENTS

CONTENTS

CONTENTS

CONTENTS

CONTENTS

CONTENTS

CONTENTS

INTRODUCTION

"A lot of time has been wasted on arguing over which came first—the chicken or the egg. It was undoubtedly the rooster."

—*Theodore C. Achilles*

In the beginning there was no sex. Long before Adam and Eve got down to business, al fresco in Eden, there was the lonely, lovelorn single-celled organism that reproduced by cloning it-self—an adult splitting in half to produce offspring cells that would, in turn, grow and split themselves. Not much of a Saturday night, granted. How sex entered the equation is not clear, but some think it developed as a result of predatory activity carried out by small, undernourished cells. According to this theory, these predatory cells (protomales) would seek out fat well-nourished cells (protofemales) and merge with them to consume their nutrients. This merging also led to a combination of the genetic material of both cells. Mixing genes like this accelerated evolution tremendously, it being a quick way of introducing variety into a gene pool that would otherwise have to depend on random mutations. Cells practicing sexual reproduction could evolve to suit changing ecological conditions much faster than their sexless neighbors and prospered at their expense. Sex continues to be a winner. Although there are many animals that can reproduce without sex (the American timber rattlesnake, for example)—a process known as parthenogenesis—of the three million species that have been discovered so far, only a thousand or so have adopted nonsexual reproduction as the way to go.

So in line with more primitive life, humans have traditionally indulged in sex to improve their gene pool and ensure the prosperity and survival of the tribe and species. This is, though, a claim with limited success as a come-on these days. Artificial cloning techniques have recently opened up the possibility of human parthenogenesis, though it's doubtful this will act as the death knell for sex. In our largely prosperous and well-appointed modern existence most human sexual activity is solely for pleasure—as much an act of complex psychological welfare as one of procreation. Sexual pleasure can take many forms; most people have their quirks (some banal, some bizarre), and numerous attempts have been made to explain them using some sort of "psychosexual" framework. Ever since Sigmund Freud lit his first phallic cigar at his Vienna practice, psychoanalysis has told us that sex, whether we like it or not, underlies many of our most deep-seated motivations and actions in life.

Freud broke down human sexual development into five stages. A primary *oral* stage is seen in babies under one year old, where pleasure is derived from sucking. A secondary *anal* stage is seen in infants between two and three years old, where most pleasure is derived from defecating. And a third *phallic* stage starts when a child is four or five years old, where pleasure is associated with the genitals. According to

Freud, this stage is complex and leads to boys developing a sexual attraction to their mothers (the Oedipus complex) together with castration anxiety, while girls are attracted to their fathers (the Elektra complex) and develop penis envy. After the upheavals of the phallic stage, a fourth *latent* stage follows, during which nothing much happens until puberty and the final *genital* stage begins. Freud believed that humans are equipped with a certain amount of sexual energy—the libido—that is used up while passing through each stage. If too much time is spent in a certain stage of development, the libido becomes exhausted and the personality is stuck there forever. For example, Freud believed that men who never got past the phallic stage overidentified with their mothers and developed homosexual traits.

During the twentieth century, psychoanalysis—the process by which these sexual dysfunctions are identified and worked through—became something of a religion for many. But, though widely accepted as a valid psychosexual template, Freud's theories are almost impossible to prove or disprove and are inherently unscientific. Some academics have stopped looking for underlying reasons altogether and have concentrated on accurately gauging what people do rather than trying to explain why. These researchers have included Alfred Kinsey, Masters and Johnson, and Shere Hite among others; their mass sexual observations have helped to dispel many myths and provide scientists with a solid bedrock of data on which to plan the research of the future (though if it's actually worth finding out why Uncle Gerald enjoys covering his genitals in peanut butter is another question entirely). This book draws on the findings of these researchers and many others, but does not pretend to be a work of serious scholarship. Instead it's best regarded as a brief—and hopefully enjoyable—dip into the huge and murky pond of sexual practice, fact and fable, past and present. The chapters, while following a tentative logic, can be enjoyed in any order, so feel free to strike up a casual relationship with the book, dipping into it when and where you choose.

SEX:

* A User's Guide

BIRDS DO IT, BEES DO IT

Sex in the Animal Kingdom

Sex is often thought of as an animal activity ("You're a tiger!"), and the animal kingdom is as good a place as any to start a comparative sex education. Evolution has thrown up innumerable sexual variations in the living world. Some creatures, like aphids, manage to do without sex at all and reproduce using a cloning process, while others can't seem to get enough of it, the humble single-celled paramecium evolving into (somewhat extravagantly) eight sexes rather than the more usual two. Some creatures (many species of reef-living fish, for example) have distinctly shaky sexual identities and will change gender at the drop of a hat. Others like spiders and bristle worms combine sex with cannibalism. Indeed, compared to many animals, the sex lives of the most infamous human libertines seem positively lackluster.

The Naked Ape

As might be expected, when compared with animals, human sex lives most closely resemble those of our nearest relatives—the chimpanzees—rather than gorillas and our more distant cousins the monkeys. Gorillas have tiny penises compared to body size; on average they come in at 1¼ inches. Orangutans aren't much bigger at 1½ inches, while the relatively small chimps are a whopping 2¾ inches. Humans come out best with an average of 5½ inches, but there seems to be no reason for this relatively huge size; a 2-inch penis would do the job just as well. Gorillas don't need to be well equipped in this respect because a dominant male keeps a harem of females. This means there's very little day-to-day competition with other males. In contrast, chimps live in large groups where females mate with a number of different males every day. Chimps need a relatively large penis and a high volume of sperm production to compete. The sperm acts as a douche, washing out the sperm left by a female's previous lovers. It's the male chimp who produces the most sperm who will father the most children. This is why chimp testicles weigh around 4 ounces each, while the more monogamous humans clock in at only an ounce and a half.

Proportionally the largest testes in the primate world be-

THE record for most reproductive organs goes to the tapeworm. The bodies of tapeworms are made up of hermaphrodite segments equipped with the organs of both sexes. The largest tapeworm on record was 70 meters long and made up of more than 11,000 segments, giving it a grand total of 22,000 individual organs.

long to the woolly spider monkey. Females of the species have been known to mate as many as eleven times a day when in heat and literally overflow with sperm. This excess is treated as a nutritious snack, and spider monkeys lick it up by the mouthful.

👣 Giving Him the Bone

An interesting difference between humans and animals is the lack of a human "penis bone," also known as an *os penis*. The majority of mammals, including bears, cats, dogs, weasels, moles, shrews, and most primates, possess such a bone, and why humans don't is a mystery. The size of these bones varies. Walruses have os bones two feet long, resembling ivory truncheons, while bats have tiny ones. As a rule, fish lack an os bone (which would spoil their streamlined shape), as do most birds (where they'd be an unnecessary weight).

👣 Bird Penises

Some birds have penises; these are usually found among flightless birds (where the extra weight isn't a disadvantage) and aquatic birds like swans, ducks, and geese (where aquatic mating means there's a chance of sperm being washed away). It's probably a coincidence that penis-owning waterfowl seem to be the ones that most commonly indulge in rape. Male ducks have a reputation for this sort of thing and often take part in "gang bangs"—large numbers of drakes mobbing a female for sex and sometimes drowning her as a consequence. Bird penises tend to resemble mammalian penises but do not contain a urethra to drain the bladder. Some can be remarkably

> ♀ Female moorhens will often fight each other for the favor of fat males. It's the males that incubate the eggs, and the larger the better.
>
> ♂ Chickens can reverse their sex from female to male, but not the other way around.

long; the Argentine lake duck commonly has an 8-inch penis, but the largest reach 16 inches.

For those who'd like to see one, fresh ostrich penises can be bought over the Internet as an aphrodisiac.

 ## Big Penises

The record for the world's largest penis is held by the world's largest mammal, the blue whale, which has an organ just over ten feet long and one foot in diameter. The sperm whale (named after *spermaceti*, a mysterious white oily substance found in its head) comes a close second with a nine-footer. A whale's penis is known as a *dork*, which is where the insult comes from.

Among land mammals, giraffes have erections reaching four feet long, while elephant erections can reach five or six feet. One enterprising biologist has even gone as far as to calculate the average weight of an elephant penis—59.5 pounds (with testicles at 4.4 pounds each). Rhinos tend to be shorter in this department, their penises being around two feet long; however, they make up for it by being prodigious ejaculators, some coming as many as ten times during a half-hour session. These genitals have been put to some unusual uses in the past. In India golf bags have been made from elephant penises, while in Africa rhino and hippo penises were often stretched and dried to make whips.

Weird Penises

Smaller animals may be less impressively equipped, but many make up for it by having bizarre penis shapes. Some animals, like marsupial opossums, have two—one for each of the female opossum's paired vaginas.

Pigs have corkscrew-shaped penises; the male pig makes semirotary motions to literally screw himself into his mate. Spider monkeys have barbed penises to help them hang on during mating. Tomcats also have barbed penises; the pain caused by withdrawal is the stimulus that causes the female to release her eggs. Like pigs, some bulls have corkscrew penises, though in this case it's an undesirable medical condition that makes mating difficult.

Insects have unusual penises. For example, dragonflies have shovel-shaped organs designed to scoop any previously deposited rival semen out of a female. One of the most bizarre boners belongs to the European rabbit flea, which has a penis consisting of two coiled rods, with sperm wound around the smaller one like springs. Some earwigs have two penises—they are very brittle and a spare is needed in case the main one breaks off. Male bees (drones) have alarming-looking genitals. Even more alarming is the fact that they explode. Once the drone has mated with a queen bee in flight, his genitals burst with a pop that can be heard some distance away. The explosion blocks the queen's genitals so she can't receive sperm from any other male.

Barnacles have developed a penis to help solve their

immobility problem. Once it's glued itself to something solid, a male barnacle is stuck for life; however, its penis is commonly 150 percent longer than its body and is able to snake out and molest any female within striking distance.

👣 Super Sperm

We're used to thinking of sperm as numerous and tiny, but many creatures produce a small number of relatively enormous sperm cells. The house centipede produces a sperm cell that is as long as its body (commonly over 4.7 inches), and some beetle species go one better and produce sperm that are longer than their owners, coiling them up like springs inside the body. An unfortunate side effect is that after fertilization the female often has to waddle around with a sperm tail sticking out of her rear end. Proportionally, the record for the longest sperm belongs to the fruit fly, *Drosophila bifurca*; it has sperm 2.4 inches in length, twenty times longer than its entire body.

Some creatures produce spermatophores, dense packets of sperm coated with protective gels. Octopi use spermatophores that are three feet long and as thin as a pencil. Some octopus spermatophores have barbs to stop them from being withdrawn once they're placed inside the female, a necessary precaution, as unbarbed spermatophores are often removed and eaten. Katydids (relatives of the grasshopper) also make use of sperm as food; here females have to be bribed with sperm food parcels before they'll allow their eggs to be fertilized.

👣 Perverts of the Animal Kingdom

Bedbugs have extremely unsavory sexual habits. Female bedbugs are born without vaginas, so sperm is passed on during an act of "traumatic copulation." The bedbug's penis is a swordlike rod stabbed into the female's body, depositing sperm into her gut. The sperm then travels via the bloodstream to a special storage gland, where it is kept for further use. This system has a benefit for the female, as in hard times she can use this sperm as a free meal. Some African bedbugs play a variation to this game by indulging in "male rape." They stab other males in the hope that, when the attacked male mates with a female, some of their sperm will be passed on as well. To obtain a free sperm meal, some males deliberately invite an attack by disguising themselves as females.

Some bean weevil species are equally repellent, having spine-covered penises that deliberately cripple the female. The lacerations caused by these penises are often fatal: the female lives long enough to lay her eggs but not so long that she has a chance to mate with rival males.

Coming in a close third in the pervert stakes are banana slugs. Slugs are hermaphroditic, and some pairs mate as equals, playing both male and female roles. Others use this moment of intimacy as an opportunity to gnaw off the penis of their

---

♀ The clitoris of the female gibbon is often longer than the penis of the male.

♂ The average boar ejaculation consists of a pint of fluid.

♀ The female hyena has scrotal pouches beneath her clitoris.

FOR some animals the sex act is over in a blink. The mosquito only spends two seconds on the job. Swedish seed bugs, on the other hand, copulate continuously for hours. The bug sex record-holders must be the Bibionid flies: they only live for a few days but sometimes copulate for up to 56 hours. Among mammals, minks and sables are renowned for their marathon sex sessions, while in the reptile world the record for a pair of rattlesnakes is 22.75 hours.

Among primates the common chimp wins in the speed stakes with 7 seconds; in contrast, the pygmy chimp takes a leisurely 15 seconds, gorillas average about a minute, and orangutans 15 minutes (roughly three times as long as humans).

The record for the largest number of matings must go to Shaw's jird, a type of gerbil; one individual was seen to mate 224 times in 120 minutes.

sex partner, forcing them to become exclusively female. These penises represent a hearty meal; banana slugs are commonly 5 inches long but may have penises as long as 30 inches.

Another animal with kinky habits is the American slipper snail (*Crepidula fornicata*). Here a male snail attaches itself to a rock and becomes a female. Another male snail will then settle on the female and mate with her; should a third male land on the second snail, then snail number two will change into a female and be mated with. This might carry on until up to fourteen snails are welded in a tower of lust.

Vaginal Plugs

After mating, many male organisms seal up the vaginal canal of their sex partners. Some parasitic worms exude a glue that seals the female's organs shut. Other animals leave fluid deposits that harden to form a plug. It's thought that many animal penises have such odd shapes because they're designed to get around these vaginal plugs. Male rats are said to be particularly effective at this and can dislodge 68 percent of these obstructions. Female moles plug up their own vaginas to prevent earth from getting inside; secretions from various glands mix into a gummy mass that sets like epoxy resin.

HELLO, I LOVE YOU

Sexual Attraction

Just what it is that makes one individual irresistible and intoxicating to another has been a question posed in more than the odd pop song down the years and in more scientific arenas, too. Some people believe there is no overall standard of beauty. They point out that what rates as attractive differs around the world and often changes over time. Standards of beauty will also differ from person to person; as one Japanese saying puts it: "In the eyes of the lover, pockmarks are dimples." Despite these factors many researchers think that sound scientific principles must underlie human attraction, and a number of theories have sprung up to explain just what makes the perfect mate.

👣 You've Got the Cutest Little...

One popular theory is that attractive faces are "babyish," with small lips, high foreheads, small chins, and big eyes. The idea is that these faces remind us of children and trigger a protective response. Unfortunately this theory does not take into account the fact that men often cite high cheekbones as being attractive, while women rate a broad jaw as an attractive male feature. Neither of these is a "baby" feature. Added to this is the fact that babies usually have large fleshy cheeks, which have never been rated as attractive in adults. Having a "baby face" is also disadvantageous in that it suggests incompetence—not a desirable feature in a breeding partner. Babies are cute but extremely inept; you wouldn't want one servicing your car.

👣 Hormone Balance

Another theory is that attractive facial features are ones that indicate a correct hormone balance. A broad jaw is a sign of high testosterone levels, so a broad-jawed man is attractive while a broad-jawed female is less so. A sign of low testosterone in women is a fine head of hair. Testosterone leads to hair loss, so a woman with long silky tresses is unlikely to have much.

Another factor is that the by-products of hormones are often toxic, so the fact that you're good-looking (i.e., have the correct hormonal balance for your sex) and in good health would also suggest that you have an excellent immune system capable of dealing with these poisons.

🐾 Exotic Allure

One theory has been developed to try and explain why people are often attracted to the exotic and unusual. In these cases it's thought that people are seeking out "rare genes." The idea is that in any population parasites have evolved to take advantage of the "average" person. If you can produce nonaverage children by having sex with someone with nonaverage genes, then your children will be better able to resist parasites. According to the theory, this is why blondes have more fun. Natural blond hair is not common in most societies, so it represents a rare genotype.

🐾 Symmetry Is Sexy

Symmetry has also been cited as a factor in attractiveness. If you take a portrait, split it down the middle, and match each half with its mirror image, you get two perfectly symmetrical faces. Usually both symmetrical faces are more attractive than the original. It's not known why a symmetrical face is more attractive than a lopsided one. Perhaps the more regular your features, the better the genes you're carrying. Many famously good-looking people (Tom Cruise, for example) have a high level of facial symmetry.

🐾 Averageness Attracts

Human brains seem to like storing information as simple models. When we're young, we build up a model of an "average" face in our minds, based on the faces we see around us every day. If we come across a new face, we compare it to the average and add some distinguishing features to tell it

THE optimum age of reproduction for women is twenty-four; co-incidentally this is the age at which women gain their highest scores for "attractiveness."

apart from all the others buried in our memory. It's been discovered that "average" faces (created on computers by overlaying multiple portraits) are usually rated as being highly attractive. The theory is that we find familiar people attractive, and the computer's average face will often closely match the average, attractive face we carry in our memory.

The theory of averageness seems to be borne out by the fact that many people marry someone who resembles one of their parents. This isn't the result of psychological Oedipus and Elektra complexes; rather their average, attractive face will be based on the faces they saw most often as children—their parents. Since most children resemble their parents, this is also why many people choose a partner who resembles themselves.

This idea of parental "imprinting" is borne out by some animal experimentation. For example, when male rats were raised by mothers who were artificially lemon-scented, they tended to be attracted to similarly scented females later in

WHEN talking about human attraction, researchers are careful to make a distinction between casual sex partners and marriage partners. When sleeping around, people tend to choose partners who are physically attractive. However, when it comes to marriage, factors like personality, religion, and interests tend to be more important than looks.

life. White geese reared by parents dyed pink later went on to prefer pink partners over normal white ones.

🐾 Smelly Stuff—*Pheromones*

In many animals hormones released in female urine indicate whether they're sexually receptive. In fact, most of the life of a stallion, stag, or male camel consists of drinking his harem's urine to see who's fit to diddle. If a female isn't in the mood to pee, she's often kicked until she does. When drinking, these animals pull a curious face (known as *flehmen*), in which the lips and nostrils are pulled back to help pick up the full flavor of the urine. To help spread pheromones, deer will often pee on the ground, then wallow in it, while male goats have the charming habit of peeing and ejaculating into their beards to create a distinctive perfume.

In humans pheromones are spread by the hair in the pubic and underarm region. Although little is known about human pheromones, they are thought to be by-products of hormone production. Three are currently recognized: androgen, estrogen, and progesterone. Both sexes produce these hor-

♂ An Australian study has shown that men who snore tend to have more testosterone.

♂ Sunlight activates the pineal gland to produce melatonin, a substance that enhances the sex drive.

♀ Cold showers boost the production of sex hormones in men and women.

mones, but men produce more androgen and women produce more estrogen and progesterone.

These pheromones aren't confined to humans. Androgen is present in the saliva of boars, and a sow needs to smell some androgen before she'll assume the mating posture. Androgen is a general name for a group of male pheromones that include the steroids androsterone and androstenol. Apart from in hog saliva, they are also found in truffles, caviar, celery, and parsnips (most of which have been widely touted as aphrodisiacs).

Androsterone smells musky, like sandalwood, but it also strikes some people as having a rank urinelike smell. Androstenol is much nicer, having a flowery yet musky scent. Although both sexes can detect minute quantities of these chemicals, women are far better at it: 70 percent of women are able to detect androstenol (only 30 percent of men can), while 92 percent of women can detect androsterone (54 percent for men).

Women's sense of smell is worst at the beginning of menstruation but rises at ovulation. For example, women are a thousand times more sensitive to musky smells than men, but this sensitivity rises to one hundred thousand times at the time of ovulation. This heightening is connected with the menstrual cycle; if a woman has her ovaries removed, it disappears completely.

Androstenol has some powerful effects. In men its production increases fivefold in late December, its female-attracting qualities resulting in plenty of September babies. In one test, spraying androstenol on a seat in a dentist's waiting room resulted in more women sitting on it, while men tended to avoid the area. Another test found that androstenol

A MEDIEVAL tale tells of two sisters who devised a novel method of making themselves unattractive to potential rapists: they hung bits of rotting chicken between their breasts.

sprayed in a men's toilet cubicle made it unattractive to men. While men don't like androstenol, it does get their blood up. If asked to rate pictures of women for attractiveness, the marks go up if they're wearing a mask treated with the pheromone. Regular contact with women also triggers extra androgen production and results in increased beard growth.

Male hormones also have an effect on the female reproductive cycle. Without men the cycle tends to be longer and more irregular, but when men are on the scene, periods become regular and shorter. Women also affect other women. For reasons that aren't properly understood, a group of women who spend a lot of time in each other's company find that their menstrual cycles start to synchronize. Moreover, there are some women who seem to have dominant hormones—the cycles of the other females synchronize with the most hormonally dominant female.

⚥ In men testosterone levels are highest in the summer.

♀ Women experience a surge of testosterone after drinking alcohol.

⚥ Men's testosterone levels are highest at dawn.

 BO Rules OK

Bacteria are another source of odors. The armpits are sites of pheromone production, but the aerobic diphtheroid bacteria found in armpits also seem to be involved. Human sweat is odorless and only begins to smell once bacteria have started to work on it. This bacterial breakdown results in musky odors that many people find pleasant. Sweat only starts to stink when it is trapped in clothing and becomes stale. Some have suggested that the traditional hands-behind-head pose used by models is sexy because it exposes the armpits and liberates the musk.

The Smell of Female

The vagina is also a source of smells, some nice, some not so nice. A woman's sexual odor has been given the name *cassolette*. (This means "perfume box" in French, though bizarrely, it's ultimately derived from a Spanish word meaning "saucepan.")

According to scientists, vaginal odors consist of more than thirty compounds, many of which smell like Limburger cheese. These compounds are released by various organs: some come from the sebaceous glands surrounding the vulva, others from glands in the ducts of the ovaries, while

ELIZABETHAN ladies were aware of the attraction of armpit odors. One trick involved peeling an apple, hiding it in the pit of your arm, then presenting it to your beau. Presumably this could be taken as a compliment or an insult, depending on how often you washed.

IN some zoos the staff aren't allowed to wear perfumes, as the civet musk they contain sexually excites the animals.

still more come from the lining of the uterus. Some of these compounds are volatile fatty acids called *copulins*. When present in large concentrations, these acids have a rank "fishy" smell but are otherwise innocuous. In clinical tests it's been shown that men like the smell of copulins and are likely to rate women as being more attractive if asked to look at a picture while smelling them. It seems that vaginal odors are great levelers; smelling copulins results in a small increase in the rating of women already described as attractive, but large increases in women who had previously been rated as less attractive.

It's been suggested that copulins could be the basis of a devastating perfume, and patents have been taken out for commercial production methods. Unfortunately copulins are an equal turn-on for animals like monkeys and goats, and court cases might ensue if one of these uninhibited creatures got hold of a woman wearing a copulin scent.

Keep It in the Family

An obvious problem with the "averageness" theory described earlier is that of incest. If you're so strongly attracted to close relatives, why not breed with them and ignore everyone else? This sibling sexual attraction is sometimes seen in cases where brothers and sisters who were separated early in life are later reintroduced. Thankfully nature has provided its own solution to the problem. No one is sure why, but incest is rare, and even nonrelated children raised together rarely marry each other. It seems there's a built-in regulator in most higher animals which means that, while we're attracted to people who resemble the individuals we grew up with, if they're too much alike, it's a turn-off.

How this evolutionary anti-incest "brake" developed is not certain, but any species that didn't develop one would have soon died out thanks to accumulating defects in the gene pool.

Numerous studies have shown that incest results in genetically inferior children. For example, the child of a brother and sister is five hundred times more likely to suffer genetic defects than a nonincestuous baby. In one Czech study 160 children born through incestuous relationships were compared with another 95 children produced by the same mothers and nonrelated fathers. Of the 95 nonincestuous children, 95 percent went on to have children of their own, while only half of the incest children were able to reproduce.

Marriage with first cousins also causes problems. In Sweden it's been shown that 4 to 6 percent of nonincestuous children have genetic defects, while the figure for children from first-cousin marriages is 16 to 28 percent. In France and Japan similar studies have shown that the children of first-cousin marriages are twice as likely to die in childhood. A famous example of a child from a first-cousin marriage was Toulouse-Lautrec. His stumpy stature wasn't a genetic malformation in itself, but his below-par genetics meant his fragile legs were unable to heal properly after he broke them in a childhood fall.

The problems associated with incestuous marriages have been known for years. The Bible forbids sex with a sister, a son's daughter, or a daughter's daughter, the penalty being death by stoning. It even prohibits the marriage of nonblood relatives like an adopted daughter, or her daughter. Even very distant relatives like a maternal grandmother's brother's wife are covered. Some cultures took it to extremes; in ancient China to marry someone with the same surname was sometimes considered incestuous.

The neighbors of the Hebrews, the Assyrians and Hittites, also had anti-incest laws, but the ancient Egyptians actually made a habit out of incest, at least as far as royalty was concerned. As an example of the complexities of Egyptian royal marriages, we can take the pharaoh Akhenaton (Ikhnaton), who lived around 1350 B.C. First he married his mother, then his maternal cousin. His third and fourth wives weren't blood relatives, but his fifth wife was the third daughter of his second wife. His son and heir, Tutankhamen, was born of the fourth wife, and he eventually went on to marry his half-sister. From the records it seems that the incestuous marriages of the pharaohs tended to produce daughters. The pharaohs usually had plenty of illegitimate sons from nonincestuous relationships, and one of these sons would be chosen to be the next pharaoh. Unfortunately the son would normally be married to one of the pharaoh's legitimate daughters to strengthen his claim to the throne, and their incestuous marriage would produce more daughters, starting the whole cycle again.

Incestuous royal marriages occurred in countries as diverse as Iran, Peru, and Hawaii. These arrangements tended to be seen in societies where the royal bloodline was passed on through the female line. In these cases a king whose royal queen died would have a shaky claim to the throne and would often marry his eldest daughter to legitimize his rule.

Other factors have encouraged incest. In societies where a bride was married with a dowry, a girl would sometimes marry an uncle to keep the cash in the family. People living in isolated communities have often taken to incest when no other mates were available. Inuit men in remote communities often married a daughter if their wife died, though this was always considered a last resort.

THE Roman emperor Caligula had sex with three of his sisters. Nero is reputed to have had sex with his mother Agrippina while they were being carried in a litter.

LET'S GET IT ON

Dressing for Sex

Leather and latex fetishists and endytophiliacs (people who are aroused by having sex fully clothed) aside, most sex happens as nature intended it—in the nude. So you might ask, what exactly do clothes and fashion have to do with it? But of course only the central sexual act takes place finally disrobed of our worldly finery. What is of equal importance is the long, merry, and infinitely complex social dance that leads us there. For these preliminary acts of ritual display, clothes, demonstrating social standing and sexual worth, have been very important props (sometimes quite literally).

Europe only started dressing "fashionably" in the fifteenth century, when an increase in wealth and the breakdown of tradition (both spurred on by the Black Death) meant people had the opportunity to be more flamboyant in their appear-

> AN extreme style of the late eighteenth century was "naked-ness." After the upheavals of the French Revolution, daring young women took to covering themselves in wispy muslin veils that in many cases verged on the transparent. These outfits provided little protection from the elements, and it was reckoned that women frequently died from pneumonia in the name of fashion.

ance. Before that time dress was determined by longstanding local custom, and style changed at a snail's pace.

Given the freedom to dress how they liked, people tended to emphasize their social status by buying the most sumptuous garments they could afford. Those looking for a partner used clothing to show off their more attractive features. The assistance of padding, corsetry, girdles, and brassieres could be used to effect some remarkable changes, though some of the "alluring" outfits worn by our ancestors now appear rather bizarre. A good example is seen in the female costumes of Venice of around 1580. Here women wore gowns padded before and aft and had their dyed-blond hair raised into six-inch horns. These horns supported a black crepe veil that hung over the shoulders while, at the front, dresses were slashed to the navel to expose the belly and breasts. As a final touch these women used to totter about on platform shoes that were often twelve inches high.

 Corsetry

Corsets have been known since ancient times—some of the earliest examples cropped up in ancient Crete around 1600

> IN the eighteenth century women spent fortunes trying to keep up with the rapidly changing fashions, and some respectable ladies even turned to prostitution to pay for their wardrobes. Other women made fortunes out of the fashion craze; Mrs. Abingdon, a famous London actress, charged £1,500 a year for her services as a personal shopping consultant.

B.C. The modern corset came into vogue around 1750 and reached the height of its popularity at the end of the nineteenth century, before being superseded by the liberated flapper styles of the 1920s. The supposed benefits of corsetry were numerous: they compressed the waist, raised the bust, flattened the stomach, rounded the hips, and straightened the back. Immobilizing corsets were also a status symbol, as wearing one showed that you were rich enough not to have to work for a living. Some women (and men) wore them constantly. Corsets were devised for sports like swimming and tennis; there was even a special maternity corset. Part of the appeal of the corset was the "wasp waist" it produced (indeed, *The Wasp* was the name of one of many Victorian magazines devoted to corsetry), and some women aimed at measurements in the 14- to 16-inch range (the smallest verified waist was 13 inches). This type of constriction was extreme, however; most Victorian and Edwardian corsets had a minimum waist of 20 to 22 inches.

Underpants

Underpants have had a relatively short history, as few women wore them before the twentieth century. In the nineteenth century King Victor Emmanuel I of Sardinia remarked that he was "delighted to see, Madame, that your ladies do not wear drawers, and that the gates of paradise are always open"— this after one of the ladies-in-waiting of the French empress fell over in front of him during a state visit. Many humorous prints of the eighteenth and nineteenth centuries show tumbling ladies being exposed without the benefit of underwear.

Female underwear only took off in the late nineteenth century, when women started to take up energetic sports like cycling, where a fall might result in bystanders getting an eyeful. Ankle-length trousers called *bloomers* started to be worn under skirts at this time, and as skirts got shorter, underpants became increasingly necessary. Their adoption was also helped by the production of cheap elastic in the early twentieth century, making underwear far more comfortable than the previous bulky drawstring models.

👣 A Glimpse of Stocking . . .

Foot and leg coverings were worn as early as 400 B.C.—the ancient Greeks sometimes turned to them in the winter. Most of these early coverings were made of woven cloth, but this

> ♀ In 1993 a Japanese mail-order service was started allowing customers to buy the used panties of schoolgirls, housewives, nurses, and widows. Bottles of schoolgirl saliva were also on offer.
>
> ♀ A "lingerie museum" in Hollywood has exhibits donated by Cybill Shepherd, Madonna, and Zsa Zsa Gabor.
>
> ♀ A recent survey of New York women aged 16 to 25 found that 30% rarely wore underwear.

changed in the sixteenth century when hand-knitted stockings came into vogue. The fashion spread when William Lee, an English minister, invented a stocking-knitting machine in 1589. By the seventeenth century almost everybody wore stockings: poor people wore cheap woolen ones, while the better off chose cotton or silk. For centuries stockings, or *hose*, were worn by both sexes. Women's stockings were hardly ever seen, as long skirts rarely gave anyone a chance to look at their legs. Only "immodest" women like prostitutes revealed themselves below the waist. One of the earliest examples of provocative legware comes from the fourteenth century, when London prostitutes mimicked the fashion for long, wide dresses but added a split up the side to reveal their calves and thighs encased in tight, brightly colored hose.

Of Busts and Bras

It's not certain why large breasts should be admired by so many. In the past breasts were recognized as an important reservoir of calories, and big breasts have also been equated with higher milk production (though this is not actually the case; female chimpanzees are extremely flat-chested but

> In 1988 two Texas women were found fighting in a parking lot armed with a hammer and a tire iron. They were arguing over who had the biggest breasts.
>
> In Victorian times bathing in fresh strawberries was thought to tighten up flabby breasts.

have no problems breast-feeding). Some researchers believe that human breasts took over from buttocks as prime sexual signals when mankind first started walking upright, and since those early days breasts have tended to evolve on a "the-bigger-the-better" basis.

Not all cultures have preferred big breasts, however. In Europe the fashion in the early Middle Ages was for a small bust, and the Chinese have traditionally preferred small breasts. In the past big boobs were regarded as coarse, the mark of prostitutes and "bad" women. In an effort to inhibit their bust size, developing Chinese girls were sometimes strapped into corsets that resembled straitjackets.

Elsewhere corsetry and tight bodices were used to enhance the bust, not suppress it. In fourteenth-century Europe a fashion for bigger breasts developed—bodices were laced so high and tight that boobs sometimes stood out horizontally, forming a shelf. As one horrified medieval cleric observed, "A candle could be stood upon them."

In Roman times a favored method of breast support was the *mamillare*, a sort of prototype brassiere. Bras in one form or another have been around for a long time, though most were simple bindings. The modern underwire bra is a more recent French invention, though the word *brassière* actually means "arm protector" in French. The French call a bra a *soutien-gorge*, or "throat support."

In the late eighteenth century corsetry went out of fashion, and breasts were held by simple pockets built into the fabric of a dress. This lack of uplift presented problems for the less well endowed, a lack that was sometimes remedied by the use of wax falsies. On one occasion a young English bride fainted at her wedding party and woke up to discover that her fake waxwork bust had slipped out onto the floor.

👣 Busting Out

To increase bust size, some women have adopted extreme methods. In Abyssinia (present-day Ethiopia) women would sting their breasts with bees, sometimes resulting in three- or fourfold increases. In other parts of Africa the fashion was for pendulous breasts. The women of the Nadi tribe artificially flattened their breasts by strapping boards to them, and the Bagandi of central Africa used to hang weights from theirs to lengthen them.

Today women usually resort to implants if they want to increase their measurements. Thomas Cronin and Frank Gerow were the first surgeons to successfully implant silicone gel bags into a woman in 1960, and by 1973 more than fifty thousand operations had been carried out. Today implants consist of saline or silica-filled bags placed behind the breast tissue or under the chest muscle. Placing implants behind the muscle is more painful but has the advantage of not interfering with mammograms.

A less drastic alternative is to use a recently invented enhancer called a "Bust Booster." This is a gel that stimulates the capillaries in breast tissue, making blood rush to the area. Apparently the gel works very well—a small amount increases the bust by a whole cup size. Unfortunately the effects wear off after five hours.

👣 Bizarre Breasts

Women with little or no breast development are said to be suffering from *hypoplasia*, while those with very large breasts have *hyperplasia*. Some hyperplasia sufferers can grow breasts in excess of eighty inches. What's too large or too

MANY large-breasted ladies (both natural and artificial) are found among the ranks of the porn stars. Famous examples are: Alyssa Alps (56FF), April Chest (67HHH), Ashley Juggs (38DD), Donita Dunes (44GG), Pandora Peaks (72HHH), Penelope Pumpkins (72HHH), Plenty UpTopp (127PPP), Tawny Peaks (38DDD), Tiffany Towers (70FFF), and Wendy Whoppers (55EE).

small is often a matter of opinion, but women with very large breasts often suffer from backache and from shoulder and neck pain, and may opt for breast reduction. Sometimes the breasts themselves are painful.

Some breast abnormalities are not size-related. For example, *tuberous* breasts are those shaped like a cylinder. Here the base of the breast is so narrow that the breast is cylindrical rather than conical.

Gynecomastia is an odd breast condition suffered by men. Here a hormonal imbalance causes male breast growth and, in rare examples, milk production. In most cases a natural excess of estrogen is the problem, but some hormone-based drug therapies can also result in unwanted chest development.

Nipple Rings

Rings worn through pierced nipples were a popular accessory in the late Victorian era. The fashion started in Paris and may have been an import from France's North African possessions, where the practice was a local custom. In England they were known as "bosom rings," in France they were called *anneaux de sein,* in Germany *Busenringen* or *Brustwartzenringe,* and in Sweden, *intimsmycke,* meaning "intimate jewelry." Many were very expensive, made of gold and set with brilliantines. Some women suspended chains between the rings, and one celebrated Gaiety Theatre actress was famous for having a string of pearls tied between her nipples. Apart from their decorative aspect, rings were worn because it was believed they improved the size and shape of the breasts. They also helped make the nipple stand out under heavy fabric and produced a titillating sensation when they rubbed against clothing.

Another example of Victorian piercing is the "Albert," a type of foreskin ring supposedly first worn by Prince Albert to allow his penis to be strapped down out of sight when wearing tight clothing. In fact this story was invented in the 1970s to help publicize a string of California piercing parlors.

 ## Fat

The distribution of female body fat is an important sexually dimorphic trait—that is, one of the things that helps us tell men from women. In women a large proportion of body weight is fat, deposited in prominent places like the breasts and buttocks. In men most body weight is muscle, concentrated in the arms, shoulders, and chest.

According to one widely held theory, fat is attractive on a woman because it indicates she is likely to be fertile. Girls cannot reach menarche (the first menstruation) unless they accumulate a certain amount of fat. Typically fat should make up 17 percent of body weight, though the ideal percentage for a successful pregnancy is 22–28 percent. This is enough to see a woman through nine months of pregnancy and three months of breast-feeding. (A human pregnancy consumes

50,000 calories, lactation burning 1,000 calories a day.) In poorer parts of the world it might take a woman half her life to reach menarche, due to an inadequate diet. In contrast, the richness of the Western diet is thought to be responsible for the decreasing age of puberty in girls. In 1780 the average age of menarche was 17, and since 1830 it has dropped by three to four months in every decade, bottoming out at the current age of 12.5 years in the 1960s.

Today large ladies tend to be more appreciated in poorer, politically unstable countries, where extra pounds are regarded as insurance against hard times. In these countries fat is a status symbol, appreciated not necessarily for itself but for the wealth it represents.

Many societies have appreciated the connection between weight and fertility, and in some cultures young girls are encouraged to eat calorie-rich food as part of puberty rituals. In Sierra Leone and Ghana girls coming of age are expected to eat lots of oily stews. The same happens in Sri Lanka, where Tamil girls are fattened up on rich sesame oil curries, cakes, and puddings.

You can of course take things too far. In 1861 the explorer John Hanning Speke (1827–64) visited East Central Africa and was amazed at the size of the royal wives. Speke recorded that most of the women were so fat, they couldn't walk—their arms hung down like "loose stuffed puddings." Speke took measurements of one of the larger royal wives and discovered she was 23 inches around the arm, 52 around the chest, 31 around the thighs, and 20 around the calf. The wives kept their weight up by consuming milk. Young brides always had a milk pot in their hands and were beaten if they didn't drink constantly.

Since many men like a fuller figure, some women have

resorted to artificial aids to help plump themselves up. In ancient Greece some skinny girls walked around with padded bottoms, and in the eighteenth century some English girls resorted to wearing pads over their stomachs to simulate a rounded belly. Some of these contrivances were made out of metal, earning them the nickname "tin pinafores."

Hair

Body hair has been fashionable in some times but not in others. In ancient Egypt both sexes had their pubic hair removed, as did the ladies of Greece and Rome. In Greece the house slave responsible for hair removal was called the *paratiltria*.

There were many methods for getting rid of hair. Some people rubbed it away with soft sand or pumice, while others preferred to use a blade, or a plucking method. The Romans and Anglo-Saxons used metal tweezers to pull out individual hairs, while Native Americans used clamshells as makeshift tongs.

Faster methods involved covering an area with hot wax or resin and pulling it off when it hardened. The same was done with hot pitch, a method known as *dropax*, from the ancient Greek *dro-pakizo* (pitch plaster). A popular plucking method

Nudists who remove all their body hair are called "smoothies."

Charles II had a wig made from the pubic hair of his mistresses.

In sixteenth-century France pulling out pubic hair was sometimes recommended as a cure for hysteria.

IN some Islamic societies women are stripped of all body hair in a prewedding ceremony. Girls are left hairy before marriage as it's thought it will help put off unwanted male attention. The removal of the pubic hair is also thought of as removing the "veil of nature," an act that echoes the lowering of the bride's veil by her husband on the wedding night. Oddly enough, the denuded privates are often thought to look too bare after the hair has been removed, and the pubic area is sometimes dyed with henna to camouflage it. All these worries disappear in Paradise, however; there all "immodest" body hair falls away of its own accord.

invented by the Egyptians involved the use of sugar—usually in the form of honey—diluted with lemon juice. The juice and honey were boiled down into a toffeelike mass that was then smeared onto the area and stripped off when it dried. The medieval Turks did something similar with a mixture of honey and turpentine. This process was known as "sugaring" and is still carried out today, though it is now usually known as the "warm wax" method.

An unusual plucking method from the Middle East is known as "threading," where a lacework of cotton thread is run over the skin to encircle and pull out hairs.

Depilatories that dissolved or burned off hairs were sometimes used. A famous Roman concoction was called *psilothrum* and consisted of melted resin in oil, while others used ingredients as diverse as starch, vine gum, ass's fat, she-goat's gall, bat's blood, and powdered viper. Extreme methods relied on potions containing arsenic, quicklime, and lye. One eighteenth-century recipe called for a mixture of powdered cat dung and strong vinegar.

👫 IN 1990 a Gillette survey found that 92% of women in the United States shave their legs (67% shaving the entire leg and 33% shaving from the knee down), and 98% shave their underarms, but only 50% shave their bikini line.

A modern method of hair removal is electrolysis, where individual follicles are killed off with the application of an electrified needle. This is a development of a nineteenth-century method where a needle was used to burn out follicles using drops of sulfuric acid. More recently lasers have been used to kill follicles with heat.

Shaving remains a favorite with many, though people are advised to test out small quantities of shaving creams and soaps to make sure they're not allergic to them. You should be warned, however, that once the pubic area has been shaved, it should be kept shaved—the chafing caused by pubic bristles growing back can be unbearable. There are advantages to nude naughty bits—some shavers report that the sensitivity of their genitals increases tenfold after a shearing.

🐾 Feet

Many people have a strong attraction to feet and footwear. Perhaps the most extreme example of foot fetishism was the Chinese practice of foot binding. Foot binding was carried out for over a thousand years until it was banned by imperial decree at the turn of the twentieth century. Around 40 percent of Chinese women who lived during this period had "lotus feet" or "golden lilies," as bound feet were known. Feet were bound at around five years old, the object being to reduce the adult foot to a length of around four inches and a width of two inches.

The origins of the practice are unknown. One legend attributes the custom to an emperor with a liking for tiny-footed women; another puts the blame on a clubfooted eleventh-century empress called Taki who demanded that all court ladies bind their feet to resemble hers. Whatever its origins, it soon became an integral part of Chinese life; all respectable women had their feet bound, as did courtesans and prostitutes (both female and male). The size of a woman's dowry often depended on the size of her feet.

Binding was carried out using strips of cloth around ten feet long. The toes and heel were bent under the sole to form a fold of flesh. This fold was sometimes used as a second vagina, and some sex manuals were devoted exclusively to foot sex. Foot fetishists licked feet, drank the water used to clean feet, and ate food from between the toes. Bound women were said to get pleasure from these activities too— apparently some orgasmed when their feet were licked. Given this sexual aspect, it's not surprising that only a husband was allowed to see his wife's feet unbound.

Apart from making the foot small, binding was thought to have other advantages. The hobbling gait it produced, known as the "willow walk," was thought to develop the muscles and internal folds of the vagina. The binding was also meant to force blood up into the thighs, hips, and buttocks and make them more voluptuous.

 ## These Boots Weren't Made for Walking

Today many foot fetishists are more interested in the shoe or boot than in the foot itself. In particular many people are

DURING the Middle Ages a popular type of shoe was the *poulaine*. These had enormously long pointed toes that were often stuffed with moss to stiffen them. Apparently one of the attractions of wearing poulaines was a variation on the game of footsie you could play under the table. It's said that men often wore them to banquets so they could stick them under the dress of a woman sitting opposite and tickle her between the legs.

excited by high heels. These heels help sculpt the body by increasing the height of the wearer, making the legs appear longer, and bunching the muscles of the calves to improve their shape. However, if such shoes are worn for long periods, the tendons in the lower leg can become deformed, making it impossible to put the heel flat on the floor.

The acme of high heels is the seven-incher, sometimes known as the ballet heel (because only the tips of the toes touch the ground). Ballet heels are rarely seen outside of window displays and static photo shoots for the simple fact that they are impossible to walk in.

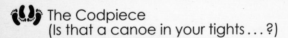 The Codpiece (Is that a canoe in your tights…?)

Throughout history there have been few examples of overtly "sexy" fashions for men. An exception are the penis sheaths or *phallocarps* often worn by island tribesmen in the Far East. These sheaths are extremely long, up to four feet in some cases, and are tied upright around the waist to create a giant *faux* erection. Most men have a wardrobe of sheaths and will put on a different one every day.

> **THE** armor of Henry VIII in the Tower of London has the largest codpiece of any suit in the collection. It was often rubbed by visitors for good luck.

In Europe something similar was seen in the codpiece (sometimes called the *braguette*). The codpiece gets its name from the Old English word *codd,* meaning "bag" or "scrotum." It started life as a simple flap, a covering for the fly, which was a fourteenth-century invention allowing a man to urinate without having to pull down his hose. Another good reason to cover this area was the medieval fashion for short jackets that revealed the loins and buttocks. The codpiece preserved your modesty in these situations and, with the help of padding, was also handy in disguising any deficiency in the crotch region. Even when hemlines dropped in the Tudor period, the jutting codpiece was revealed via a central split in the fabric.

In some cases the codpiece was used as a pocket for valuables, and some devil-may-care fellows kept fruit in their codpieces so they could offer lucky ladies a nibble.

> **SOME** sources claim that the Italian duke Fabrizio of Bologna did much to popularize the stuffed codpiece in Tudor times. Legend has it that the duke (on an ambassadorial mission to England) had to appear before King Henry VIII and Anne Boleyn. The duke dashed into court after a hurried romantic encounter, and his state of excitement was obvious to all. Apparently the king looked at the duke's bulging codpiece and decided he wanted one just like it.

Codpieces were popular from the fourteenth century onward but died out in the seventeenth century with the adoption of large doublets that puffed out to obscure the crotch region.

The style of codpieces varied from country to country. They were so distinctive that historians can often date a male costume and tell the nationality of its wearer just by examining the bulge. The German codpiece was like a heavily padded pillow, the English pointed upward, the French covered theirs in gold buckles and trinkets, and the Italians seem to have made theirs as conspicuous as possible by minimizing the rest of their clothing. Some codpieces were as much as four inches long, and a few were even decorated with little gargoylelike faces.

Not surprisingly, nations of non–codpiece wearers found the fashion a little ridiculous. Apparently Turks were fond of waylaying Western travelers where possible and stripping them to see if the contents lived up to the packaging.

Fetishes

Outfits made from leather, rubber, and PVC are often referred to as *fetish clothing*. PVC (a plastic called polyvinylchloride) is not flexible, and PVC outfits have to be cut and stitched rather than molded and glued like rubber. (A good example is the Catwoman suit from *Batman Returns*.) In the past rubber fans had to make do with commercially made raincoats and galoshes to satisfy their cravings, but these days most waterproof garments are made from plastics, and the majority of rubber-fetish clothing is specially manufactured from versatile sheet latex, a substance developed in the 1970s. There is a wide variety of rubber-fetish wear available today, including rubber corsets, leggings and stockings, miniskirts, bras, and

FOR the man who has everything, why not buy him a pimp hat? A specialty shop in Hermosa Beach, CA, claims to have cornered the market in the type of pimp headgear seen in films such as *Superfly* and *Shaft*. Going for around $40 each, these wide-brimmed, floppy, furred, and feathered headpieces are most often bought by clubbers and for costume parties.

vests, as well as more exotic items such as restraints, hoods, and masks. Some rubber outfits even come with built-in dildos. Some have three: two internal ones, and an external one to use on a friend.

As to the attraction of fetish wear, rubber and PVC clothing encourages erotic interest because, while a sheer, skintight garment covers everything, it effectively conceals nothing. Thus a wearer can be fully clothed but effectively naked. Rubber and PVC also show off the wearer to their best advantage. Fetish wear is flattering as it supports and lifts the bits and pieces that would otherwise sag, and covers blemishes and wrinkles. An aging, wrinkled, spotty bottom covered in rubber immediately becomes taut, smooth, and "youthful." These garments are by their nature very tight and constrictive so they offer an added bonus to those who enjoy bondage.

Some leather garments are worn for the same reasons as rubber and PVC, but this material has an important extra dimension in that most devotees are primarily attracted by its masculine connotations. Indeed, in the 1960s, leather, chains, and handlebar mustaches were adopted by many gays as symbols of ultramasculinity, often as part of the gay S&M scene. Not all leather has the same erotic impact, however. Few people are sexually attracted to suede or colored leather—the vast majority of leather lovers only wear it shiny and black. Many people are attracted to fetish clothing because of its shiny, glistening quality, and there are at least two magazines devoted to this form of clothing: *Shiny International* and *Shiny Rubberist*. The reason why shiny is sexy is unclear, but it's been suggested that taut materials like latex and leather are sexually suggestive because they resemble (superficially at least) the taut glistening surface of aroused genitalia and/or sweat-drenched skin. Black seems to be a favorite because shiny black clothing offers a more reflective surface than colored items. This, and the fact that black emphasizes body contours, is probably why the majority of latex and leather garments come in the one shade.

YOU SHOW ME YOURS

The Ins and Outs of the Vital Organs

 His

Most men would consider their penis their most valuable possession. This sentiment was captured perfectly in an ancient mural of Pompeii depicting the hugely endowed god Priapus (see Chapter 16) weighing his mighty organ against a pile of gold—the inference being that it's "worth its weight."

Medically speaking, the head of the penis is known as the *glans* (a name derived from the Latin for "acorn"), with an opening at the tip called the *meatus*. Joining the glans to the shaft of the penis is the *corona*, and the two are connected by a thin stringlike flap of skin called the *frenum*.

Internally the penis shaft consists of three tubes: a pair called the *corpora cavernosa* and, between them, the *corpus spongiosum*, containing the urethra, the tube that carries urine and sperm.

When a man is sexually aroused, nerve messages cause the spongy blood vessels in the corpora cavernosa to dilate and fill with blood. As these blood-filled chambers expand, they exert pressure on the veins that would otherwise drain blood from the penis. More blood starts to flow in than go out, and the penis becomes erect.

The mechanics of an erection were not understood until recently. In the past there were many odd theories about erections. Some doctors thought they were pneumatic effects caused by eating gassy foods (see Chapter 7). The thirteenth-century physician Albert the Great thought that heat generated in the testicles by lustful thoughts turned body humors into steam and expanded the penis like a hot-air balloon.

 ## Size

Penis size has been of interest to both sexes for centuries. As the Roman writer Martial recorded, "When you hear clapping in the baths, you know some moron with a giant dick has arrived."

Something that often causes confusion is the relationship between soft and erect penis dimensions. Some men have penises that are always full of blood. In these cases erections don't result in any increase in size—the penis just becomes stiffer and upright. Other men have penises that hold very little blood when flaccid and are tiny shriveled objects. In these cases erections usually result in a significant size increase. Some erections are more than ten times larger than the flaccid member.

In humans the penis reaches its adult size at the age of seventeen, and the size can vary a great deal. The largest medically verified penis on record was 13½ inches long and 6 inches in circumference; the smallest was around ⅜ inch long. Many surveys have measured penis size, but perhaps the most famous investigator was the French army doctor Jacobus X (thought to be a pseudonym of Louis Jacolliot). Jacobus devoted twenty-eight years of his life to penis measurement, carrying out most of his work in the early 1900s. Jacobus concluded that Africans had the biggest, the average size being 7¾ inches long and 2 inches in diameter. Among Africans the doctor rarely came across penises less than 6¼ inches long and 1¾ inches in diameter, and frequently encountered 9- to 9½-inch penises that were 2¼ inches in diameter. One gentleman from the Sudan possessed a polelike monster that was 13 inches by 2.

According to Jacobus, Hindus are at the smaller end of the scale. A sixteenth-century Hindu text called the *Ananga Ranga* describes three types of men: Hare men with a penis 6 finger-breadths long (3¼ inches), Bull men of 9 finger-breadths (5 inches), and Stallion men of 12 finger-breadths

---

⚥ A Frenchman left his monster 9¾-inch penis to a friend in his will.

⚥ The male stripper troupe Dreamboys has insured its members' genitals for $1.2 million in case of accidental damage by female fans.

⚥ In *Antony and Cleopatra* Shakespeare makes a joke about penis size: "If you were but an inch of fortune better than I, where would you choose it?" "Not in my husband's nose."

⚥ If you suffer from Peyronie's disease, your penis is shaped like a boomerang.

MOST male porn stars are often well endowed (this being the prime qualification for the job), and at least one has claimed that erections make him dizzy due to the volume of blood taken out of circulation. But according to insiders, the organs of male porn stars often have inflated reputations; their real sizes do not live up to the hype. Techniques to make them look bigger include shaving off pubic hair, using penis development pumps, and "cock rings."

(6¾ inches). In Jacobus's experience most Hindu men were Hare men, but a twentieth-century survey put Asian men at the bottom of the league, with an average penis length of 5½ inches.

There have been numerous surveys measuring penis size among white males, but few seem to agree. One study found an average of 6 inches and another 6½. Another survey of Western men found that most unerect penises are between 3½ and 4 inches long (2½ to 4¾ inches in circumference) and that an erection increases these dimensions by approximately 30 percent. The same survey said that only 1 percent of men had a penis larger than 9 inches, and 5 percent had one shorter than 3½ inches. "Normal" is anywhere in between.

Surveys probably differ because different researchers have measured the penis in different ways. The correct way is to put a ruler at the base of the penis's topside and swing the penis through horizontal to vertical; the longest length is the measure you write down.

MEN with two penises suffer from a condition called *diphallas-paratus*. It's very rare, and fewer than eighty cases have been reported. In some men the penis splits into two; in others there are two distinct organs, one above the other or side by side. There is usually a dominant, larger penis, though often both work equally well. Testicles can also come in bonus packs, a condition known as *polyorchidism*. Sufferers often have three testicles, but four or five have been recorded.

Making It Bigger

There have been many methods for increasing penis size, some of them painful. In 1503 the Spanish explorer Amerigo Vespucci reported that native women in the New World used to make poisonous lizards bite their husbands' penises. Apparently the treatment was often successful, but the occasional swelling penis burst through "lack of attention." Some cultures have tried the same trick with bee stings.

Dr. Jacobus recorded a penis enlargement method he encountered in Guyana. Here an eggplant was split in half and the halves hollowed out to make deep grooves. Bark from the *nux vomica* (strychnine) tree was boiled in water and mixed with flour to make a paste. Added to this were the heads of 6 to 12 phosphorescent matches, 2 or 3 small pimentos, 12 peppercorns, 12 cloves, and a few vanilla beans. This gunk was then spooned over the erect penis and the stiff member encased in the eggplant. The penis was left inside for "many minutes" before being taken out and washed. The mixture inflamed the penis, temporarily increasing its size and improving the quality of the erection. A young French officer tried this treatment and discovered that his penis tripled in size. Unfortunately his foreskin didn't grow correspondingly, and immediate surgery was required to remove it.

Over the years numerous concoctions have been touted as penis growth creams. In 1848 one New York quack called William Early sold a cream that was based on manure.

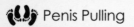 ## Penis Pulling

In the 1770s a British envoy in Russia said most Russian men were well hung because Russian nurses constantly pulled on the penises of babies to stretch them. In northern Uganda some tribesmen hung stones from their penises to stretch them, and some modern penis enlargement devices involve something similar. There's even one contraption (looking like a leg caliper) that can be used to apply constant tension to the penis.

Stretching can have its drawbacks. The members of one Hindu sect hung stones from their penises from a young age, resulting in superlong organs that brushed the ground. In this case penis enlargement was carried out to make them chaste,

---

🔮 In the nineteenth century the Aboriginal Wallabi tribe shook penises instead of hands on ceremonial occasions.

🔮 In some parts of New Guinea pulling someone's penis is a sign of goodwill.

🔮 In 1992 a Cincinnati surgeon was fired for drawing smiley faces on the penises of two unconscious patients.

as stretching a penis to these lengths makes it impossible to have an erection.

Vacuum Developers

Most modern penis enlargement kits consist of a hollow tube and a hand-operated vacuum pump, and similar devices have been around since the early 1900s. The tube is placed over the penis, and the air is pumped out, the partial vacuum causing the penis to expand and blood to rush in to fill the additional volume. The theory is that over time the blood vessels and spongy tissue of the corpora cavernosa will be expanded permanently. Some tubes also incorporate a set of weights that can be used to stretch the penis.

In some cases these penis-developers are used to cure impotence. A tight "cock ring" is placed over the base of the penis to prevent blood escaping after it's been drawn in by the vacuum. Some kit manufacturers claim increases in length by as much as 2½ inches and increases in circumference by 1½ inches.

 Surgery

The only certain way to increase penis size is by surgery. There are two surgical procedures, one to increase length, the other to increase circumference. To increase length,

ELEPHANTIASIS, a disease caused by parasitic worms, can cause the testicles to swell to the size of watermelons. The largest on record belonged to an African whose two-foot-wide scrotum weighed 154lb.

ALTHOUGH it doesn't contain a bone, the human penis can snap if treated roughly. A sudden wrong move can cause the blood-filled corpora cavernosa to break with a loud cracking sound. The old treatment involved a splint, an ice pack, and drugs to inhibit erections while it healed. Today more effective surgical methods are employed.

suspensory ligaments at the base of the penis are cut. There is a significant amount of penis hidden inside the body (as much as 2¾ to 3¾ inches), and cutting these ligaments allows it to come forward. Lengthening is encouraged by the use of postoperative weights or extensors to stretch the organ. The amount of extra penis length gained in this way depends on the individual, from 0 to 2¾ inches; there's no way of knowing beforehand.

The record for an extension is said to be held by a Danish plastic surgeon who increased a 1¾-inch penis by an additional 5¾ inches. Some men have tiny working penises less than ⅜ of an inch long, a condition known as *micropenis*. This occurs in approximately one in fifty thousand births and is due to low hormone levels in the developing fetus. Even though they are genetically male, many micropenis babies are operated on to make them female. In cases where the baby is left as a boy, later surgery can often stretch the penis to around 2½ inches.

To increase circumference, fat cells are taken from other parts of the body and injected into the shaft of the penis. Increases in girth by as much as 50 percent can be achieved, but this thickening isn't permanent as the injected fat will eventually melt away.

These surgical procedures are very popular. In 1994 one

SOME people think the size of a man's nose indicates the size of his penis; others think the size of a woman's mouth indicates the size of her vagina. As one Arab saying puts it, "A maiden's mouth shows what's the make of her chose [vagina]. And by a man's mentule one knows the length of his nose." One subscriber to this theory was Queen Johanne I of Naples (1326–82), who married the huge-nosed Andrew of Hungary in 1343. Sadly, Andrew proved to be poorly equipped, and—for this and other reasons—Johanne had him strangled.

U.S. clinic reported that it had carried out fifteen hundred *phalloplasty* operations in the previous eighteen months. In China there have even been experiments to try and improve the quality of erections by transplanting arm muscle into the penis shaft.

Penis Splints

The *Kama Sutra* mentions a number of devices called *apadravyas* that could be used to increase penis size, or help stiffen an inadequate member. Some were made of metal, others from buffalo horn or wood. They ranged from hollow cylinders that fitted over the penis to increase girth, to one or more "erection stiffening" braces or splints, to rings that fitted over the base of the penis to help maintain erections. Rubber "cock rings" are still made today, and rubber and metal penis splints were sold into the twentieth century under brand names such as Robut-Man, Monster Auto Man, and The Wimpus.

PRACTITIONERS of *chi kung* (an ancient Taoist art of body control) attempt to gain sexual nirvana by lifting heavy weights with their penises. A device looking like a coat hanger is attached to the base of the penis and fitted with weights. Practitioners then work out with various swinging and lifting motions. Some are able to lift 250 lbs 2 feet off the floor.

Making It Smaller

You can have too much of a good thing. The vagina is usually between eight and nine inches deep, so a large penis can make intercourse uncomfortable. A number of devices have been invented to help solve this problem. One seventeenth-century French doctor developed a *bourlet*, a thick doughnut-shaped piece of padded cork that slipped over the end of the penis and rested at its base to reduce its effective length.

All Dicks Great and Small

The ballet dancer Nijinsky didn't fill a pair of tights too well, and the authors Hemingway and Fitzgerald were both said to be underdeveloped in the trouser department (Hemingway's was said to be the size of a little finger). He and Fitzgerald are said to have compared sizes on one occasion.

Others have been more fortunate. The English king Charles II was said to have a penis the length of his scepter (though this might have been poetic license). The French painter Toulouse-Lautrec was so well endowed, his prostitute friends described him as a *verge à pattes*, a "walking penis." Rasputin's penis was reputedly over twelve inches long. After his poisoning he

♂ In 2000 three martial arts masters in Taipei pulled a truck holding eighty people using ropes attached to their penises (though they only dragged it 12 inches).

♂ In 1989 a 28-year-old Indian man tied his penis to a car and pulled it along as part of a protest against rising oil prices.

♂ In Asia there is a phenomenon called the *koro epidemic*. During one of these epidemics large numbers of men convince themselves that their penises are shrinking and tie objects to their organs to stop them from retreating inside their bodies.

was castrated; his preserved penis was said to resemble a dried black banana a foot long. In Hollywood Gary Cooper and Errol Flynn were famously large gentlemen, the latter broadcasting the fact by playing the piano with his penis at parties. Ultimately the matter is of no importance—as the Roman satirist Juvenal said, "If you've run out of luck, it doesn't matter how long your penis is."

Circumcision

The earliest record of a circumcision is in Egypt around 2300 B.C. It's been suggested that it developed as a male counterpoint to puberty in females. The onset of womanhood was marked with menstrual bleeding, so it was decided to mark male puberty with something similar. This theory is borne out by the fact that nearly all tribal circumcision rites occur when boys are in their early teens.

Another theory is that primitive societies thought the folds of the foreskin looked like the skin surrounding the vagina.

IN Malaysia it's been proposed that the mass circumcision ceremonies organized by some religious sects be promoted as tourist attractions.

Cutting the foreskin away helped accentuate the difference between males and females.

Hygiene has also been cited as a factor for circumcision. *Preputial glands* under the foreskin (prepuce) extrude a substance known as smegma. If not cleaned away regularly, this can get nasty, leading to an infection known as *balanitis*.

The foreskin can cause other problems. *Phimosis* is the name given to a condition where the foreskin cannot be pulled back due to the growth of connective tissue between the foreskin and the glans. This is usually easy to solve surgically, as is *paraphimosis*, where the foreskin is so tight it cannot be rolled back.

Most circumcisions involved only the removal of the foreskin, but some Arab circumcision ceremonies involved the removal of all the skin on the penis at puberty. If the boy cried out, he was killed on the spot.

Sometimes circumcision is accompanied by *subincision,* where the underside of the penis is slit. Sometimes this incision is only half an inch long; at other times a cut is made along the whole length of the penis. One Aboriginal tribe split the penis entirely to mimic the sexual organs of the tribe's totem animal, a lizard with a naturally bifurcated penis.

In some cases the main purpose of circumcision is to act as a mark of identity. This is the principal reason for Hebrew circumcision, which is carried out in infancy. This ceremony is known as a *bris*, and a rabbi qualified to perform the circumcision is called a *mohel*.

Circumcision is common in America. Hygiene is the main reason given, but the more cynically minded point out that doctors charge a great deal for what is essentially a simple procedure and sometimes do it without consulting the parents.

Some say the practice became common after the First World War, men having the operation as a preventive measure against "trench rot" of the foreskin. A more likely reason is that it was thought to prevent the evils of masturbation—against which many U.S. health experts undertook a crusade in the nineteenth century.

These days so many men are circumcised in the United States that most American women have never seen an "uncut" penis. Now, however, the practice seems to be in decline. One source estimates that over 60 percent of American boys are no longer circumcised at birth.

Some men are circumcised later in life, for medical or religious reasons or because their partners prefer it. Because the head of a circumcised penis is constantly exposed, it is less sensitive than an uncut penis, so it takes longer to reach a climax. Some women appreciate this extra time, though for others it can go on too long and result in soreness. Recently, circumcised men have also complained about the difficulty in masturbating. The postoperative phase of an adult circumcision can be very painful; unwanted erections sometimes lead to burst stitches.

👣 Penile Inserts

In Borneo and many parts of the Far East it was the custom to bore a hole through the head or shaft of the penis and insert a metal rod or wire called an *ampallang*. During intercourse this metal appliance was said to be very stimulating for the female partner.

A similar trick involved implanting objects under the skin of the penis. In Burma men often cut open their penises to insert small bells, while the men of the Malaysian Peninsula did the same with metal balls. Some rural tribesmen used the dried tongues of adders, the Japanese inserted pearls, and the men of Sumatra made do with small stones. As with the ampallang, these objects were designed to pleasure women, though some early Western travelers theorized that the practice was started to discourage anal sex.

The bells used by the Burmese were useful as they announced their presence. The more bells you had, the better lover you were thought to be, and the more noise you made when walking. The rich had bells made with silver, while the poor made do with lead. If a king wanted to honor someone, the best gift he could offer was to have one of his bells cut out and presented as a gift. Some of these bells were as large as hazelnuts, and many men had three or more.

🔞 Teenage erections can last for an hour. Between age 66 and 70, you're lucky to get seven minutes.

🔞 According to a U.S. health survey, Miami men have the hardest time getting erect, while Phoenix men have the least trouble.

Penile inserts were also found in India. These had many names depending on their shape: for example, the wooden mortar, the elephant's goad, or the heron's bone. One fifteenth-century traveler reported that many old Indian ladies made a living by inserting small bells of gold, silver, and copper under the skin of the penis. Depending on the size of the inserts, some men had half a dozen or more. Boys would have bells inserted after puberty, then have their "junior" models changed for larger ones as they grew up.

Today implants are sometimes used to cure impotence. Two bendable rods are surgically inserted into the penile shaft, and when an erection is required, the organ is simply bent upright.

Sperm—*A Drop of the White Stuff*

Sperm has been regarded as a magical substance. Alchemists called it the "blood of the red lion," and in classical times it was believed that sperm coagulated in the womb to form a baby. In Hindu tradition it's thought that one drop of sperm contains the distilled energy of forty drops of blood and takes forty days to produce.

♀ A transsexual from Birmingham, England, is planning to store his sperm so that, with the use of a surrogate womb, he can eventually be the mother and father of a baby.

♂ In 2001 it was decided that San Francisco prisoner William Gerber had a constitutional right to mail his sperm home to his wife.

IN medieval times it was believed that some spirits stole semen. Nocturnal demons in female form called *succubi* visited young men to encourage wet dreams. The female succubi then turned into male *incubi* and used the stolen sperm to impregnate sleeping women.

Taste

Sperm consists of a large number of substances, including ascorbic acid, chlorine, cholesterol, citric acid, lactic acid, pyruvic acid, urea, uric acid, vitamin B_{12}, and zinc. Considering what's in it, it's not surprising that most people don't like the taste. In one survey women described sperm as tasting like Ajax cleanser, Brie, Clorox bleach, dirty socks, and salty soft snot.

Different foods can affect the flavor of sperm, as can smoking. A protein-rich diet is said to give sperm a fishy, bitter taste, while a diet high in dairy foods is said to produce very unpalatable ejaculations. The worst-tasting sperm is said to be produced after a meal of asparagus; garlic comes in a close second.

Vegetables good for sperm flavor are celery and broccoli, while sweet fruits such as pineapples, bananas, and papayas are also said to have positive effects. Some alcoholic drinks also improve the flavor, the good news for real ale drinkers being that naturally fermented alcohol produces the best results.

An American company has recently started selling a drink powder called Semenex that apparently makes semen taste sweet. As one satisfied customer charmingly put it, "I've per-

SPERM FACTS

⚤ An ejaculation contains between 5 and 15 calories.

⚤ The average human ejaculation contains around 400 million sperm.

⚤ The average volume of ejaculate is 0.11 fluid ounces.

⚤ The average speed of a human ejaculation is 17 mph.

⚤ The average distance covered by a human ejaculation is 6.9 inches.

⚤ A human spermatozoon is 4 microns long and can travel an inch an hour.

sonally used it, and my girl grins instead of cringes when taking a big load of skeet down her trap."

 ## Sperm Power

Many love potions included a dose of sperm, and in the Far East sperm was thought to be full of yang energy. Old men prized the sperm of the young, as they believed it would rejuvenate them. According to a journalist working in Shanghai in the 1930s, there were male brothels where old men could go to suck off youngsters. The young men stood behind a screen, poking their privates through a hole, while old gentlemen queued up for a drink. On one occasion a youngster fell asleep on a train and awoke to discover that his fly had been opened by an old man sitting opposite. Granddad had the youngster's penis in his mouth, hoping for a free sample. Apparently these incidents were not uncommon on Chinese public transportation.

The belief that a loss of semen was debilitating was also popular in the West. As recently as the 1920s Eugene Steinach of Vienna performed vasectomies on older men to try and preserve their vigor. Two men who had this procedure carried out were Sigmund Freud and William Butler Yeats.

 Hers

Some people have been very uncomplimentary about the vagina. Saint Augustine bemoaned the fact that man was "born between feces and urine," while the eighteenth-century French physician André des Laurens wrote, "How can this divine animal which we call man be attracted by those obscene parts of a woman defiled with juices and located shamefully at the lowest part of the trunk?" Others have been more upbeat: Eve Ensler's *The Vagina Monologues*, a recent theatrical phenomena, is a series of stories and reminiscences that celebrate the organ in all its facets.

Taking a gynecological view, the vagina is essentially a tubular canal sitting between the bladder and the rectum connecting the uterus with the outside world. The average vagina is eight to nine inches long and extends from the cervix at the mouth of the uterus to the vaginal opening. The opening is surrounded by folds of skin that form the inner and outer labia. At the upper junction of the inner folds there is a budlike clitoris, which normally hides under a hood of skin. Lubrication is provided by glands around the vaginal orifice, the most important being the Bartholin glands.

Clitoris

There's been a lot of discussion about clitoral sizes. For years it was thought that lesbianism might be due to an abnormally sized clitoris, and some medical authorities reported clitorises as long as 2¾ inches. A French medical encyclopedia of 1813 even claimed the existence of a 12-inch clitoris.

On average most clitorises are stubby and less than ⅙ inch across, growing to about ⅜ inch stimulated. Perhaps one woman in five hundred has a clitoris larger than a peanut.

The clitoris and penis develop from the same fetal tissue and are similar in many respects: they're sited in the same place, are packed with nerve endings, and swell up when they're stimulated.

Recognizing its importance as the seat of female pleasure, the clitoris has been given names such as the "gadfly" and the "bonbon of lust." The witch-finders of sixteenth-century England had another name for it—the "devil's teat," an organ supposedly used to suckle a witch's familiar spirits—black cats, imps, toads, and the like.

Labia

In some cultures large protruding vaginal lips were very desirable. Hottentots were said to have very large labia, which they lengthened by rubbing and pulling on them. The women of the South African Venda tribe and the Benin of West Africa did the same. Sometimes they helped each other out by pulling their friends' lips, stretching them by as much as 2¾ inches. The results were tucked inside the vagina to keep them out of harm's way.

The Ponapeans of the Caroline Island group also appreciated large labia and clitorises. Here one method of increasing their size was to apply stinging ants to the area. Less painfully, elderly gentlemen could be employed to suck and pull on them.

Today some plastic surgeons specialize in *vaginoplasty*. Many patients want a vagina similar to that of a typical *Playboy* centerfold and request a reduction of inner lips so they don't protrude. Another common procedure is a "vagina lift," where sagging outer labia are rejuvenated by taking up excess skin. "Fat" vaginas can also be treated; liposculpture can remove unsightly bulges.

Female Circumcision

A more brutal form of surgery is female circumcision or female genital mutilation (FGM), which is still practiced in many parts of the world, particularly in Africa, the Arabian Peninsula, Indonesia, and Malaysia. There, surgery is often carried out with rudimentary tools, the object being either to remove the tip of the clitoris (*Sunna circumcision*), the removal of the entire clitoris (a *clitoridectomy*), or the removal of the clitoris and all or some of the labia (*infibulation* or *pharaonic circumcision*). In the latter case the vagina might be sewn up, leaving a small opening for urine and menstrual blood. The vagina is often opened again on the woman's wedding night by her husband, using a double-edged dagger. If the husband goes away for any length of time, he might have his wife sewn up again to prevent her from committing adultery.

According to one source, about six thousand girls and women undergo these operations every day, and it's been estimated that up to 130 million women worldwide have had the operation. Various reasons are given for the practice. In some areas the clitoris is regarded as a dangerous organ that will cause impotence or death in a man who touches it. If it touches a baby during childbirth, some think the mother's milk will become poisoned. Others believe the operation removes genital odors, prevents lesbianism and nervousness, or stops the face from turning yellow. Some fear that without the procedure a man will not be able to match his wife's sexual drive in old age. In most cases the real reason appears to be an attempt to de-sex females in the hope they will be chaste before marriage and faithful to their husbands afterward.

 ## Female Ejaculation

The fact that some women release fluid at orgasm (in addition to normal vaginal secretions) has been recognized for centuries. In ancient Greece both Aristotle and Galen knew of it, and some thought that babies were produced by mixing male and female ejaculate in the womb. A recent survey suggests that approximately 40 percent of women "ejaculate." A prime suspect for the origin of this fluid is the Skene glands, on the anterior wall of the vagina near the urethra. These glands were named after the American doctor who described them in the 1880s, but they've been known of since the seventeenth century, when it was assumed they were the female equivalent of the prostate gland (the site of semen production in men).

Later researchers noticed that there appears to be erectile tissue surrounding the urethra, and this tissue became known as the *G-spot*, after Dr. Ernst Gräfenberg. To call it a "spot" is a misnomer, though, as the tissue usually forms a

THE youngest authenticated mother was a five-year-old Peruvian called Lina Medina, who delivered a 6lb boy by cesarean section in 1939.

ridge under the anterior vaginal wall. Current research suggests that female ejaculation is caused by the G-spot and Skene glands working together.

Many modern doctors and sex researchers like Alfred Kinsey and Masters and Johnson have rejected the idea of female ejaculation, believing "ejaculate" was urine released from the bladder during orgasm. To get to the bottom of the mystery, researchers drained the bladders of female volunteers, fitted them with catheters, and got them to masturbate to orgasm. All the women were copious "ejaculators" who managed to produce between 1.7 and 30.4 fluid ounces. Interestingly, 95 percent of this fluid did come from the bladder but was not normal urine, containing only 25 percent of the normal levels of urea. Of the remaining fluid, some consisted of normal vaginal secretions, though in other cases there was also a small milky discharge from the Skene glands.

To summarize, it seems that whereas most female "ejaculate" is modified urine, ejaculation is not simply a question of losing bladder control. Something else is going on, but no one is quite sure what.

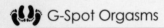 G-Spot Orgasms

The Gräfenberg spot is a famously elusive erogenous zone responsible for very powerful female orgasms. The majority of female orgasms are due to clitoral stimulation that only produce vaginal contractions, but orgasms produced by stimulating the G-spot produce contractions of the uterus and are more powerful and prolonged. For those who need directions, the G-spot (the size of a thimble) is just beyond a rough patch of tissue on the anterior wall of the vagina, approximately three to four inches up the vaginal canal. To manipulate it, firm pressure is required, and although there's an initial urge to urinate, this soon disappears. To facilitate masturbation, there are many vibrators on the market designed to hit the G-spot, all of which have a right-angled kink at the end of the shaft.

 ## Kegel and Kabazzah

Keeping the vaginal muscles toned can help ensure a happy sex life by ensuring they clamp down on the penis for a "tight fit." To help women exercise this area, a Los Angeles gynecologist called Kegel developed a workout program in the 1940s. The first step is to try and halt urination in midflow by tightening the muscles of the pelvic floor. Once this initial muscle control has been developed, it can be refined by rhythmically contracting the vaginal muscles while keeping the muscles of the abdomen and buttocks relaxed. To help your exercise routine, one company has even invented the Kegelmaster (analogous to a Thighmaster), a sprung plastic device that can be inserted in the vagina.

In the past the women of Abyssinia (modern-day Ethiopia) were famous for the agility of their vaginal muscles. Using these muscles, a woman could bring a man to orgasm by straddling him and using vaginal contraction alone. The practice was known as *kabazzah* (meaning "holder"). Not surprisingly, Abyssinian concubines were worth three times more than any other. Another term for this practice is *cassenoisette* (meaning "nutcracker"). Strong muscle tone is also the secret behind the famous "ping-pong" trick often demonstrated at Bangkok bars, where a girl will shoot table-tennis balls from her vagina. Other legendary tricks performed by a "trained" vagina include playing the harmonica, drinking glasses of whiskey, and peeling a banana.

Penis Captivus

Sometimes the muscles of the vagina can grip the penis so tightly, it can't get out again. This condition is called *penis captivus* and occurs when the vagina goes into an involuntary spasm (*vaginismus*). This has given rise to many urban myths, but there are few reliable medical records of it occurring, and many doctors refuse to believe it can happen at all. Anecdotal stories of penis captivus usually involve sex in a public place, with the woman so nervous that the penis becomes trapped for hours or even days. A tale told by the fourteenth-century French writer Geoffroy de la Tour-Landry involved a soldier having illicit sex with a woman on a church altar, doggy-style. They became trapped and spent all night and the next day locked together. They became something of a tourist attraction, the locals trooping into church to pray that "such a horrible sight be removed." They were eventually separated and had to undergo severe penance for three Sundays.

LOSING IT (HIS)

Castration

Ever wondered what it would be like to part with the family jewels? It goes without saying that the process itself would be a turn-on for only the smallest minority, but what about after the chop—heaven or hell? Would you be a ball of sexual frustration without an outlet or maybe as contented as a neutered cat? After all, Socrates described reaching the age where sexual appetite no longer has a hold over you as like being finally unchained from a madman. Thankfully it is a question few of us are asked to research and answer personally.

Castration involves the removal of the testicles and/or penis; a castrated man is known as a eunuch. Past castration methods involved the destruction of the testicles by crushing them, or twisting the scrotum to destroy the connecting tubing. Another technique involved tying a thong around the scrotum, cutting off the blood supply so it would gradually wither and fall off. In most cases cutting was the preferred method as there was less risk of infection.

The Assyrians seem to have started the eunuch habit, and in time most cultures of the Middle East and Orient employed them. The Persian emperor Darius (558–486 B.C.) demanded a tribute of 1,000 talents of silver and 500 castrated boys from Babylon every year; these unfortunates were employed in every palace position from doorkeeper upward. Eunuchs were popular as servants because they were considered docile, unambitious, and loyal.

He Who Has Charge of the Bed

The word *eunuch* is from the Greek meaning "he who has charge of the bed," and in ancient times eunuchs were often employed to guard the king's harem. The Ottoman sultans were famous for the army of eunuchs they employed; those

THE Hebrews took enemy foreskins as battle trophies, and the ancient Egyptians and Ethiopians took penises in the same way. In 1300 B.C. the Egyptian pharaoh Menephta celebrated a victory over the Libyans by collecting 13,240 penises from their dead soldiers. Assuming an average flaccid length of three inches per man, the penises would have stretched over half a mile. The practice was also common in later centuries. In 1058 King Henry I of France castrated prisoners he took in his wars with the Greeks. On one occasion a prisoner's wife begged him to spare her husband's penis, saying she needed it. She suggested the king let her husband go and cut out his eyes if he was caught a second time.

serving the sultan in the *selamlik* (men's quarters) were white, but it was death for any white male (eunuch or otherwise) to be found in the women's quarters (*haremlik*), where all the eunuchs were black. The sultan employed only the ugliest black men he could find for harem duty and removed both their penis and their testicles. (White eunuchs lost only their gonads.) Apart from being a painful operation, having your penis removed was also inconvenient, as "total eunuchs" had to urinate with the help of a quill. This type of castration had a mortality rate of around 90 percent. For years the Sudanese town of Tewasheh was the largest supplier of eunuchs in the world—more than 30,000 African men died each year to meet an annual quota of 3,000.

Not all harem guards were castrated. Old men and warrior women usually guarded the harems of Indian princes; Hindus had a horror of eunuchs, who were regarded as unclean. There are many eunuchs in modern India (known as *hijras*, "impotent ones")—a recent estimate puts their number at 400,000. Shunned by society, these eunuchs live in mutually supporting "families" that often recruit new members by kidnapping boys and forcibly castrating them. Eunuchs usually dress as women and make a living as dancers. Others operate a kind of protection racket, gate-crashing weddings or hanging around shops and businesses until they're paid to clear off.

Imperial Eunuchs

The eunuchs of the Chinese imperial court also had their penis and scrotum "shaved," as the removal was termed. Chinese eunuchs came in two varieties, the *ching cheng*, who were castrated as adults, and the *tung cheng*, who were castrated as small boys and often spent their early years as the pets of court ladies. The operation required four large men to hold the arms and legs of the victim while the surgeon sliced away with a fan-shaped blade dipped in lime juice. The wound might then be cauterized with a hot poker or tar. After a few days' healing, the patient was forced to drink a huge quantity of water so that emptying the bladder would clear the urethra of scar tissue. A small plug was then inserted to prevent the urethra from closing over.

Once the penis and testicles had been removed, the "precious," as they were known, were pickled in a jar and presented to the eunuch as his credentials. In future the eunuch would have to present his pickled privates for inspection whenever he received a promotion, and they would eventually be buried with him.

Some surgeons prided themselves on not leaving a stump, but some did, and on one occasion this had unfortunate consequences. The story goes that an eighteenth-century official of the Chinese court was insulted by the chief eunuch, and, determined to get revenge, he told the emperor that severed penises could grow back. The emperor had all the eunuchs inspected and found that most of them had a significant stump. These must have been left over from the original operation, but the emperor was convinced they were regenerating. To stop the process he had all the stumps sliced off, and many eunuchs died as a result.

Amazingly, despite these drawbacks there was fierce competition to become an imperial eunuch. In 1644 20,000 men applied for 3,000 eunuch positions doing jobs as diverse as engineering, interior decorating, and looking after the emperor's cats. For many being a eunuch inside the palace was better than starving outside.

In China the creation of eunuchs carried on into the twen-

♂ In 1982 a Welsh preacher cut off his own penis and threw it in a fire.

♂ In 1983 a Malaysian man had his penis bitten off by a turtle when swimming naked in a pool.

♂ In 1991 a 64-year-old Turkish man cut off his penis to prove to his wife he was not having an affair with a neighbor.

tieth century; the last imperial eunuch, Sun Yaoting, died in 1996 aged ninety-three. After the emperor was deposed, many jobless eunuchs were cared for by the state. A traveler in the 1930s reported coming across a hostel called the "Refuge for Distressed Eunuchs," next to the Pa Pao Shan Golf Club in Beijing. It had thirty-three inhabitants aged between sixty and eighty.

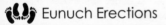 Eunuch Erections

The reason many harem guards had their penises removed as well as their testicles was the fact that, in some cases, even a man without testicles can have an erection; he can even ejaculate, most seminal fluid being produced in the prostate. Some Roman women prized adult eunuchs as lovers for their incredible stamina, though to be a stud you had to be castrated after puberty, as those castrated before didn't develop properly.

The source of eunuch erections is the small but significant amount of testosterone produced by the adrenal gland. Most testosterone is produced in the testicles, but enough comes from this gland to "start your motor," and some eunuchs can be as active as normal men.

👣 Prostitutes and Choirboys

Some eunuchs ended up as the inmates of a harem rather than its guards. Male brothels often kept castrated boys, as the removal of their testicles kept them soft and feminine. In ancient Greece an unsavory character called Panionius was notorious for kidnapping good-looking boys and castrating them for the export market. As late as 1845 the explorer Sir Richard Burton came across a male brothel in India staffed by eunuchs and boys. Apparently the boys were preferred, as their testicles gave customers something to hang on to.

In Europe eunuchs were prized as choirboys and opera singers. In Renaissance Italy the operatic *castrati* (many of them ex-choirboys) performed all the female roles onstage, and such was their popularity that crowds used to shout "Long live the knife!" during ovations. One estimate put the number of Italian boys castrated at about four thousand a year, and in some Italian antique shops it is still possible to buy old signs reading "Boys castrated here for a modest price." The practice began to be discouraged in the eighteenth century, and church choirs started to refuse boys who'd been deliberately castrated. As a result a black market in castrati developed. Doctors carried out back-street castrations; the results were passed off as "accidental." The last of these eunuchs sang in the Papal Choir until 1878.

👣 Religious Castrators

Castration has been a feature of many religions. One famous castrating sect were the worshipers of Cybele, an ancient Greek earth goddess. The sect was strong in Syria, and here new priests castrated themselves on the *Dies Sanguinis* (Day of Blood). The priests hacked off their own genitals with a ceremonial sword, then ran through the streets clutching them in their hands. When they were exhausted, they'd fling their bloody privates through the window of a house; the lucky homeowner was obliged to look after the priest until he recovered. The priests of Cybele in Rome seem to have been more dignified; their chopped-off nether parts were buried in the earth as part of a fertility rite.

Castrating for Christ

Many people have interpreted certain New Testament passages as being in favor of castration. For example: "If your hand causes you to sin, cut it off," "Blessed [are] the barren," and "Put to death your members."

This pro-castration belief is in direct contrast to the Old Testament, which says that any man "wounded in the stones" cannot enter heaven. In medieval Rome any new pope had to sit on a bottomless chair so a priest could feel his privates. Some believe this was done to check that the pope was really a man, others that it made sure all his equipment was present and correct.

In the East castration was popular with some Christian sects. Around A.D. 250 a castrating sect was founded by an Arab Christian called Valerius, who believed that mortal suffering led to spiritual happiness. In the Byzantine Church many priests were castrated. Eight senior church positions were exclusively reserved for eunuchs, as they were believed to be more holy and trustworthy. Some Byzantine families had a son castrated early in life to prepare him for a career in the Church. The popularity of the practice is seen in the fact that seventy-two eunuchs can be found in the list of Christian saints. One of them, Saint Jerome, castrated himself.

A more recent castrating sect, the Skoptzy, was founded in Russia in 1757 by André Ivanov, a former member of a fla-gellant sect. André castrated himself and thirteen disciples and was promptly arrested and packed off to Siberia, where he died. The sect flourished, however, and one of Ivanov's original disciples, Kondrati Selivanov, was declared to be the new Christ. The Skoptzy preached that "everyone can be a tsar through this conversion." The sect grew in size, prestige, and wealth, with many converts coming from the middle classes and nobility. Factory owners who joined the Skoptzy often forced their workers to be castrated, and orphan chil-dren were cared for on condition they joined up.

Skoptzy castration usually occurred after the birth of a member's second child. For men the first step originally in-volved burning the testicles off with a red-hot poker, though later they were simply given the chop. The second stage was carried out a few years later, when the entire penis was hacked off, the deed being accompanied by a ritual dance. A variety of tools were used for the job, including pruning knives, chisels, sheet metal, broken glass, sharpened bones, and hatchets. To stop the bleeding, the wound was packed with ice and sealed with resin; a metal tube was pushed up the urethra to keep it open.

For women the first stage involved amputation of the nip-ples. The second stage was the cutting away of the breasts and some or all of the external sexual organs. Although the Skoptzy were persecuted in Russia, they persisted well into the twentieth century. The Bolsheviks outlawed them in the 1920s, but as late as 1970 around a hundred Skoptzy were found living in the Crimea. For a short time emigrating Skoptzy even took their creed to Canada.

Modern Castration

Castration can be good for you, adding an average of thirteen years to a man's lifespan (though it probably seems longer). In the past it was often cited as the solution for a variety of ailments. In France it was believed to cure leprosy, rheumatism, and gout, while in the United States it has been used to treat insanity and epilepsy. Sex offenders were often "cured" with castration, and sex criminals were sometimes given a choice between castration and a long jail term. In California between 1955 and 1975, 397 sex offenders chose castration over prison, and in Denmark 300 had the chop between 1929 and 1959. Today some violent criminals and sex offenders in Germany can opt for the knife in return for a reduced sentence, while chemical castration (the use of drugs to suppress testosterone output) is carried out in many U.S. prisons.

These days many individuals are castrated as a first step toward a sex change. Some men have a psychological compulsion to be castrated and try to do it themselves. A few use tools such as the Burdizzo clamp emasculator, used to castrate animals. A Burdizzo device doesn't break the skin but pinches the spermatic cord within the scrotum and severs it. As you can imagine, castrating yourself with one of these

PETS that suffer postneutering trauma can be supplied with artificial testicles made of plastic—they're known as Neuticles.

⚢ In 2001 transsexual Tammy Lynn Felbaum was found guilty of involuntary manslaughter after botching the DIY castration of her sixth husband.

♂ In the time of Alfred the Great a male servant who raped a female servant had to "make bote with his testicles," i.e., pay the fine with his nuts.

♂ To try and avoid a long prison sentence, a Texas child-abuser recently castrated himself by shooting off his testicles with a shotgun.

takes nerve. Doctors report that many self-emasculators try to do the act slowly and end up deforming the testicular cords rather than cutting them cleanly with a quick hard nip. According to one man who paid a back-street castrator to clamp him, the pain—though excruciating—lasted only twenty seconds per testicle.

For those who want their testicles surgically removed, it's a quick and easy job that will only set you back around $1,500. After a local anesthetic, two small incisions are made in the scrotum, then the testicles are popped out and cut away.

👣 Knife-Wielding Women

The most famous case of a man losing his penis to a woman is that of John Wayne Bobbit, but these occurrences are nothing new. One well-known Japanese case involved a woman called Sada Abe who killed her lover, Ishida, during a sex game and cut off his penis as a keepsake (the story was told in the 1976 film *In the Realm of the Senses*). More recently a Chinese housewife cut off her husband's penis with a knife. Apparently she hoped a bit of pruning would make it grow back bigger and better and restore their marriage. Two Thai wives made sure their husbands' severed penises would not be reattached; one threw it out of the window, where it was grabbed by a duck; the other tied the severed member to a helium balloon. In 1992 a German man auctioned off his penis at his local bar after it was cut off by his wife. For those interested, the going rate for a German penis was $40 and a bottle of schnapps.

LOSING IT (HERS)

Virginity

Female virginity has been a much-prized commodity throughout the ages, and today many cultures still take it very seriously. In fact, it's only recently that Turkey has tried to ban the forced virginity testing of unmarried girls. The practice is most common in Turkey's rural Sanliurfa district, where local custom demands that a bridegroom pay for a bride, rather than the bride's father providing a dowry. Bride prices range up to $40,000, but nonvirgins are worthless and girls with sullied reputations are sometimes killed by their relatives.

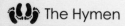 The Hymen

The most obvious sign of female virginity is the presence of a *hymen*. This is a fold of membranous tissue that partly, or almost wholly, covers the opening to the vagina. The presence of a hymen is an imperfect test of virginity, hymens often being rather fragile (according to one source approximately 11 percent of women have "weak" hymens), and boisterous pursuits like horse riding often lead to a premature rupture. In fact, respectable girls in ancient China were taught to walk very daintily, moving their feet a fraction of an inch at a time in case the action broke the hymen. On the other hand some hymens are as tough as old boots and may require surgery (a *hymenectomy*) to open them up.

Virginity Tests

Because hymens are unreliable virginity indicators, people have tried to devise other tests over the centuries. In South America the Incas believed that the breath of a virgin could ignite a smoldering fire (a nonvirgin would put the fire out). In Rome Vestal Virgins had to prove their virginity by carrying water in a sieve, a task that sounds impossible until you learn the trick that a well-greased sieve carries water very well. In the Jewish Talmud an odd method is outlined in which the woman under scrutiny stands over an open cask of wine. If the investigating rabbi could detect the smell of wine on the

---

In the USA 46% of youngsters are said to be against premarital sex.

One Northern California provirginity group is called Clean Teens.

Isaac Newton, Hans Christian Andersen, Immanuel Kant, and Lewis Carroll all died virgins.

The early British sex educator Marie Stopes was a virgin during her first five years of marriage.

woman's breath, she was not a virgin. Presumably it was thought that rising wine fumes would be able to waft up the vagina of the nonvirgin and travel through the body. In ancient China girls had to take the pigeon egg test: if the vagina was taut enough to resist the egg being pushed up it, the girl was a virgin; if it slipped inside, it was bad news. Another Chinese test involved wrapping a finger in white linen and rubbing the remains of the hymen (usually present as a ridge of tissue) until it bled. If this bloodstain could be removed from the cloth by washing, it was a sign the girl was not a virgin; the blood of a virgin was considered magical and could not be washed away. Chinese girls who lost their virginity (called *po xie* or "old shoes") were often expected to kill themselves. "Chastity Arches" were built where a young girl could go and hang herself and restore her family's good name.

In medieval Europe many supposedly infallible virgin tests were touted. Musical instruments were thought to play out of tune if a nonvirgin came near. Virgins were able to catch salmon with their bare hands, successfully hold on to the shaved, greased tail of a bull, pass through fires without burning, happily hold poisonous snakes, and were never molested by bees. Other tests highlighted the supposed supersensitivity of the virginal. A feather placed over a doorway would make any passing virgin blush, and a virgin was sure to

ZULU traditionalists in South Africa, who routinely test females for virginity, are trying to extend testing to males. Signs of a nonvirgin male are spraying while urinating, the lack of a visible penile vein, and looseness of the underside of the foreskin.

TODAY Chinese women in Hubei Province have to pay a fine of up to 2,000 yuan (in some cases the equivalent of a year's wages) if they are found to be nonvirgins. A medical examination is required before women can get official permission to marry, and this is where they are unmasked. According to a local official, the fines are necessary to stamp out "immoral trends."

detect a pea if it was placed under a mattress (though the fairy tale "The Princess and the Pea" cites this as a test of royalty rather than virginity).

Compared to the above, other medieval virginity tests sound almost scientific. In the thirteenth century Italian physicians believed that the urine of a virgin was always clear and sparkling, while the nonvirgin produced muddy urine that had been contaminated by blood and sperm. Other tests involved feeding a girl ground-up lily flowers, or washing jet stones in water and giving it to her to drink; in both cases an immediate desire to urinate would prove she was a nonvirgin. Another test required the girl to be fumigated with burning dock flowers—if she went pale, she was a virgin. Last but not least, the act of urination in a virgin was expected to make a high-pitched hissing sound.

In many cases virginity was often determined by a panel of experts. The girl would be laid out on a bed while matrons, midwives, and doctors prodded and probed her private parts. Sometimes the tightness of the vaginal canal was tested with a wax penis. As contemporary commentators pointed out, if the girl was a virgin before the examination, she certainly wasn't one afterward.

👣 Blood Virgins

Throughout much of recorded history people have relied on bleeding to determine virginity. If the bride stained the sheets on her wedding night, all was well. If not, there could be trouble. In ancient China the father of the bride often had to sign a contract assuring his daughter's virginity and was liable to a hefty fine if it proved otherwise. The fact that all had not gone well was usually announced on the third day after the wedding, when the married couple traditionally visited the bride's parents for a feast. A roast suckling pig was usually taken as a gift, but if the pig was presented with its tail or ears cut off, it was a sign that the bride's honor was suspect. Not surprisingly a mutilated pig at the dinner table was a source of great shame. As a last resort the bride's parents might demand a "lemon test." It was believed that some girls had white vir-

---

THE chastity belt is thought to have been invented in the Middle East and imported to medieval Italy, where it became known as the "Florentine Girdle." The oldest known model in existence dates back to 1388 and is displayed in the armory of the Doges' Palace in Venice. It belonged to Francesco II, ruler of Padua, who required his wife to wear it constantly in his absence. Padded with leather, the belt covers the pubic region and is equipped with razor-sharp teeth at each orifice.

Other surviving belts look far too bulky to have been worn for extended periods. Some were probably put on women to save them from rape during long journeys; others were used on female corpses to stop their bodies from being despoiled.

♂ A Sicilian father once tried to insure his daughter's virginity at Lloyd's of London.

♀ Cleopatra reputedly lost her virginity at age twelve.

♀ In Rome the Vestal Virgins (guardians of the eternal flame of the goddess Vesta) were recruited at age ten and were not allowed to marry till they were forty.

ginal blood that couldn't be detected on a sheet; only rubbing the linen with lemon juice could make it visible.

The bloodied bedsheet has been used since biblical times. In Deuteronomy it states that, in case of disputes, a bloodied blanket should be produced for the inspection of the city's elders. In the case of a false accusation, the father of the bride was paid a hundred shekels of silver; if the accusation was upheld, the daughter was stoned to death at her father's doorway, "because she hath wrought folly in Israel, to play the whore in her father's house."

This quaint tradition is still strong in many Middle Eastern countries. In rural Morocco a marriage is not considered legal unless there's a public showing of the sheet, and it's said that in Iraq, Baghdad hotels often have their sheets stolen by honeymooners so they can take them home to show their older, more traditionally minded relatives. In the past some Indian Muslims even insisted on public defloration to show the bride was pure.

If there were concerns that the bride wasn't going to put on a sufficiently bloody display, there were ways to solve the problem. Some scams involved tying off a portion of dove's intestine, filling it with blood, and pushing it up the vagina.

Others did the same with a fish bladder or a small sponge. Some recommended putting powdered glass in the vagina, while others used leeches. In this case the leech would be applied to the mouth of the vagina before the wedding night. The leech's bite would form a scab, which would then be rubbed off during sex to produce a satisfactory flow. In other cases women with regular cycles were able to time the wedding so it coincided with menstruation.

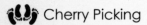 ## Cherry Picking

In some cultures the defloration of a bride was seen as a hazardous business best left to someone else. Contact with a virgin's blood was thought to lead to impotence; many societies believed there was a link between virginal blood and taboo menstrual blood.

To prevent a bridegroom's penis from coming into contact with potentially harmful female blood, a number of measures were adopted. The Phoenicians had their daughters deflowered by a servant before the wedding. In ancient Greece virgins were often deflowered in a temple by a priest using an artificial phallus made of ivory, stone, or metal. The priest, because of his heavenly connections, was thought to be immune to the ill effects of virginal blood. Even in recent times Buddhist priests in Cambodia have been called upon to deflower local virgins. In some cultures kings and lords were also held to be immune from potential ill effects. The kings of Mesopotamia apparently found defloration so onerous, they charged for the service and forbade any nonpayer from marrying.

In ancient Rome brides sat on the organ of Priapus, a fertility god whose statues all had huge erections. Some believe

NOT all cultures have valued premarital chastity. The Quito Indians of Ecuador and the men of Tibet never married a virgin if they could help it, girls having numerous partners before they married. In Tibet a group of foreigners arriving near a village would be approached by local women offering their daughters as bedmates. Girls would be given a trinket or token by each of their male lovers, and these would be displayed on a necklace. Any respectable young woman was expected to have collected a score of these trophies before she could consider herself a marriage prospect. By contrast, a married woman was expected to be absolutely faithful, it being considered a grave offense to touch another man's wife.

the bride sat astride the penis as a symbolic fertility rite; others suggest that the statue's organ was used to break the maidenhead.

In the Samoan Islands a bridegroom would avoid trouble by carrying out the defloration in public by using two fingers of his right hand. This tradition did not apply to the bride of a chief, however—she was deflowered with the help of a shark's tooth.

In other cultures a random male was chosen from the wedding guests to deflower the bride, as it was thought a disinterested stranger would be able to shake off any resulting bad luck more easily than the husband. The inhabitants of the Marquesas Islands took this a step further and obliged all the male members of the wedding party to have sex with the bride—bad luck was shared out and diminished. The same custom was observed by the ancient Nasamonians, mentioned by Herodotus.

In ancient Peru the task of defloration was left to the

bride's mother or an older female relative, while in other primitive societies it was the father's job. This superstition lasted
until recent times. Some Egyptian husbands were paying
other men to deflower their wives well into the twentieth
century.

Born-Again Virgins

Apart from blood, another supposed proof of virginity was the
tightness of the vagina. So if necessary, a slack vagina could
be tightened with the help of astringents. The steam from
boiling vinegar was said to be good, while acorns, myrrh,
roses, and Cyprus nuts have all been included in potions. An
eleventh-century recipe called for sugar, egg white, and alum
to be put in a bath. To this was added rainwater in which pennyroyal and calamint had been boiled down. This solution
was then used to bathe the genitals.

An elaborate procedure was recommended by the
thirteenth-century physician Albert the Great. According to
Albert, you took half an ounce of turpentine, a similar quantity
of milk, asparagus sap, and a quarter of an ounce of rock
alum and steeped it in lemon juice or the juice of green apples. Fresh egg white and some oatmeal were added. The
mass was then mixed and rolled into a ball that was inserted
into the vagina, which had previously been syringed with
goat's milk and rubbed with an ointment made from white
wine. After four or five repetitions you were as good as new.
Astringent preparations are still available today—one brand
is known as China Shrink Cream.

A more drastic method of recovering your virginity is
through surgery. Hymen reconstruction is popular in many
parts of the world. In Japan one estimate puts the number of

ACCORDING to the Koran, men who get to Paradise enjoy seventy-two "bashful dark-eyed virgins as chaste as ostrich eggs with complexions like rubies and pearls." The supply of virgins is endless, as their hymens regrow overnight.

operations performed annually at around thirty-five thousand. The Japanese technique involves making a fake hymen out of sheep gut, but this membrane dissolves after a month, so it has to be done a few weeks before the honeymoon.

Many Muslim girls opt for surgical help, as the alternative is often a grisly death at the hands of outraged relatives. A recent report claimed that this sort of surgery had reduced the revenge murder of Egyptian women by 80 percent over the past ten years. Only about 40 percent of women bleed when they're deflowered, so even genuine virgins will sometimes ask for surgery to guarantee they'll put on a good show. Typically this sort of surgery involves threading a suture through the remains of the hymen (a ridge of tissue). The suture is then pulled tight, closing the vagina like a drawstring bag but leaving a three-quarter-inch opening. On penetration the suture often breaks with a satisfying *pop!* If this won't suffice, a more elaborate surgical technique involves the creation of an artificial hymen out of a strip of tissue from the posterior vaginal wall.

Defloration Mania

Whereas most virgins have been valued as chaste brides, some cultures have sought out virgin females for other reasons. For centuries a European superstition held that intercourse with a

TO advertise the arrival of a virgin, continental brothels used to hang a laurel wreath outside the front door.

virgin was a surefire cure for venereal disease. One rural Scottish doctor in the early 1900s believed that most of the sexual attacks on young children he came across were committed by sufferers of VD, and in modern South Africa there have been many recent instances of child rapes carried out by men seeking protection from, or a cure for, HIV.

Virgins have also been considered rejuvenating. In China it was thought that sex with a virgin could add two years to your life. Many rich men paid good money to deflower a virgin, some getting through hundreds a year. This was an expensive business; some men turned the act into a huge event that might cost as much as a regular wedding.

Virgins were also popular among brothel patrons in the West—the possession of a maiden was said to be the height of sexual titillation. The journalist W. T. Stead (1849–1912) wrote a series of articles called "The Maiden Tribute of Modern Babylon" in which he investigated the London virgin trade. In Stead's case a thirteen-year-old London slum-dweller was bought from her drunken parents for a sovereign by a brothel-keeper. She was then sold on to a procuress for £5 (£3 down and the other £2 on proof of virginity), and then to Stead for £20. Stead exposed the scandal, and partly as a result of his efforts, the age of consent was raised from thirteen to sixteen in 1885.

Not all virgins were young innocent girls. In 1881 a sixteen-year-old sold her own virginity and, astounded at the money to be made, started recruiting virgins herself. Most of her finds were shopgirls, governesses, cooks, nursemaids, and servants whom she befriended in London parks. Many of these young women were happy to sell their virginity as long as the price was right.

In Victorian London the trade in virgins became so extensive that a glut in the market developed. In the early nineteenth century a man could pay £100 for a virgin, but by the 1880s the price had dropped to £5. This excess probably had a lot to do with a decline in quality control. One brothel-keeper estimated that a girl's virginity could be sold as many as five times before she had to give up the charade.

PERFORMANCE ENHANCEMENT

Aphrodisiacs

Impotence has many causes, but most often it's simply a result of old age, poor health, or tiredness. Some have tried to solve the problem with rest cures, adventurous sex play, or even a change of partner. More have resorted to aphrodisiacs, and over the centuries innumerable, often unpleasant, substances have been swallowed to try and revive a lagging libido. To bolster confidence in their effectiveness, some aphrodisiacs have been given encouraging names, a good example being the nineteenth-century French "Corpse Reviver." One of the oddest aphrodisiac names is the "Bald Chicken Drug": according to Chinese legend, the drug turned an aged gentleman into a veritable sex machine, but his wife's privates were so sore she was unable to sit down. To end her misery, the woman threw the potion out of the window, where it was swallowed by a cockerel. The cock then jumped on the near-

> 👫 IN the past impotence could affect more than your love life. In Europe one of the few accepted reasons for divorce was nonconsummation. A husband accused of impotence often had to prove himself by getting an erection in front of witnesses. In 1572 Baron Charles de Quellenec was divorced after failing to produce an erection in court, but it was more usual for a couple to be put in bed together and the woman to be examined for signs of penetration afterward.

est hen and started having frantic sex, pecking at her head as he did so. By the time the cock was finished, the hen was completely bald—hence the name.

👣 Fruit and Veg

In many cultures phallic-shaped foods like mandrake roots, bananas, cucumbers, zucchini, and carrots are regarded as aphrodisiacs. A recent American study has suggested that women are aroused by the smell of cucumbers. Asparagus tips also fall into this phallic category, and in nineteenth-century France a bridegroom was expected to eat large quantities of it at his wedding feast. Avocados also have a suggestive shape, this time of testicles—which is what the Aztec name for the plant, *ahuacatl,* actually means. They were considered so powerful, they were off limits to virgins. The Spanish missionaries were also aware of the resemblance and would not let the trees grow on church grounds.

Fruits like pomegranates, figs, and quinces have a reputation for fertility because they contain many seeds. In ancient Rome nuts were fertility symbols, and Roman newlyweds were pelted with walnuts to ensure fruitfulness. Pine nuts (actually pine seeds) were considered aphrodisiacs by the ancient Greeks, and an old Arabic sex manual recommends a concoction of honey, twenty almonds, and a hundred pine nuts to be taken three nights in a row.

Despite its famously odoriferous effects, garlic has been used as an aphrodisiac all over the world. Onions are also widely touted in this respect, especially in the Middle East. The onion's reputation was such that celibate Egyptian priests tried to avoid it altogether.

Other fruits and vegetables have less obvious qualifications as aphrodisiacs. Fennel was considered an aphrodisiac by the Hindus and ancient Greeks; one Hindi recipe consisted of a mixture of fennel juice, honey, clarified butter, sugar, and licorice. Alternatively, fennel soup is said to do the job. Many people have considered celery to be an aphrodisiac, and it has recently been found to contain the male hormone androsterone.

The ugly artichoke is a surprising choice as an aphrodisiac, but it has been very popular, especially in France. Street sellers would tempt customers with the cry, "Artichokes! Artichokes! Heats the body and the spirit! Heats the genitals!"

Other unlikely aphrodisiacs are the turnip (recommended by the Iranians) and the sweet potato (popular in sixteenth-century Europe). In the latter case the potato was a recently introduced New World novelty. Most of these American imports seem to have been touted as aphrodisiacs, perhaps to encourage people to try them. The tomato was another new arrival, though its alternative name "love apple" is probably due to a misunderstanding. The theory is that the first tomatoes to reach Italy arrived via Spain and were called *pomo dei Mori* ("apple of the Moors"), but were then mistranslated into French as *pomme d'amour* ("apple of love").

Beans might not appear sexy, but they have a centuries-old reputation as aphrodisiacs. The ancient Greeks thought beans resembled the shape of immature fetuses, and ever since they've had associations with fertility, so much so that nuns in the early Christian Church were forbidden to eat them. For many years it was also believed that gassy foods like beans were responsible for lustfulness in men, as erections were thought to be the result of a strange pneumatic effect.

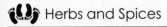 ## Herbs and Spices

Hot spices such as ginger and pepper had a reputation for "heating the blood." Ginger was either rubbed on the genitals or taken internally; an Indian recipe mixed ginger with honey and half-boiled eggs. Even gingerbread men might have been aphrodisiacs—the original gingerbread men were made as love charms to help girls find a husband.

Other herbs and spices with a sexy reputation are chiles, cardamom (mixed with boiled milk and honey), saffron, cinnamon, cloves, and nutmeg (mixed with honey and half-boiled eggs). Basil is also meant to be potent. In Haiti voodoo lore claims basil is a gift from the love goddess Erzulie, and it turns up in many local aphrodisiac recipes.

Vanilla is supposedly a powerful aphrodisiac. The name *vanilla* is derived from the Latin for "vagina"—Spanish explorers noted the resemblance between the vanilla bean and the female organ. It seems to do the job—the sex researcher Havelock Ellis once visited a vanilla processing factory and found that all the men had permanent erections.

In South America vanilla was often drunk with chocolate, yet another New World aphrodisiac. Montezuma is said to have drunk fifty cups of chocolate and vanilla before tackling his huge harem.

Another South American aphrodisiac is *quebracho* (sometimes known as Paraguay tea or South American holly), similar to the *yohimbe* tree found in West and Central Africa. Both are said to increase blood flow to the genitalia in men and women and may help stimulate the nerves responsible for erections. Curiously, yohimbe is sometimes used to treat angina, the heart condition that Viagra was invented to help. Another tree, *ginkgo*, is also said to be a great erection booster.

Honey

Honey has a worldwide reputation as an aphrodisiac, probably due to the energy rush it produces. Honey features in many marriage customs around the world, perhaps the most famous being the "honeymoon." This Anglo-Saxon custom required a newlywed couple to drink honey-rich mead for a lunar month to promote fertility.

Truffles

Truffles are a famous aphrodisiac, and it's been discovered they give off chemicals that are similar to human sex hormones. The same hormones are given off by pigs, which is why they're so good at tracking them down. Both Louis XV of France and George IV of England thought very highly of truffles; Louis demanded that his mistress, Madame de Pompadour, keep herself permanently aroused by eating truffles, vanilla, and celery.

Booze

Alcoholic beverages have a two-edged reputation as aphrodisiacs—a little alcohol strips away inhibitions, but too much makes you incapable. Some beers are recommended as aphrodisiacs (usually by brewers) as is the Japanese rice wine, sake. Two liqueurs that have also been touted as knicker-droppers are Green Chartreuse and Benedictine. Both were invented by monks.

Seafood

The ancient Greeks regarded mussels and crabs as aphrodisiacs, and almost all seafood is considered good for you in

IN the past many doctors tried to restore the sex drive with animal transplants. In 1889 the French doctor Charles Brown-Séquard injected himself with ground-up extracts of dog and guinea pig testicles, and in the 1920s and '30s the Russian doctor Serge Voronoff transplanted tissue from chimpanzee and baboon testicles into human patients. Monkey ovary transplants were even tried on women to treat menopause. These operations grew so popular that the supply of chimps and baboons started to dry up. Similar operations were carried out in America by the famous quack Dr. John Brinkley. In 1918 a farmer called Stittsworth came to Brinkley to be treated for impotence, and Brinkley, aware of the European experiments, suggested an implant of goat testicle tissue. The operation was declared a success when the farmer later fathered a son (named Billy). Brinkley went on to charge $750 for goat testicles and $5,000 for human ones (acquired from death row prisoners). Though often denounced as a charlatan, he died a wealthy man.

this respect, caviar in particular. Oysters are famous aphrodisiacs (at his peak Casanova ate fifty oysters a day), though this might be due to their resemblance to the female sex organs. Eels are another popular aphrodisiac worldwide; the Japanese sushi dish *unagi* (raw sea eel) is famous for putting lead in your pencil. Like certain vegetables, the eel's reputation probably hangs on its phallic appearance. The sea slug is another phallic-shaped animal touted as an aphrodisiac; it's known to Italian fishermen as "sea Priapus."

 ## Meat

Although all meat has a reputation for "inflaming the lust," some parts of the animal were considered better than others. In Algeria and Morocco lions' testicles were said to be effective, while in Europe the testicles of bulls and rams have been popular. Other animal recipes had a more "magical" aspect to them. In China the bones, liver, fat, and penis of the tiger are considered very beneficial, as are the ground horns of deer and rhino. In the latter cases the benefit was purely symbolic—practitioners hoped to develop a "horn" as powerful as the one they'd just eaten.

So What Makes a Good Aphrodisiac?

Meat probably works as an aphrodisiac because of its high protein content. After eating meat, amino acids are released in the bloodstream, and these heighten the senses and increase activity. In the past many people had low-protein diets, so a sudden boost of amino acids did their love lives a world of good. It's perhaps no coincidence that many aphrodisiac recipes incorporate high-protein foods (such as milk, fish, meat, or beans), often in combination with an energy source like honey or fat. (A mixture of camel's milk and honey was popular in the Middle East.)

Apart from being protein-rich, many seafoods have an additional benefit in that they also contain many of the minerals (phosphorus, iodine, and zinc) necessary for a happy sex life. Eggs are also high in protein and as an added bonus contain choline, an important precursor to neurotransmitters that boost your nervous system. Eggs also contain lecithin, a component of sperm. Many male porn stars dose themselves with lecithin in the form of eggs or lecithin supplements to increase sperm production and make sure their "money shot" "makes a splash."

 ## Spanish Fly

The most notorious of all aphrodisiacs must be the blister beetle (better known as Spanish fly), an insect found in southern Europe. The effects of Spanish fly were known to the Romans, but it was largely forgotten in Europe until the eighteenth century. Spanish fly is actually very toxic—as little as .05 ounce of powdered beetle can kill you. In 1758 a Frenchman from Caderousse was killed when his wife gave him Spanish fly to try and cure a fever. According to the doctor's report the man had a permanent erection and tried to mount his wife forty times in one night. The patient was wrapped in vinegar-soaked sheets to try and calm him down, but he soon died. Another nineteenth-century case involved a group of French soldiers in North Africa who developed excruciating erections after eating frogs' legs. It was later discovered the frogs had been feeding on blister beetles.

Blister beetles contain a substance called *cantharidin,* an extremely caustic chemical often used to burn off warts. If swallowed, cantharidin passes through the kidneys and irritates the lining of the urethra. Blood flow to the region increases, often resulting in prolonged painful erections. Similar cantharidin-rich beetles are found worldwide. In southern Africa these beetles are used in potions called *vuka-vuka* (meaning "wake up, wake up") and *squirrel's jump* (the local squirrels being notoriously randy).

In India another insect-based technique involved stripping the irritating bristles off poisonous caterpillars and rubbing them on to the penis to make it swell.

Viagra

Viagra is the sex wonder-drug of the twenty-first century. According to some figures, over 80 percent of Viagra users notice an improvement in their erections. Originally the drug was developed to help angina sufferers by increasing the blood supply to the heart, but its aphrodisiac qualities soon stuck out a mile. Viagra acts by relaxing certain tissues in the penis, allowing a greater flow of blood. More blood enters than leaves, so the penis fills, and an erection develops. The drug has even been shown to have sexual benefits when prescribed for women by increasing the blood supply to the vagina. It's not all good news, however—an FDA report has recorded a number of minor but unsexy Viagra side effects, including hiccups, abnormal hair growth, and belching.

Magic

In ancient Rome powdered frog bones were thought to be an excellent aphrodisiac, while wearing the right testicle of a

AN old Hindu charm for prolonging an erection involved making a candle out of frog's fat. Once it was lit, the erection was meant to last as long as the candle.

donkey on your bracelet was meant to guarantee fertility. In Java it was customary to hang a pair of crocodile testicles over the bed of an old man marrying a young girl. Semen was a popular ingredient in many love potions and aphrodisiacs.

One Chinese aphrodisiac consisted of deer blood, human semen, and hawk excrement. Putting semen in food was also a love charm. In 1012 a German bishop wrote out a list of banned love charms that included sperm swallowing, adding semen to food, kneading bread with your naked buttocks, and putting menstrual blood in food and drink. Some charms survived until relatively recently. In the late nineteenth century it was not uncommon for a French peasant woman to preserve her daughter's placenta so it could be used in later years as part of a love potion.

Some spells were extremely grisly. In Ireland one charm was to cut a strip of skin from a man buried for seven days, then tie it to the leg or arm of a sleeping lover. Another Irish recipe recommended eating the brains of a murdered man as a cure for impotence. Some magical cures involved living people. In India barren women would travel for miles to kiss or touch the penis of a "potent" guru. If all else fails, try a Barry White album—it never fails.

Anti-aphrodisiacs

While there were many magical cures for impotence, some people had a stock of charms to do exactly the opposite. In ancient Egypt a favorite curse of soothsayers was to cause a man's virility to "melt away before his partner." One European charm required a sprig of the herb vervain to be put under a man's pillow. This, apparently, made it impossible for him to have an erection for seven days.

In the past many men who lost their virility assumed the local witch was responsible. Some believed that witches could actually steal penises, which were then kept in boxes or baskets, where they hopped around like chickens pecking on grain. One story from seventeenth-century Scotland tells how a man had his penis "magicked away" and asked the local witch how to get it back. The witch told him to climb a tree, where he'd find a nest full of them. The man could choose any one he wanted except the largest, which belonged to the parish priest.

Many people, especially the religious, have looked for ways to reduce desire. The Roman writer Pliny the Elder (A.D. 23–79) had many anti-aphrodisiacs up his sleeve, including liniments made out of mouse dung and snail excrement, and pigeon droppings mixed with oil and wine. Another charm required blood from a black bull's tick to be rubbed into a woman's loins. Years later the physician of Pope John XXI

IN medieval Germany it was thought a woman could destroy a man's love for her by putting some of her feces in his shoe. Alternatively it was thought a young bride could ensure her husband's love by peeing in his coffee.

(1276–77) said that excessive lust could be cured by tying hemlock to a man's testicles or bathing them in camphor oil. Another cure of this period was to eat lily roots, a remedy used by many monks and nuns.

More recently, the entire breakfast cereal industry was founded in an attempt to smother the sex drive. Dr. John Harvey Kellogg (whose brother started the famous cornflake company) developed cereals as bland vegetarian alternatives to the more inflaming bacon and eggs. Kellogg was so keen on his cereals, he recommended taking them as an enema if they couldn't be eaten. In the same way, the Graham cracker was originally invented by Sylvester Graham (1794–1851) as a bland, unspicy anti-aphrodisiac.

Other anti-aphrodisiacs are thought to include licorice, coffee, and marijuana, but there is conflicting evidence. In the case of coffee it's thought that small quantities act as a stimulant but too much depresses the sex drive, though in one survey it was discovered that coffee drinkers were almost twice as likely to describe themselves as sexually active as nondrinkers. Licorice also has a mixed press. The results of one study suggested that licorice increased penile blood flow, while another clinical trial found that 8.8 ounces of licorice a day reduced male testosterone levels by 44 percent. It also contains small amounts of estrogen, which would tend to reduce the sex drive. With regard to marijuana, a little strips away inhibitions, while too much plays havoc with testosterone levels. Fat, too, is an anti-aphrodisiac. A high-fat diet is a major cause of impotence, high cholesterol levels being one of the main causes of penile erectile dysfunction.

ON THE JOB

Methods, Manuals, and Marital Aids

👣 Sex Manuals

The earliest sex manuals were written by the Chinese over five thousand years ago. One of the first was *Hsuan Nu Ching* or *Manual of Lady Mystery*, which offered advice to the mythical Yellow Emperor. These works often combined mysticism with medicine, the Taoists of the period believing that sex was health-giving and cultivated yin-yang harmony. Many had long-winded titles like *The Explanation of the Meaning of the Cultivation of Truth, by the Great Immortal of the Purple-Gold Splendour*, or *The True Classic of the Complete Union, by All-Assisting Lord Ch'n-Yang*. Others were short and to the point: *Visiting the Fairy Cave*, *Prayer-Cushions of the Flesh,* and *The Handbook of Sex for the Plain Girl*.

Other sex manuals followed. Two of the best known were the Indian *Kama Sutra of Vatsayayana* (written around A.D. 100)

THE males of the island of Tikopia, near the Solomons, aren't allowed to touch any genitals, even their own. Penetration is entirely handled by the females.

and the *Ananga Ranga*, written in the sixteenth century by the poet Kalyan Mall. Another sixteenth-century work was *The Perfumed Garden* by Shaykh Umar ibn Muhammed al-Nefzawi, a nobleman living in Tunis who started the book as a time-consuming exercise to try and avoid a stint in the civil service.

Many of these books provided step-by-step instructions and useful tips. In Japan and China they were sometimes known as *pillow books, bride books*, and *trunk bottoms* and were often placed in young women's dowry boxes for their instruction.

In Europe one of the most famous early sex manuals was Pietro Aretino's *I Modi* (*The Ways*) also known as *Aretino's Postures* (see Chapter 12), a sixteenth-century work describing sixteen basic sexual positions. Another famous sex education book was *Aristotle's Masterpiece,* a seventeenth-century work that was reprinted innumerable times. Aristotle certainly didn't write it, and no one knows who did or even where it was first printed. The *Masterpiece* has been described as a "midwives' handbook" and contains useful information on "the use and action of the genitals" and "advice to both sexes in the act of copulation." This work remained a popular reference book into Victorian times, when it was often sold via mail order.

The nineteenth century saw sex manuals aimed at women containing contraceptive advice. Early examples were *Every Woman's Book,* written in Britain in the 1820s, and *Physical,*

Sexual and Natural Religion, written in 1855 by George Drysdale, a medical student from Edinburgh. Other titles followed, for example, *Plain Facts for Old and Young: Embracing the Natural History and Hygiene of Organic Life* (1886), *What a Woman of Forty-Five Ought to Know* (1902), and in 1918 *Married Love,* penned by Dr. Marie Stopes while she was still a virgin. Since then the bookshelves have been full of them: *Ideal Marriage* (1929); *Love Without Fear* (1940); *Living with a Husband and Liking It* (1942); *Everything You Always Wanted to Know about Sex—But Were Afraid to Ask* (1969); and in 1972, *The Joy of Sex.* Many have been best-sellers—*The Joy of Sex* has sold over 12 million copies in twenty-four languages.

Red-Hot Lovers

Fatafehi Paulah, king of Tonga from 1770 to 1784, had the job of deflowering every virgin on the island. He claimed to have eight to ten women a day, bringing his total to over 37,800. The Saudi king Ibn-Saud (1880–1953) is said to have had sex with three different women every night, making his lifetime total 20,000, a figure claimed to be equaled by basketball star Wilt Chamberlain (1936–2000). The porn star John Holmes (1944–88) racked up 14,000 conquests on and off the screen in his forty-four years, while King Edward VII (1841–1910) got through only 7,800 (estimating three different women a week for fifty years). King George IV (1762–1830) is thought to have had at least 7,000 lovers, as he took a lock of hair from each conquest and 7,000 hair-filled envelopes were found amongst his possessions after he died.

Julia the Elder (39 B.C.–A.D. 14), daughter of the Roman Emperor Augustus, is thought to have had 80,000 men. She started her exploits in childhood and would reputedly offer herself to anybody, often dragging men off the streets. The eighteenth-century French actress Mlle. Dubois kept a catalog of all her lovers over a twenty-year period. After she died, the final count was 16,527, roughly three a day. Valeria Messalina (A.D. 22–48), wife of the Roman Emperor Claudius, is said to have had around 8,000 lovers, once turning a palace bedroom into a brothel. On one occasion she challenged a famous prostitute to a sex contest and won, taking on twenty-five men in twenty-four hours.

Though not such high-scorers in the sexual partner stakes, there are others who deserve a mention for their amatory pursuits. Perhaps the best-known lover is Giovanni Giacomo Casanova (1725–98). This Venetian-born adventurer trained as a priest but was thrown out of school for bad conduct. He later became a secretary, a soldier, an alchemist, a gambler, a violinist, a lottery director, and a spy, finally ending up as a librarian. His diaries reveal that he made love to over 132 women, the youngest eleven and the oldest fifty, of whom thirty-one were virgins. He seems to have had remarkable stamina, once giving a woman fourteen orgasms with one erection.

A famous Spanish seducer was Don Juan, but he is entirely fictitious; the character emerged from a Spanish folk legend that became popular in the seventeenth century. His story was immortalized by the writer Molière in 1665 in the play *Don Juan* and later by Mozart in the opera *Don Giovanni* (1787). According to the legend, Don Juan (a famous lover with over a thousand conquests) tries to seduce a young beauty when he is discovered by her father. The two fight a duel, and the father is killed. Don Juan later visits the father's tomb and contemptuously invites the dead man to dinner.

This grim joke backfires, however, when the father's funerary statue comes to life and, taking hold of Don Juan with an icy grip, leads him off to hell.

It's not certain how many lovers Mae West (1893–1980) had, but she started working in vaudeville at the age of five, and her doting mother seems to have encouraged her natural promiscuity from an early age. Old age didn't slow her down, and Mae was demanding daily sex well into her sixties. Stamina seems to have been a key requirement for a West lover; in her 1959 autobiography *Goodness Had Nothing to Do With It,* she wrote that she and a beau named Ted once made love for fifteen consecutive hours.

Anaïs Nin (1903–77) was cast in the same mold as Mae, though she was a less earthy, more highbrow version. Anaïs was born in Paris, then moved to America in 1914. She studied as a dancer and worked as a model before marrying a New York banker in 1923. In 1935 she returned to France and self-published erotic literature based on her own sexual adventures. She had numerous sex partners of both sexes, including Henry Miller and his wife, June. She became best known for her erotic diaries and the books *The Delta of Venus* and *The Little Birds*.

Oral Sex

Oral sex comes in two main variants: fellatio (for him) and cunnilingus (for her). Cunnilingus is the probing of the vagina (in Latin *cunnus*) with the tongue, while licking the vagina should more properly be called *cunnilinctus*. In the same way some people refer to fellatio as *penilinctus*. Two additional varieties on oral sex are *anilinctus* and *anilingus*, which are,

> In a Victorian book of 1897 it was said that cunnilingus could give a husband cancer of the tongue and result in the death of his wife.
>
> In ancient China oral sex was called "mouth music."
>
> Fellatio is illegal in fifteen U.S. states.
>
> Cleopatra and Eva Perón were both famous for their blow jobs. Eva was said to be "good on her knees," while the Greeks called Cleopatra *Meriochane,* "the Gaper."

respectively, the licking and probing of the anus. Another curious variant is *oculolinctus*: eyeball licking.

Fellatio is derived from the Latin *fellatus,* "to suck," and a woman well versed in the art was known as a *fellatrice*.

For Him—*Fellatio*

Fellatio has a long history, the first recorded blow job occurring in ancient Egypt. According to legend, the god Osiris was cut into pieces by his brother, who then threw the bits in a river. Most of him was reassembled by his sister Isis, but the missing penis had to be replaced by a clay one. Isis then blew life back into Osiris via his new earthenware member.

The Chinese called fellatio "playing the jade flute," and the Greeks also used "flute playing" as a euphemism. The Indian *Kama Sutra* devotes a whole chapter to the art, which it called *auparishtaka* or "oral congress," other terms being *mukhamethuna* ("oral churning") and *ambarchusi* ("mango-fruit sucking"). According to the *Sutra,* everyone was at it; male servants did it with their masters, some masters did it with each other, and barbershops had eunuch shampooists who paid more attention to your crotch than your split ends.

In Rome fellatio seems to have had many fans. The Roman poet Martial told an aging friend that to revive his member, he should "gain but the heights" rather than "plague in vain unhappy vulvas and posteriors." In some cases fellatio was levied as an on-the-spot fine for minor transgressions such as petty theft. In these instances the culprits fell on their knees, and the standing Roman thrust his penis into their mouth, a practice known as *irrumatio*.

Although not approved of by the Koran, fellatio has been widely practiced in North Africa and the Middle East. Many local connoisseurs believed that fellatio (known as *qerdz*) was far more pleasurable than vaginal or anal sex, and many brothels specialized in the practice.

👣 Fellatio Technique

There are two main methods of fellatio: the shallow suck, where the penis is held in the mouth, and the more penetrative version sometimes known as "deep throat." The former might be accompanied by a technique known as the "Shirley Temple," where the penis is licked as if it were a lollipop. The deep throat technique is trickier, as the throat bends almost 90 degrees behind the tongue. A way of getting around this is

IN seventeenth-century China an enterprising craftsman built a "Hall of Joyful Buddhas" as a sex education theme park. Here models of male and female Buddhas with moving parts demonstrated the various lovemaking positions for the sons and daughters of the nobility.

IN some cultures fellatio is disdained, as the mouth is regarded as a sacred object that should not be sullied. Many sub-Saharan African tribes feel this way, as do the Inuit, who even rub noses rather than involve the mouth in any oral intimacy.

IN one New Guinea tribe a male initiation ritual required the young men of the tribe to perform fellatio on the tribe's warriors. In this case the swallowed sperm was meant to pass on the virility and power of the elders.

for the oral partner to lie on a bed with their head bent back over the edge of the mattress. In this position the mouth and throat are almost in line, and full penetration can be achieved. According to some, the sensation is heightened if the oral partner makes swallowing motions. This deep penetration can overcome the body's natural gag reflex, as it bypasses the sensory nerves that trigger it. Some practitioners train themselves to ignore the reflex by sticking a finger or toothbrush down their throat. Needless to say, this method does carry the risk of suffocation if carried to excess. Alternatively some might only want minimal penetration, in which case a fist, or fingers, wrapped around the base of the shaft limits the amount of intrusion. One oral technique also involves the testicles; here the active partner takes the testicles in their mouth and makes a humming sound.

With regard to semen swallowing, the best advice seems to be to swallow it quickly if you're going to swallow at all. The less time it's in the mouth, the less the taste. One way to drown out unpleasant flavors altogether is to rinse the mouth with crème de menthe beforehand. Not only does this neutralize nasty flavors, but the mintiness in the liqueur is said to make the penis supersensitive.

👣 For Her—*Cunnilingus*

Like fellatio, cunnilingus has been around a long time. The *Kama Sutra* mentions it as a habit of harem women, and the T'ang empress Wu Hu (683–705) was apparently so fond of it she demanded that visiting dignitaries bow before her to "lick the lotus stem."

Regarding technique, most sources recommend avoiding the clitoris in the early stages, as it is often too sensitive to take direct stimulation. Some also recommend mixing tongue action with manual stimulation of the G-spot and anus. The *mons pubis* (the mound at the top of the vaginal opening) also responds to massaging. The usual position for the active partner is between the female's legs, but a side-on position is also useful, as it allows the hands easy access to the breasts and vagina. Alternatively the woman can squat on her partner's face and help stimulate herself with pelvic thrusts.

⚢ A recent survey found that 66% of women have faked an orgasm.

♀ In seventeenth-century France female sexual excitement was sometimes considered a sign of mental illness.

⚢ In Japanese the word for orgasm translates as "die and go to heaven."

♂ A recent study found that only 1% of heart attacks are triggered by sex.

ORAL condoms called Dental Dams have been invented to prevent the spread of diseases from vagina to mouth and vice versa.
They resemble a condom split lengthways but few people use them as the
chances of catching anything nasty this way are said to be remote.

Some women enjoy the sensation of being "filled," and in
these cases oral sex can be combined with a dildo or
vibrator.

The quality of tongue action is an important factor. A variety of motions and textures seems to be the key to success.
One handy hint is to probe the vagina with the letters of the
alphabet, the tongue tracing out an "A" shape, then a "B,"
etc. Although it sounds eccentric, this technique is said to be
effective as it teases the area with a regular but subtly changing rhythm. If the tongue tires, the area can be brushed with
the lips.

A technique similar to the crème de menthe method mentioned earlier is to insert a presucked menthol or mint cough
drop into the vagina during oral sex. This has the advantage
of masking any unpleasant tastes and odors, and like crème
de menthe, the cough drop causes a tingling sensation.
Spectacularly titillating results are said to be had with Altoids,
a brand of super-strong peppermints. Those with a sweet
tooth can also try candy, always remembering that sugar can
feed any existing yeast infections.

Apart from sweets, there are numerous substances on the
market designed to improve vaginal flavors, such as Kama
Sutra Honey Dust; alternatively, honey or whipped cream are
good stand-ins.

Getting It On

The humorist Gershon Legman once calculated there are 14,288,400 sexual positions, though how he reached this figure is not certain. One of the earliest Chinese sex books, *Manual of Lady Mystery,* describes nine basic positions. These are:

The Dragon Turns: The woman lies on her back and opens her "jade doorway" to admit the man's "jade stem." He lets it reach a depth of five inches, stirring slowly. He then thrusts, penetrating shallowly for eight strokes, then deep for two.

The Tiger Slinks: The woman kneels on the bed with her head down. The kneeling man takes her from behind, thrusting deeply thirty-two times before taking a rest.

The Monkey Wrestles: The woman lies on her back. The man puts her legs on his shoulders and pushes her knees over her chest. He then penetrates her to a depth of three inches.

The Cicada Clings: The woman lies on her stomach and opens her legs. The man lies over her back, penetrates her, and thrusts fifty-four times.

The Turtle Stirs: The woman lies on her back and bends her

COITUS obstructus (aka *coitus reservatus*) is a method that requires a man to press hard between the anus and the testicles before ejaculation. The pressure blocks the urethra, forcing semen into the bladder. The ancient Chinese thought this action squirted invigorating semen into the brain. Other cultures used it as a method of birth control.

ACCORDING to the Kinsey report, standing is the least popular sexual position.

knees. The man pushes her feet until her knees reach her chest and then enters her.

The Phoenix Hovers: The woman lies on her back and holds her legs apart with her hands. The man kneels between her thighs and penetrates to a depth of four inches, thrusting twenty-four times.

The Rabbit Nibbles the Hair: The man lies on his back. The woman kneels over him facing his feet. The man then enters her to a depth of one inch.

The Fish Interlock Their Scales: The man lies on his back. The woman sits lightly over his body, her thighs open, to enable him to enter her slowly to a depth of two inches.

The Cranes Entwine Their Necks: The man sits on the bed with the soles of his feet facing each other. The woman then straddles him.

The sex manual writers of the Orient and Middle East were fond of inventing intricate positions and giving them flowery names. Examples from various Chinese and Arabic sex manuals include: Cat and Mouse in the Same Hole; Congress of an Ass; Driving the Peg Home; The Donkeys of Late Spring; Fixing a Nail; Hovering Butterflies; Jade Stem in Flower Heart Runs; Old Man Pushing a Wheelbarrow; Phoenix Sporting in the Cinnabar Cleft; Pounding on the Spot; Shooting the Arrow While Running; Splitting the Bamboo; Swinging Monkey; The Monkey Shakes; The Mutual Shock; The One Who Stays at Home; The Rooster Perches on a Stick; The

Screw of Archimedes; The Toothpick in the Vulva; The White Tiger Leaps; and The Winding Dragon.

It wasn't only Orientals who enjoyed making up names. In ancient Greece one position requiring a woman to crouch with her buttocks in the air was called The Lioness on the Cheese Grater.

To describe many of these positions without the benefit of illustrations would be irresponsible and might lead to serious back injury. Suffice to say that most are subtle variations on a few basic positions. For example, in the Indian Congress of the Cow the woman stands on her hands and feet, and the man mounts her like a bull; however, by acting out the roles of different animals, this simple position can also be transformed into: The Congress of a Dog; The Congress of a Goat; The Congress of a Deer; The Forcible Mounting of an Ass; The Congress of a Cat; The Jump of a Tiger; The Pressing of an Elephant; The Rubbing of a Boar; and The Mounting of a Horse.

Most positions found in these manuals are fairly practical, but a few verge on the ridiculous. One position found in both Chinese and Arab manuals is The Dog Barks in the Autumn

♂ In 1995 the owner of a Mexican restaurant in California was arrested for serving his own semen as a condiment.

♂ Some people are allergic to semen.

♂ In some Catholic hospitals the ban on masturbation means that sperm samples to test fertility have to be taken from the wife's vagina after sex. Other hospitals use an "un-erotic" vibrating machine attached to the testicles.

♂ In the USA most sexual encounters take place at 10:34 P.M.

♀ On average, European women expect sex four times a week.

♀ Catherine the Great advocated sexual relations six times a day.

♂ In 1657 a French general, the Prince de Condé, made love twelve times in one night. To commemorate the event, all his clothes and possessions were thereafter marked with a twelve.

or, as the Arabs knew it, Reciprocal Sight of the Posteriors. This position requires penetration when both partners have their backs to each other.

Basic Positions

Man on Top: Of all the positions, this is the one most practiced worldwide. In Tuscany, it was known as the Angelic Position, while the Arabs called it Mating in the Manner of Serpents. No one is quite sure how it got labeled the Missionary position (a name it seems to have acquired in the 1960s), but it does have a religious connection, as for centuries it was the only position officially approved of by the Catholic Church.

Woman on Top: Here the woman can control the depth of penetration and rate of thrust. The position is said to be comfortable for larger or pregnant women. Both partners have their hands free, and the man has to do very little work. This is probably how Homer and Marge do it.

Rear Entry: Also known as Doggy Style or, as the French say, *à la vache*. Here penetration can occur while standing, lying, sitting, or kneeling. This position is described as being "physiologically natural," as the penis and vaginal canal are in alignment, suggesting this is the way humans are designed to mate. Some women prefer this position as the penis stimulates the G-spot, but to do so effectively, she has to crouch with her buttocks higher than the head. One sexologist suggested that this position's popularity lies in the fact that it lets the testicles knock rhythmically against the clitoris.

Spooning: The rear-entry position (where both partners lie on their sides) is good for longer periods of sex. Penetration can be made deeper with changes in position, and there are a number of variations that can be achieved by moving the legs and upper body. This less physically demanding position is often appreciated by the elderly and infirm.

Nonpenetrative Sex: There are a number of techniques that do not involve penetration at all, and many are used by gay couples to avoid HIV. For example, the Princeton Rub involves rubbing the penis against various parts of the body. Another variant is "interfemoral sex" (also known as Oxford Style), where the penis is inserted between the thighs. The same can be done between a pair of buttocks (in Greece this was known as *pygisma* or "buttockry") or in the fold of the knee or elbow.

Group Sex

In the *Kama Sutra* a man enjoying two women at the same time is said to be having United Congress. If he has more than two, it's called, unflatteringly, Congress of a Herd of Cows. Where the man is sporting in the water with his lady friends, it's referred to as The Congress of an Elephant (presumably because elephants enjoy bathing). In some regions

> ⚲ According to *The Hite Report*, 74% of women are keenest on sex just before menstruation.
>
> ⚲ A medical journal has suggested that 30% of women are more sexually active at the full moon.
>
> ⚲ According to some studies, women enjoy sex more in their thirties and forties. It's thought that childbirth increases blood supply to the genitals, making them more responsive.

of India men used to share their wives with their friends. As the *Sutra* puts it, "Thus one of them holds her, another enjoys her, a third uses her mouth, a fourth holds her middle part, and in this way they go on enjoying her several parts alternately." For some reason the act of simultaneous sex with multiple partners is often called a Mongolian Cluster.

Midair Sex

Hammocks and swings have often been used for sex, the woman usually being suspended so the man can stand upright. A recent invention is the "Sex Swing and Bondage Stand," a portable self-assembly frame that avoids the need for ceiling and wall hooks. You can even take it on vacation with you.

The Physiology of Sex

There are a number of stages to the sexual encounter. In the arousal or excitement stage, the erectile tissue in your nose becomes engorged, creating eddies in the nasal air currents.

This improves the sense of smell, enabling you to pick up stimulating olfactory signals.

In men, a plateau phase follows, where the blood flow to the penis and scrotum increases, causing the penis to become erect. This congestion also makes the scrotum's skin appear smoother.

In women, increased blood flow to the vagina stimulates the release of lubricating fluids. The cervix and uterus become elevated, so the cervix doesn't get prodded too much when the vagina is penetrated by the penis. At the same time the clitoris begins to become engorged, and the breasts get 20 to 25 percent larger. A phenomena that might strike at this point is the sexual flush, a blush that spreads over the breasts, chest, belly, and buttocks. This is seen in half to three-quarters of women and a few men. In the final moments of the female plateau stage, the clitoris might actually start to shrink, as blood is drawn away from it into the swelling vaginal lips.

The next step is the orgasmic phase, followed by resolution. According to one survey, the average man takes two minutes to get to orgasm. Women take around four minutes

A *Cosmopolitan* survey said that foreplay usually lasted fourteen to seventeen minutes for the average married couple, the man typically reaching orgasm after six minutes of sex.

IN 1992 an East African truck driver was forced to wear incontinence pants after he started spontaneously ejaculating. For reasons never determined he came more than forty times a day for over a month.

♂ Hindu women called Western men "village cocks" because their lovemaking (like that of cockerels) was over so quickly.

♀ In the *Kama Sutra* the "69" position is called the Congress of a Crow.

ACCORDING to Saint Jerome, having sex with a menstruating woman would result in deformed, blind, lame, and leprous offspring.

through masturbation, and between ten and twenty minutes through intercourse.

People vary hugely in their ability to orgasm. In a recent scientific study one woman could orgasm 134 times in an hour, and one man was able to come sixteen times in the same period. Men's orgasms tend to be shorter, lasting between three to five seconds, while women's last five to eight seconds. Some women are capable of achieving a drawn-out *status orgasm* that might last much longer. In one test a woman had a forty-three-second orgasm consisting of twenty-five "spastic contractions." Some status orgasms last more than a minute.

Bottoms Up

The Chinese called anal sex "bringing the flowering branch to the full moon," the Indians referred to it as "lower congress," while a quaint eighteenth-century English term was "to navigate the windward passage." More often the practice is known as sodomy or buggery, both words having religious origins.

We get the word *sodomy* from Sodom, one of the "cities of the plain" mentioned in the Old Testament. According to the Book of Genesis, the townsfolk had a reputation for anal sex and once besieged the house of Lot trying to get their hands on two of his male visitors.

The word *buggery* has its origins in eleventh-century Bulgaria, the home of a Christian sect called the Bogomils. The Bogomils practiced anal sex (both homosexual and heterosexual) as a contraceptive measure. The word *buggery* probably entered the English language around 1550 through the French word *bougrerie*, their name for the "Bulgarian heresy."

Heterosexual anal sex was practiced in many parts of the world, most often as a form of contraception. Many Roman women used this method, and the Emperor Tiberius had a wall painting in his palace depicting the act. Anal sex was also depicted on the tomb paintings of the Etruscans. In ancient Greece high-class prostitutes, the *hetaerae,* usually insisted on it.

In pre-Columbian South America acts of heterosexual anal sex are frequently found immortalized in pottery. One survey of acts depicted on these clay pots had man-woman sodomy as the front-runner with 31 percent; oral sex came second at 14 percent; and normal intercourse third at 11 percent. The score for homosexual sodomy was 3 percent.

Medieval Italy was said to be a hotbed of heterosexual anal sex. The Spanish used to say that a Spaniard and an Italian could both love the same woman without jealousy as each worked in a different area. Despite its popularity the act was often illegal. To try and stamp out the practice in Venice, a law was passed in 1467 requiring a doctor to report any woman who had a "break in the rear parts caused by a member." Some women got rid of unwanted husbands by accusing them of sodomy, and one Venetian fisherman was beheaded for the act in 1481.

In more recent times anal sex has supposedly thrived in those countries without access to contraceptives, such as Catholic Ireland—hence the expression "doing it Irish fashion." Another common term is "Greek style," which might have its origins in the ancient Greek fad for pederasty. In many Western countries heterosexual anal sex was illegal until recent times. One of the last prosecutions in the United States was in 1965, when an Indiana man admitted to having anal sex with his wife and served three years in prison.

Bottom sex gives pleasure to many for a variety of reasons. Nature tries to make necessary functions pleasurable, and bowel movements fall into this category. Some rectal stimulation is probably enjoyable because it mimics the expulsion of a stool; indeed, Samuel Johnson once said that a good bowel movement was better than intercourse. The anal sphincter and the perineum (the area between the anus and genitals) are also criss-crossed with nerves that connect the sex organs to the spinal cord. In men the prostate gland (found at the base of the bladder) is responsible for producing seminal fluid and acts as a "middleman" between the testicles and penis. It's quite sensitive (some describe it as the male G-spot) and is most easily stimulated by sticking an object up the rectum. Some practitioners report that the anus contracts naturally on orgasm, and if this is prevented by the insertion of an object, it can prolong and heighten the pleasure.

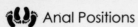 Anal Positions

Those who know recommend a position where the passive partner lies on their back with their knees drawn up over the chest. Apparently this position allows deep entry and good access to the prostate. Other popular anal sex positions include doggy style and rear entry, both face down and standing up.

An alternative to penile penetration is *postillioning,* where a finger is inserted to massage the prostate manually. An extreme variant on this is *fisting*, where a whole hand and forearm can, with patience, be inserted into the rectum. Obviously care should be taken, as the rectum is very fragile and damage can lead to a fatal case of peritonitis. Yet another variant is oral stimulation, sometimes known as *rimming*.

Help Is at Hand—*Marital Aids*

DIY sex aids are dealt with in Chapter 13, but there are a few devices on the market designed specifically for use by couples during penetrative sex. A good example is the clitoral stimulator, a textured rubber or plastic tongue attached to a ring that slips over the base of the penis. There have been many versions of this around the world. The ancient Chinese had a "bracelet of caoutchouc studded with points" that did the same job. Some were made of jade or ivory and held in place by ribbons.

In the thirteenth century one Oriental inventor came up with a ring made of goats' eyelashes. These were attached to a thread tied under the head of the penis and pointed outward to stimulate the inside of the vagina. The Indians of

Patagonia had a similar device called a *guesguel*, made from stiff hairs taken from the mane of a mule.

 The Joy of Fat Sex

Given the increasing incidence of obesity in Western society, more attention should be paid to the topic of "fat sex." Despite the obvious problems faced by plump partners, the good news is that, according to an expert in the field, "no woman is so fat that her vagina is inaccessible."

Man on Top: This position is unsatisfactory, as big women find it hard to breathe lying on their backs and large gentlemen find it exhausting. The overweight male is advised to sit back on his haunches; this posture leaves both hands free to lift the woman's stomach out of the way.

Woman on Top: Good for the fat man with a skinny partner, but risky with an obese woman. One man who had sex with a 500-pound woman reported that her stomach spread out so much, it tucked itself under his chin. He enjoyed himself but found it difficult to breathe. Where both partners are fat, it helps if the woman sits facing the man's feet, as this keeps their stomachs apart.

Rear Entry: Recommended for plump lovers. As a bonus, the woman's buttocks make a convenient platform for the man to rest his stomach on.

Sim's Position: Named after the gynecologist who invented it, this position is designed for the obese woman with a slim partner. The woman lies on her side and draws up her free leg, and the man penetrates her from behind.

Upside Down: According to one source, belly-to-belly

contact is best avoided by having sex in a "reverse missionary style," the man lying over the woman with his head at her feet.

T-Square: Another belly-avoidance maneuver. The T-Square requires the woman to lie on her back with her legs spread wide and raised. The man then lies back, positioning his hips under the arch of the female's legs, and penetrates her.

69: This can be tricky. As one person put it, a fat couple can do "6" and they can do "9," but they can't do "69."

As a final resort, the idea of vaginal intercourse can be abandoned altogether, the male partner inserting his penis into any convenient fold of skin.

ORANGES ARE NOT THE ONLY FRUIT

Gays, Lesbians, and Transsexuals

Although many people regard homosexuality as an aberration, it's a common phenomenon in the animal kingdom. Young apes of both sexes indulge in homosexual behavior, as do dolphins. Homosexual behavior is often a sign of dominance. Among male rats, weaker ones play the role of females for stronger ones; this behavior is also seen in some birds.

The absence of the opposite sex often results in a "gay day." If birds of different species, but the same sex, are kept together long enough, they will often attempt to mate with each other. Male dogs and cockerels will mount each other if deprived of female company for long periods, and cows exhibit lesbian tendencies if kept from a bull. This behavior can get ingrained, and if members of the opposite sex are introduced at a later date they are often ignored.

👣 In the Navy . . .

These "enforced" homosexual tendencies are often seen in human single-sex environments. There are many tales of nuns, monks, and boarding-school inmates supposedly having homosexual affairs (though confirming these stories is often impossible). Homosexual behavior does seem to have been a feature of life in the Royal Navy, however. Churchill is frequently misquoted as saying that the history of the navy was that of "rum, sodomy and the lash," though this expression was actually coined by his assistant, Anthony Montague-Browne. Evidence for this behavior is seen in the Royal Navy's Articles of War: Article 29 orders death for the "unnatural and detestable sin of buggery or sodomy with man or beast." However, the Articles were designed to cover every conceivable crime at sea, so the fact that buggery was proscribed doesn't mean it was common. This is in contrast to prisons (in America at least), where some prison psychiatrists have estimated that 70 percent of men in correctional facilities take part in homosexual relationships, many heterosexual men recruiting—often by force—an "old lady" or "punk" to be a bedmate for the duration of their sentence. This seems to be less common among women. In one 1978 study of juvenile females in detention homes, only 14 percent indulged in homosexual behavior.

👣 Tribal Homosexuality

Some primitive societies accept homosexuality as normal. One anthropological survey found that forty-nine out of the seventy-six societies it examined tolerated homosexual behavior.

In many of these cases turning gay may be a necessity if there's a shortage of females. Among the Aboriginal Aranda tribe, a shortage of females was solved by marrying youths to older bachelors. In other cultures same-sex relationships are part of everyday life. In New Guinea the men of tribes like the Sambia and Keraki have sex with young boys until the boys are old enough to get married (and start buggering boys themselves). In the case of the Sambia the men wear peglike devices on their noses during sex with their wives to keep themselves from becoming polluted by female odors.

👣 The Ancient World

Some South American societies accepted homosexuality, and homosexual acts were often depicted on local pottery and jewelry. Among the Maya a wealthy boy might be given a male slave as a sex partner until he was old enough to marry.

Not all cultures shared this relaxed attitude. The Aztecs and Incas organized regular witch-hunts to root out sodomites. Among the Aztecs homosexuals and transvestites of both sexes were killed. For men this might involve tearing the entrails from the passive partner, tying them around a log, and setting them alight. The dominant partner was also tied to a log, but he was buried in ash till he suffocated.

A fiery fate also awaited the homosexual victims of the Incas. In these cases even flimsy circumstantial evidence was enough to secure the death penalty. After the Incas conquered one northern coastal region, they killed so many suspected sodomites, they left fifteen women to every man.

Similar attitudes existed in the ancient societies of the Middle East. According to an Assyrian law of 1350 B.C., any man guilty of lying with another male was castrated. The

Bible is very scathing of gay practices. In Exodus it says, "If a man lie with mankind as he lieth with a woman, both of them have committed an abomination: they shall surely be put to death."

Greek Pederasts

For roughly two centuries (up till the second century B.C.) it was the custom for older Greek men to have homosexual relationships with youths. This practice, known as *pederasty*, probably spread from the sexually segregated society of Sparta. The Greeks regarded these relationships as manly and were often shocked by male effeminacy. Being gay in the "camp" sense was referred to as *pedomania*.

It was rare for Greek males to have same-age relationships, and illegal for men to have a relationship with a boy below puberty. The sixth-century-B.C. lawmaker Solon ordered any unauthorized adult male found on the grounds of a school to be put to death.

One Greek physician who tried to puzzle out the difference between heterosexuals and homosexuals hit on the idea that sexual enjoyment was linked to the production of semen. He reasoned that in homosexuals semen production occurred in the rectum rather than the genitals.

Roman Scandals

In Rome homosexuality was frowned upon in the early days of the republic—a law against "abominable sexual practices" prohibited sodomy (then referred to as the "Eastern vice"), and there is at least one account of a soldier killing his superior for making an indecent proposal.

IN Rome a man who "exercises his member in the anus" was called a *pedicon*, a *pederast*, or a *drawk*. The man on the receiving end was a *cinedeorm*, *catamite*, *minion*, or *effeminate*. If he was elderly, he might be called an *exolete*.

Many emperors had homosexual tendencies. The enemies of Julius Caesar accused him of being gay, though others made fun of his huge appetite for women. One of the popular jibes against Julius was that he had a "shaved" ass, it being the habit of homosexuals to pluck out anal hairs to make access easier.

The emperor Nero (A.D. 37–68) was bisexual. Nero regretted the fact that he'd kicked his pregnant wife to death and, finding a youth called Sporus who resembled her, married him after having him castrated. Later Nero married another youth called Doryphorus. Nero played the submissive role in this relationship and, on his wedding night, imitated the screams of a young girl being deflowered.

A notorious homosexual emperor was Heliogabalus (A.D. 204–22), who took the throne when he was fourteen. Heliogabalus liked his lovers well hung, so he sent agents all

According to the Kinsey report, 37% of US men have tried homosexuality, but only 4% took it up full time.

In nineteenth-century France homosexuality was called the "German vice."

In southern India it's thought you will be turned gay if you see two snakes having sex.

over the empire to round up the biggest studs they could find. He fancied himself as an actor and on one occasion staged a theatrical performance where he, playing the goddess Venus, was buggered onstage by his latest boyfriend. People soon got tired of his antics, and after four years on the throne he was stabbed to death and thrown down a privy.

As time went on homosexual behavior fell out of favor in Rome, and by the time of the Byzantine emperor Justinian (527–65), gays were being burned at the stake.

China and Japan

In ancient China homosexuality was regarded as a fashionable vice during some periods, and many public brothels supplied boys and youths. Sodomy even had its own god, called Tcheou-wang. The act of sodomy was known as Sharing the Peach, though homosexuality came to be known as *lung-yang*, after Lung-yang-chün, the lover of a fourth-century prince. The historians of ancient China listed many emperors who were openly gay or bisexual, though in the Ming dynasty (1368–1644) homosexuality fell out of favor, partly due to the belief that bisexual fathers could sire hermaphrodite children. Despite this, homosexuality continued in the upper echelons of society during the Manchu period (1644–1912). A visitor of 1806 recorded that all the senior civil servants he encountered were habitually accompanied by a young male lover acting as a "pipe bearer."

In Japan homosexuality was also in vogue during certain periods. Some geishas were male and were often trained for anal sex by being made to sit on a series of wooden penises of increasing size.

Islam

In the Middle East homosexuality was widely tolerated even after the rise of Islam. The Koran demanded that perpetrators be publicly scourged or otherwise humiliated, but these sanctions didn't seem to put many people off, and many travelers reported pederasty as being common in Islamic countries. In Spain many wealthy Moors kept male courtesans, or catamites, and the Moors of North Africa seem to have been partial to sodomy. Any sailor who happened to get shipwrecked on the Barbary Coast was almost certain to be buggered by his rescuers. In one nineteenth-century example the French man-o'-war *Silenus* was shipwrecked off North Africa, and the entire crew was sodomized by the Arabs who found them. As one young officer later explained, it was a question of "facing a sharp sword from the front, or a large tool from behind." The practice was not universally tolerated, however, and there were many stories of Muslim men putting their homosexual sons to death.

In some Islamic countries homosexuality was seen as a vice of the city dweller. In nineteenth-century Afghanistan a popular chant went, "The worth of cunt the Afghan knows: Kabul prefers the other. Choose!" A love song of the same region contained the verse, "There's a boy across the river with a postern like a peach, but alas! I cannot swim!"

Many Afghan merchants kept boys who accompanied them on their trips. These boys were called *kuch-i safari* or "traveling wives" and were dressed like women.

According to Sir Richard Burton, many Indian Muslims were pederasts. One of his stories involves a Mogul governor who would seek out young European men newly arrived in Bombay and invite them to dinner. At the banquet they'd be plied with drugged food and wine and would wake up the next day with a sore bottom. One way or another the governor got a lot of pleasure out of backsides. A favorite party trick was to feed one of his retainers gassy foods, get him down on all fours, and stick peppercorns up his bottom. The unfortunate man was then used like a cannon: spice was forced up his nose, and his sneezes shot the peppercorns at a paper target.

Although sodomy was said to be common among Indian Muslims and Sikhs, it was rare among Hindus, even though Shiva was said to have sodomized other gods. Evidence for this distaste is found in two traditional Hindu insults, *gandmara*, meaning "anus-beater," and *gandu,* "anuser."

👣 European Gays

Since the Bible condemns homosexuality, it's surprising to discover that the early Christian Church dealt with it leniently in many cases. Indeed, from the sixth to the eleventh centuries many homosexuals were treated no more severely than heterosexual couples practicing birth control.

Attitudes against homosexuality hardened as time went on, and the inquisition developed some nasty punishments for the crime. One was known as the *chambre chauffre* ("heated room"), in which sodomites were slowly lowered onto the needlelike tip of a large heated cone.

The medieval Spanish seem to have been particularly homophobic, perhaps because they considered pederasty to be a preserve of their traditional enemies, the Moors. In contrast, homosexuality seems to have been fashionable in medieval Italy, so much so that the Spanish called it the "Italian vice." In 1610 the Scottish traveler William Lithgow recorded that sodomy was "rife" even in the smallest villages, people "making songs, and singing Sonnets of the beauty and pleasure of their *bardassi,* or 'buggered boys.'"

In France homosexuality went in and out of vogue. French gays played with fire, however; death by burning was the preferred method of execution for sodomy, the last case occurring in 1725. Homosexuality was rife during the reign of Henri III (1551–89), when it was said that "men groped each other under the very porticoes of the Louvre." This behavior might have had something to do with the transvestite King Henri, who appeared in public wearing pearl necklaces and low-cut dresses.

Another French royal transvestite was Philippe I, Duc d'Orléans and the younger brother of Louis XIV. In 1680 Philippe helped form a society called the Sacred Order of Glorious Pederasts; the club's insignia was a cross showing a woman being trampled. Many members were married, but they could have sex with their wives only with the permission of their fellow club members. The Glorious Pederasts indulged in regular homosexual orgies, and their activities eventually grew so scandalous that the society was suppressed.

Bend Over and Think of England

In England some tried to blame homosexuality on the Vikings, reasoning that the long sea voyages of these all-male raiding parties would have encouraged unnatural behavior.

Homosexuality was tolerated in the higher classes, and England had many reputedly gay monarchs. Edward II had a famous affair with Piers Galveston and died with a red-hot poker up his bottom. James I, heir to Elizabeth I, had affairs with numerous men. His personal tastes were so well known, his ascent to the throne was greeted with the words *Rex fuit Elizabeth: nunc est regina Jacobus* ("Elizabeth was king: now James is queen").

The laws against homosexuality were harsh. Until 1861 sodomy (which also included heterosexual anal sex, oral sex, and bestiality) was punishable by death, but in practice it was very difficult to convict anyone as it had to be proved that ejaculation had taken place.

Despite these laws homosexuality flourished in many quarters. In eighteenth- and nineteenth-century London there were a number of homosexual brothels and clubs (often referred to as "Mollies clubs" or "Peg houses") that catered to the needs of the gay man-about-town. One of these is described in *The History of the London Clubs*, written in 1709: "There is a curious band of fellows in the town who call themselves 'Mollies' (effeminate, weaklings) who are so totally destitute of all masculine attributes that they prefer to behave as women. They adopt all the small vanities natural to the feminine sex to such an extent that they try to speak, walk, chatter, shriek and scold as women do, aping them as well in all other respects."

One of these clubs, in St. Clement's Lane (near the Strand), was raided in 1785. Here the goings-on included transvestite role-playing, where men indulged in make-believe pregnancies, births, and breast-feeding sessions. In 1794 the Bunch of Grapes pub near Clare Market (in the vicinity of modern Oxford Circus) was raided. A contemporary witness described the scene: "Two fellows in women's attire with muffs and wide shawls and the most fashionable turban-like bonnets, silken pinafores etc. Their faces were painted and powdered, and they were dancing a minuet in the middle of the room, whilst the others were standing around watching them in the most improper attitudes."

Another Clare Market pub, the White Swan, was raided in 1810 and found to be a veritable fantasyland. One of the pub's rooms had four beds in it; another was decked out like a lady's boudoir, while another was decorated like a chapel. Here mock marriages would take place, with men dressing as brides and bridesmaids. The wedding festivities often degenerated into wholesale orgies, with male prostitutes on hand for those who didn't bring their own partner. Many of the participants turned out to be married men. These gentlemen referred to their wives as "Tommies" and boasted of sodomizing them, though one often brought his understanding missus with him. Subsequent police investigations found that the twenty-three club members were from all walks of life and operated under pseudonyms. Thus "Miss Selina" was an errand boy working at a police station, "Pretty Harriet" was a butcher, and "the Duchess of Devonshire" was a hefty blacksmith.

Seven of the men were subsequently brought to trial and given relatively light sentences of between one and three years' imprisonment. Unfortunately the sentence also carried time in the pillory, and the condemned men were roughly treated by the public. According to contemporary accounts,

The term *homosexual* was first used in 1869 by a Hungarian researcher called Bonkert.

The term *queer* was first used to describe homosexuals in a 1924 issue of the U.S. magazine *Variety*.

> IN Germany homosexuals were once known as "175-ers." 175 was the number of the paragraph of the German Penal Code that legislated against homosexuals.

the Old Bailey was besieged on the day of punishment, and carts piled high with offal and dung were dragged up from the marketplaces to provide ammunition. Vendors toured the street selling rotten apples, pears, and cabbages together with the corpses of dead cats and dogs. Rather than give the mob a free hand, the authorities allowed fifty women to form a circle around the condemned men and pelt them for an hour.

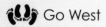 Go West

In early America the situation was similar to that in Britain. The local sodomy laws were based on English common law and covered all nonprocreative acts, including oral sex and bestiality. Illinois was the first state to drop its sodomy law, during an update of its legislature in 1962. Idaho followed suit soon after, but when a gay newspaper made it front-page news, the state legislators hurriedly made homosexual sex illegal again. Many states followed this pattern, dropping anti-sodomy laws as part of modernization programs, then creating new laws specifically against homosexual sex. It took modern America a surprisingly long time to come to terms with homosexuality—as late as 1973 the American Psychiatric Association still listed it as a mental disease.

💑 Lesbians

Female homosexuality has always been less visible than the male variety; societies tend to ignore female-to-female intimacy. According to some, Queen Victoria refused to believe it existed at all and struck out all references to lesbianism when presented with a new draft of laws on homosexuality. This well-worn tale turns out to be completely untrue. Apart from the fact that it was (and is) constitutionally impossible for a British monarch to cross out legislation passed by Parliament, the laws in question involved a reduction in the penalty for sodomy. Lesbianism wasn't mentioned because it wasn't an issue.

The ancient Greeks called lesbians *tribads* (from *tribas*, meaning "to rub"), but we get the name *lesbian* from the Greek island of Lesbos, whose inhabitants were famous for it. The most famous "Lesbian" was Sappho (or Psappho). Little is known of Sappho apart from the fact that she was born in the seventh century B.C. to a wealthy family and was an accomplished poet and songwriter. Sappho also ran an academy for young ladies and had affairs with her students. This sort of arrangement does not seem to have been uncommon; female homosexuality was accepted in the same way that male homosexuality was. In Sparta even respectable married women were said to have affairs with young girls, and in the second century A.D. the Greek writer Philaenis described lesbian sexual positions in her book *The Art of Love*.

Stories of lesbian behavior only occasionally crop up in the history books. In 1500 there's a story of two female French servants (a widow and a married woman) caught having sex on their mistress's *chaise percée* (an early inside toilet). The incident was probably memorable for its slapstick outcome—the toilet collapsed and both women were thrown to the ground.

A notorious lesbian of the seventeenth century was Miss Hobart Hamilton, a courtier to King Charles II, said to be "tender hearted to her own sex only." She became infamous for the attempted seduction of a court beauty, Miss Temple.

Lady Eleanor Butler and Miss Sarah Ponsonby were two famous lesbians of the eighteenth century. They developed an attachment after meeting at boarding school and eventually set up house together in the Welsh vale of Llangollen, becoming famous as the "Ladies of Llangollen."

Lesbianism seems to have been popular in eighteenth-century England. One writer of 1794 said that "the game of flats" (a popular term for the practice) was now as "common in Twickenham as in Turkey." Many women acquired a taste for lesbianism at boarding schools, and many cities were said to be the home of lesbian clubs (known as Anandric societies) and brothels.

Chinese Lesbians

In the past Chinese women had notorious reputations as lesbians. In most societies homosexual activity in harems was banned, but it was encouraged in China as it was believed to increase a girl's yin energy (later to be harvested by her master). Travelers reported that Chinese harems were often equipped with hammocks, each containing a pair of girls fondling each other. Their lord would recline in the middle of the room, canoodling with a favorite, while twenty or so girls enjoyed themselves in midair around him.

A more recent example of Chinese lesbianism is the

mahchehs. Still common in Singapore in the 1950s, these were a class of unmarried servant women who wore pigtails as a sign of celibacy. Some *mahchehs* swore never to have a husband and were held in very high status by their community. If commanded to marry by their parents, some *mahchehs* compromised by marrying but remaining celibate, saving their money to buy their husband a second wife. Some *mahchehs* entered into marriages with each other. These lesbian *mahcheh* couples were known as *seong-chee,* "two with mutual understanding," and the marriages were known as *moh tow foo,* after the two flat grinding-stones used to make bean curd.

 ## Transsexuals and Transvestites

Although many transsexuals are transvestites, not all transvestites are transsexual. Many transvestites are happy with their sexuality and just enjoy dressing up. Transsexuals, on the other hand, believe their "internal" sex does not match their exterior physical makeup and do all they can to change it.

Recent research has revealed that these differences may be due to a tiny cluster of cells in the brain's hypothalamus. In men—and in women who want to be men—this cluster is large; in women—and in men who want to be women—the cluster is much smaller.

 ## Intersex Babies

Contrary to what many may think, it's not always obvious what sex a baby is at birth. In the womb a penis develops from the genital tubercle if there is a male Y-chromosome. If there's no male chromosome, the tubercle turns into a

IN an extraordinary sixteenth-century case, a 15-year-old French girl called Marie ripped her crotch when leaping over a ditch and was amazed when two testes and a penis dropped through the hole. Marie was rechristened Germain and grew up to be a man with a thick red beard.

clitoris. Swellings on either side of the tubercle become the scrotum in a boy and the labia in a girl. Sometimes the chemical signals from the chromosomes get mixed up or are not acted on in the normal way—in these cases both sets of sexual organs can develop, and the baby is described as intersexed.

Sometimes an excess of the hormone androgen on a female fetus can cause the clitoris to enlarge and the labia to fuse shut (a condition seen in 1 in 10,000 births). In some genetically male babies the fetus does not respond to testosterone and develops as a female (1 in 20,000). Male babies sometimes have Klinefelter's syndrome, where an extra X-chromosome means they undergo little secondary sexual development at puberty and sometimes grow breasts (1 in 500 births).

In the West approximately 1 in 20,000 babies has surgery to tip the balance one way or the other.

Primitive Cultures

Many primitive cultures have accommodated transsexuals. Among the North American Mohave tribe men wishing to live as women were known as *alyhas*. They often married, taking the passive role in anal and oral intercourse with their husbands. *Alyhas* did their best to ignore the male nature of their sexual organs, calling their penis a clitoris, their scrotum the vaginal lips, and their anus the vagina. They went to great lengths to imitate women in other ways. When they found a husband, they would cut their inner thighs to simulate menstrual bleeding and, after sex, stuffed grass up their clothing to imitate pregnancy. Childbirth was simulated by defecating in the birthing position, the baby being treated as a stillborn. *Alyhas* were thought to be supernatural beings containing both male and female spirits, and for this reason they often became healers and shamans. Mohave transsexual women were tolerated in the same way; apart from observing menstruating taboos, they lived and worked as men.

Transsexuals were found in many tribal cultures around the world where, like the Mohave, they were regarded as magical beings. Among some Siberian tribes male transsexuals were regarded as witches responsible for influencing destructive forces. In one of these tribes there were three steps in the change from man to woman. In the first stage the man braided his hair like a woman. In the second he dressed like a woman. And in the third he lived totally as a woman. In the

♀ In 1721 a Prussian woman called Catharina Margaretha Linck was tried for masquerading as a man. She had a leather cone to let her pee standing upright and used a leather penis to have sex with several women.

♀ In 1986 a Buddhist nun was unmasked as a man after living for fourteen years in a Thai convent. It was decided to let him stay.

♀ Upon his death at age 74, the jazz musician Billy Tipton was found to be a woman. He'd kept his secret through eighteen years of marriage.

same way a woman could turn herself into a man, though in these cases the transformation was assisted by an artificial penis made out of a reindeer's leg fastened to a belt.

In some societies youngsters weren't given much choice as to whether they wanted to change sex. Even among the Mohave boys and girls were expected to choose at a relatively young age, often before puberty. In the Aleutian Islands pretty boys were brought up as girls and trained to please men. Some were married off as young as ten.

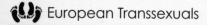 ## European Transsexuals

The ancient Greeks were familiar with transsexuals; the term *hermaphrodite* comes from Hermaphoroditos, a son of Hermes and Aphrodite, who asked to be fused with the nymph Salmacis so they would never be separated. Some men were open transvestites: the Greek poet Agathon used to entertain friends dressed like a woman, wearing a long robe, a saffron tunic and cape, a bust bodice, a hairnet, and high, tight-fitting boots. Transsexuals even had their own patron goddess, Venus Castina.

Some ancients combined a transsexual lifestyle with castration. In Phrygia (in modern-day Turkey) priests devoted to the god Attis cut off their testicles and lived as women. Some went further and removed all their male genitalia. In first-century Alexandria one writer recorded that transsexuals took "every possible care on their outward adornment, they are not ashamed even to employ every device to change artificially their nature as men into women....Some of them... craving a complete transformation into women, have amputated their generative members."

Many legends had the gods playing tricks on men by

changing their sex. One such was the legend of Tiresias, a soothsayer from Thebes who was changed into a woman for killing a female snake. Tiresias got used to his female role and discovered that women had far better sex lives, upon which he was again punished by being turned back into a man.

The Old Testament specifically forbids transvestism: "The woman shall not wear that which pertaineth unto a man, neither shall a man put on a woman's garment: for all that do so are abominations unto the Lord thy God." This biblical view colored Western thinking, and for much of the Middle Ages the punishment of transvestites and transsexuals was severe. An example of 1498 involved a Moorish transsexual known as Spanish Barbara who was arrested in Rome and paraded through the streets with his clothing lifted to reveal his genitals. Barbara was then led to the Campo dei Fiore by a city deputy who was carrying a stick with two testicles hanging from it. (They'd been cut off a Jew caught having sex with a Christian woman.) Once in the square Barbara was garroted and burned.

In later years transvestism was treated as an eccentricity. Lord Cornbury, governor of New York and New Jersey from 1702 to 1708, often dressed as a woman, even at official functions. According to Cornbury, his transvestism was due to a vow that required him to wear women's clothes for a month every year. He also claimed his dress was in honor of Queen Anne, his cousin and the head of the government he represented.

Perhaps the most famous transvestite of this period was the Chevalier D'Eon (1728–1810). Born in France, the Chevalier started life as a soldier and later became a spy for the French secret service. According to some accounts, D'Eon carried out many of his secret missions in Russia

⚥ In the eighteenth century male transvestites made fake breasts out of dried sheep's lungs.

⚥ In 1994 a Colombian actress apparently had a sex change by accident—she went in for a face-lift but was mistaken for another patient.

dressed as a woman. After securing a diplomatic post in London, rumors started to circulate that he was really a woman posing as a man. These rumors were fueled by D'Eon's lack of interest in women and by his huge collection of feminist literature. People started taking bets on his sex, and a book opened 3–2 in favor of him being a man. By 1776 the situation had reversed—the odds were 7–4 that he was a woman. Huge sums of money were wagered—one estimate put the total at £280,000—and the gambling became such an embarrassment to the French that King Louis ordered D'Eon back to France. D'Eon refused and blackmailed the French government for a state pension. In return D'Eon signed a statement saying he was a woman, and from 1777 he wore nothing but female clothing. When he died in 1810, the undertaker discovered he'd been a man all along.

👣 Trading Places—*Sex Change Surgery*

It's only in recent times that an understanding of hormones and improved surgical techniques have enabled sophisticated male-to-female and female-to-male transformations.

The first modern sex change was carried out in 1952 on George Jorgensen, a twenty-six-year-old former U.S. soldier. The operation took place in Copenhagen and turned George into Christine. Although many people were shocked, some took a more light-hearted attitude: U.S. soldiers in Korea voted Christine "Miss Neutral Zone 1953." Christine later went into show business, got engaged twice, and ended her days in a lavish L.A. home. Today there are approximately forty thousand postoperative male-to-female transsexuals in the United States.

Sex changes are usually prolonged affairs that involve initial counselling sessions followed by hormone therapy and surgery. Some male-to-female transsexuals opt for an *orchidectomy* (removal of the testes) at an early stage, as this allows for a lower estrogen intake during hormone therapy. Surgery proper involves a number of procedures; a *vaginoplasty* (construction of the vagina), *penectomy* (removal of the penis), and *clitoroplasty* (construction of a clitoris). Other treatments might include breast augmentation, rhinoplasty (nose reshaping), hair transplants, electrolysis, reduction of the Adam's apple (known as *thyroid chondroplasty*), and changes to the vocal cords to raise the pitch of the voice.

Construction of a vagina is relatively simple. The vaginal cavity is lined with penile skin or bowel tissue, and the skin of the scrotum is reshaped into labia.

For female-to-male transformations, surgical procedures include a *hysterectomy* and *oophorectomy* (removal of the uterus and ovaries), a *bilateral mastectomy* (breast removal), and a possible *phalloplasty* (penis construction). To make a new penis, a roll of skin and tissue can be taken from the abdomen and connected to the urethra, allowing it to be used for urination. In some cases this type of penis can be made erect by inserting a silicone stiffening rod down the urethra.

A more recent procedure involves the removal of tissue from the forearm and the creation of a hydraulic erection mechanism that uses a tiny hand-pump hidden in the scrotum. These state-of-the-art penises are very expensive and can cost anywhere from $15,000 to more than ten times that. Alternatively the clitoris can be enlarged as much as possible using hormone therapy and surgery to produce a micropenis, less than ⅜ of an inch long.

According to recent figures, all these transformations have a 97 percent success rate.

PROTECT AND SURVIVE

Contraception

With all this talk of pleasure, it is easy to forget that sex has other practical applications beyond self-gratification—procreation, for instance! Historically, offspring have always held mixed blessings. The ability to reproduce was obviously a sign of good health, and the larger the family, the stronger it was in many senses. Conversely, for families in poorer parts of the world the appearance of an extra mouth to feed always was and still is an insupportable burden. For prostitutes a pregnancy will often ruin business and result in penury. In some less tolerant cultures, being an unmarried mother has frequently been tantamount to a death sentence. For all these reasons it's not surprising that the prevention of conception has been a problem that has exercised minds for many centuries.

🐾 Coitus Interruptus

Historically, one of the most popular and widespread forms of contraception has been coitus interruptus. It's been suggested that this was the sin of Onan described in Genesis (see Chapter 13), but at least one rabbinical text said it was a husband's duty to "thresh inside and winnow outside" while his wife was breast-feeding, to prevent the wife from having another baby too soon after the last. This is a rare example of a pro-interruptus viewpoint; most Judaic and Christian texts condemned the practice, sex being for procreation, not pleasure. Even in the twentieth century some doctors said that coitus interruptus resulted in nervousness, impotence, and the hardening of the uterus.

Coitus interruptus isn't a very good method of birth control. Apart from the problem of premature ejaculation, spermatozoa are quite tenacious and can sometimes fertilize an egg even if they're deposited at the mouth of the vagina.

🐾 Hitting the Mark

In the past many thought that sperm had to "hit the right spot" in order to result in a pregnancy. Roman women wanting children were advised to keep still when having sex, so the seed would not miss its mark. Having rear-entry sex was thought to be particularly good for breeding purposes, as a man could aim his sperm straight and true. To avoid pregnancy, prostitutes deliberately wriggled about during sex to try and direct sperm away from the danger area. Alternatively, women could jump up and down after sex to try and dislodge the sperm. Others held their breath at the moment of ejaculation, then squatted on the ground and provoked a sneezing fit to try and expel the semen. In the same way some people have sex upright in the hope that the sperm will drain away before it can do any harm. Some women, of course, such as the prostitutes of ancient Greece, avoided the problem altogether by insisting on anal sex.

👣 Pessaries, Plugs, and Sponges

One of the earliest recorded methods of contraception is found in an ancient Egyptian document called the Kahun Papyrus. It recommends inserting a mixture of crocodile dung and *auyt* gum up the vagina. The dung probably acted like a plug and created a physical barrier, but its acidic nature might also have acted as a spermicide. Pessaries of elephant dung were touted in Islamic texts up to the thirteenth century.

Another ancient Egyptian recipe recommended a mixture of honey and *natron*, a salt found in dried-up watercourses often used as a desiccant by mummy embalmers. Again, this mixture might have had spermicidal properties as well as acting as a physical barrier. Another papyrus, called the Papyrus Ebers, suggests a more hygienic dung-free method: a pad of lint soaked in a mixture of acacia tips and honey. The acacia tips would have released lactic acid (used in many modern spermicidal jellies), while the honey would have helped trap sperm.

Olive oil was used to trap sperm by the ancient Greeks and Romans, and it was even recommended by the birth-control campaigner Marie Stopes in the 1930s. Other oils were also used. Aristotle suggested cedar oil and frankincense, while Soranus, a first-century Greek physician, swore by wool tampons soaked in oil, honey, and resin, a mixture that would have probably stopped a torpedo in its tracks. In

> ♂ Some Papua New Guinea tribespeople thought a man could give birth, an act that was usually fatal.
>
> ♀ Some Queensland Aborigines thought that a woman became pregnant after sitting over a fire on which a fish had been roasted. The giver of the fish was the father. Other tribes thought that human flesh had to be eaten to make a baby.

India similar methods existed, though here women used clarified butter (ghee) or inserted chips of rock salt dipped in oil. The salt would have created a chemical environment very hostile to sperm. Vinegar (acetic acid) was also employed in this way; many women in ancient Greece used it as a douche, while some physicians recommended dipping the penis in vinegar before sex.

Pessaries have been used all around the world. In Africa women used plugs of chopped grass or cloth, while Japanese prostitutes used wads of bamboo tissue paper. Balls of wool were a popular choice in ancient Greece and Islamic countries. The ancient Jews were very fond of sponges; their use was recommended for young brides (girls between eleven and twelve) and pregnant women. In the girls' case the sponge was designed to preserve their immature bodies from the rigors of childbirth. For the pregnant women the object was to prevent another baby—the Hebrews not realizing it's impossible for a second conception to occur during pregnancy. The sponge was popular all around the Mediterranean, where there was a limitless supply. For best effect they were soaked in crude spermicides like salt water or lemon juice. Some were treated with astringents to help shrink the vaginal canal and create a tighter fit.

Getting the sponges out could prove a problem, so they were usually equipped with a length of string or silk thread. In 1825 one English writer recorded that sponges (the size of walnuts or small green apples) were often pulled out using "penny ribbons." Synthetic birth control sponges, impregnated with spermicides, are still made today.

In Victorian times some very elaborate pessaries were invented. One doctor commented that the inside of many vaginas resembled "Chinese toy shops." An uncomfortable-sounding device was the block pessary, a six-sided wooden block with concave faces; the hope was that, once inside, one of these faces would slide into the correct position over the cervix (the mouth of the womb).

 ## Diaphragms

The most famous pessary is the rubber diaphragm. Casanova is said to have used half a lemon as a cap, but the idea was developed in 1838 by a German doctor called Mesinga. In the 1870s the diaphragm became very popular in Britain (where it was sometimes known as the "womb veil") and Holland—hence its popular nickname, the "Dutch cap." The diaphragm is a thin rubber shield that sits over the cervix and (hopefully) prevents sperm from entering the uterus. A close relative is the cervical cap, a thimble-shaped rubber cup that fits tightly over the mouth of the cervix. Both are usually used with a spermicidal cream or jelly. More recently suppositories have been invented that are inserted in the vagina, then melt to form an impenetrable cap over the cervix.

The Intrauterine Device

Better known as the IUD or coil, the intrauterine device is a small plastic T-shaped object with a thin copper wire wrapped around it. There are two popular models, the Paragard, which can be put in place for up to ten years, and the Progesterone T, which releases progesterone and must be replaced every year. Both types have small wires that project into the vagina so they can be retrieved. No one is quite sure how IUDs work, but they may alter the lining of the uterus in such a way that egg implantation is prevented.

Although regarded as a modern form of contraception, IUDs may be very old. Cleopatra is said to have used "stones" as a contraceptive, and although she may have used them as pessaries, it's possible the ancient Egyptians inserted small stones in the uterus to act like IUDs.

Herbal Remedies

Herbal remedies have always been popular; most concoctions are the equivalent of a morning-after pill, abortifacients used to kill off any recently fertilized egg. The herb pennyroyal (*Mentha pulegium*) was well known in this respect and is mentioned in a comedy play by Aristophanes—one of the characters advises it to keep his mistress out of trouble. Pennyroyal was also used in Islamic cultures alongside substances such as pomegranate pulp and willow leaves. Its use has survived until relatively recent times: pennyroyal made an appearance in an eighteenth-century midwives' handbook, where it was said it would "hasten the menses."

One of the most effective herbs of this sort was silphium. Apparently a small amount of silphium juice taken every

IN 1874 the *Medical Weekly* reported the case of a girl who was impregnated by a musket ball during the Civil War. The ball shot off the testicle of a soldier, then lodged in the abdomen of a 17-year-old girl. 278 days later she gave birth to a boy. The mother and soldier were later married.

month was guaranteed to prevent pregnancy. Unfortunately the plant only grew in a small coastal strip of North Africa and could not be transplanted elsewhere. Apart from its use in birth control, the herb was also a highly prized food flavoring, and by weight it was more expensive than silver. So much was picked it became extinct in the first century A.D.

A herb called worm root was also used by the Romans; it was later dubbed "prostitute root" by the French, prostitutes presumably being its biggest consumers. Crocuses could also do the job. A Mediterranean recipe from the third century called Cup of Roots mixed three equal measures of Alexandrian gum, liquid alum, and garden crocus with two cups of beer. The potion not only prevented pregnancies, it cured jaundice, too.

Many other plants have been thought to have contraceptive properties, including birthwort (*Aristolochia longa*), motherwort (*Leonurus*), and Queen Anne's lace (more commonly called wild carrot), not to mention rosemary, ginger, mustard, horseradish, tansy, castor oil, celery, aloe, dates, and figs. In medieval Germany teas made of marjoram, thyme, parsley, and lavender were used. Most of the herbs used in this way were mildly toxic and, if taken in sufficiently large amounts, acted as abortifacients that could cause a miscarriage. Papaya is one of the few fruits said to act in this way—eating one a day is said to prevent pregnancy.

⚣ At one time soldiers in the Russian army were kept chaste by pinning their foreskins closed with wire.

⚣ According to the World Health Organization, a hundred million sex acts occur every day, resulting in 910,000 conceptions.

⚣ A recent invention is the "panty condom," unisex panties with a two-way "reversible" condom built in.

Many of these herbs were found in nineteenth-century patent medicines designed to treat female ailments. Many quacks surreptitiously advertised their use as abortifiacients by putting a "warning" on the label, for example, "Portuguese Female Pills—not to be used during pregnancy for they will cause miscarriage."

A huge variety of nonherbal substances have also been used over the years. Turpentine, mashed ants, foam from camels' mouths, the tail hairs of blacktail deer dissolved in bear fat, quinine water in which a rusty nail has been soaked, Epsom salts, ammonia, gin with iron filings, and opium are all substances that have been sold as abortifacients at one time or another.

👣 The Pill

The oral contraceptive pill was developed from a herbal remedy, and the first commercially viable source of progesterone was the Mexican hairy yam, sometimes eaten as a contraceptive by locals. Developed in the 1960s, the pill releases estrogen and progesterone, which affect the normal release of an egg once a month and/or the attachment of an egg to the lining of the uterus. The pill is taken orally, but similar hormonal methods of birth control can be implanted under the skin. One of these, called the Norplant system, uses the hormone progestin. The system consists of six matchstick-sized capsules that are placed under the skin of the arm, where they slowly dissolve, releasing doses of hormone into the bloodstream.

Condoms

The modern sheath was invented by the Italian physician Gabriele Falloppio (1523–62) to prevent the spread of syphilis, a disease that first appeared in the 1490s. Falloppio's condom was a short linen bag that covered the head of the penis and was tied in place under the foreskin. Although this is the first recorded condom in modern times, it seems unlikely that such a useful item had not been thought of earlier. An Egyptian illustration from around 1300 B.C. shows a man wearing a condomlike sheath; the Romans are thought to have made condoms out of animal and fish guts.

Animal gut condoms were popular for centuries, and even

> ♂ Two men in Peru were recently convicted of scavenging used condoms in a local "lovers' lane" and cleaning them for resale.
>
> ♂ Egyptian investigators looking into a 90% increase in demand for birth control discovered that condoms given away free at clinics were being sold as children's balloons.
>
> ♀ In 1994 a wife in Rome put pepper in her husband's condoms before he visited his mistress. He was taken to the hospital with a severely swollen and inflamed member.

TO cash in on its famous name, the French town of Condom is opening a condom museum; however, the name of the town is actually derived from a Latin phrase meaning "the conflux of two rivers."

Casanova used them. They did have their critics, however. The French aristocrat Madame de Sévigné (1626–96) called them "gossamer against infection and steel against love." Others were equally scathing. In 1736 Jean Astrue, court physician to Louis X, said that those fearing sexually transmitted diseases "ought to arm their penises with oak guarded with a triple plate of brass." Some of these antique condoms have survived to the present day. A number of fish and animal condoms dating from the English Civil War have been recovered from a refuse dump in Dudley Castle, and an eighteenth-century gut condom decorated with a pornographic picture of a nun was recently auctioned at Christie's for $6,000. The use of animal condoms persisted for many years; indeed, reusable condoms made from sheep's intestine were manufactured well into the 1940s. Disposable animal condoms (made of lambskin) are still available today for those allergic to rubber and plastics.

Rise of the Rubbers

The first nonanimal condoms were made of vulcanized rubber. The vulcanization process was invented in 1844, and the mass production of rubber sheaths started soon after. One newspaper advertisement of 1861 sold them as "Dr. Power's French Preventatives." Like their gut forebears, these early condoms were designed to be used time and time again. In

America condom sales were healthy, but alongside all other forms of birth control, they were banned in 1873 after a campaign by the moralist crusader Anthony Comstock. Thereafter the manufacture and sale of condoms remained illegal in the United States till the 1920s.

Today the vast majority of condoms are made of latex rubber, a material first used in the 1880s. The manufacturing process involves repeatedly dipping penis-shaped glass formers into liquid latex treated with stabilizers and preservatives. The latex-covered formers are then baked in an oven to strengthen the rubber, after which they're blasted off by jets of high-pressure water. The condoms are then tested. This might involve passing a high-voltage electric charge through the rubber, or the condoms might be inflated with air or filled with water. A good condom should take about 42 quarts of air before bursting, and fluid-filled condoms are checked for leaks by rolling them on blotting paper.

Today around ten billion latex condoms are manufactured each year. But despite their cheapness and availability, there are some cheapskates who still try to wrap their lunchboxes in sandwich wrap. Needless to say, this is not a good idea.

One brand of novelty condom has a ruler printed on it. If you possess a 4-incher you're "An Average Joe," while 10 inches makes you a "Farm Animal."

Some Victorian condom brands were sold with pictures of Queen Victoria and Prime Minister Gladstone on the packaging.

The Old Glory Condom Corporation manufactures condoms decorated with the Stars and Stripes.

THE following is a nineteenth-century method of DIY condom manufacture. First you acquire a sheep's cecum (a baglike extension of the intestinal tract). The cecum is then soaked in water and washed in a weak solution of soda. The water is changed after 4 to 5 hours, and the washing repeated four or five times. The cecum's mucous membrane then has to be scraped off, after which it is dipped in sulfur and washed in soapy water. The cecum is then inflated and left to dry, after which it is cut to length and has a couple of ribbons attached so you can tie it in place.

There's still doubt as to how the condom acquired its name. Some think they were named after Dr. Conton, one of the court physicians of the randy King Charles II, but it's more likely to have its origins in Latin. There are various Latin words with the prefix *condo*, some meaning "to put away," "to put out of sight," and in the case of swords, "to sheath" and "to plunge."

Today condoms are commonly known by the names of the leading commercial brands—Trojan in the United States, Durex in the UK. The well-known term *French letter* arose as a result of Victorian newspaper advertisements for mail-order condoms that euphemistically described them as "French letters" or "French safes." The French ascribed the invention of the condom to the English, and in the eighteenth and nineteenth centuries their nickname was *capote anglaise* (English hood), or *redingote anglaise* (English riding coat). Since then many weird and wonderful names have been devised for condom brands—for example, Billy Boy (Germany), Enormex (UK), Euroglider (Netherlands), Happy Face (New Zealand), Honeymoon Super Stimulation (Germany), Jiffi Exciter (UK),

Licks (USA), Mamba (Sweden), Power Play (USA), and Skin Less Skin (Japan).

 ## Magic

Magic and superstition has always played their part in contraception. One medieval physician recommended that a woman spit in a frog's mouth three times to prevent conception for a whole year. Others suggested wearing sapphire jewelry. One superstition of the Dark Ages was that a woman could avoid pregnancy by holding a pebble during sex (some recommended a pebble of jasper), another that eating bees made you sterile ("Let a woman eat a bee and she shall never conceive"). Strapping the dried testicle of a weasel to a woman's thigh was considered a winner by many. Others suggested that a cat's testicle would do the trick if tied near the navel, or if a testicle was not available, then a bone from the right side of a black cat could be worn as an amulet around the neck. One Roman writer recommended placing the blood of a black dunghill cockerel under the marriage bed to prevent fertilization.

 ## I Got Rhythm

Almost as reliable as magic is the rhythm method, which relies on identifying a woman's fertile period and avoiding sex during this time. Unfortunately few women are very regular in their cycles, and finding out when you're likely to be fertile is tricky. One method relies on looking for changes in the mucus produced by the cervix, another monitors internal temperature. The sympto-thermal method combines both. However, factors such as sickness, emotional strain, or even a change in the weather can affect the ovulation cycle. These uncertainties, combined with the fact that sperm can survive inside the female body for up to seven days, make this method a bit of a minefield.

Vasectomy and Sterilization

A *vasectomy* is a simple procedure requiring only a local anesthetic. Two small holes are made in the scrotum, through which the vas deferens, the tubes that carry sperm from the testes, are tied off, cauterized, or closed with a metal clip. The procedure can take less than ten minutes and is said to be 99.95 percent effective. Complications are rare, and the only postoperative care required is an ice pack—or bag of frozen peas—to press against the sore scrotum. After fifteen to twenty ejaculations 80 percent of men have a zero sperm count, but for some it can take much longer to clear the semen, months in some cases.

The operation has a 70 percent chance of being reversed if carried out in the first three years, but after ten years it is almost nil. Reconnecting the tubes is not a problem, but over time some men develop antibodies that kill off sperm as they are produced.

♂ To mark World AIDS Day in 1993, a 24-yard-high, 3.8-yard-wide condom was put over the obelisk in the Place de la Concorde, Paris.

♂ A recent bottle shortage in Russia was solved by using condoms as temporary receptacles. Men buying beer on tap could carry home over 3 quarts in a condom.

♂ The EC standard condom is 6.7 inches long and 2.2 inches wide.

There are similar sterilization techniques for women called *laparoscopic sterilization*, *tubal ligation*, or *tubectomy*, depending on the technique used. This is a far more invasive operation than a vasectomy and requires the blockage of the egg-carrying fallopian tubes.

◉ Abortion and Infanticide

The use of herbal abortifacients has already been described, but sometimes physical methods were used. In A.D. 100 the Greek doctor Soranus listed a number of methods, including rides in a bumpy wagon, lifting heavy weights, taking hot baths, and having harsh enemas. The only methods Soranus disapproved of were those that introduced sharp instruments into the womb. Other methods used over the centuries have included jumping off tables, climbing trees, and drinking strong spirits. One bizarre method (first described in an eighth-century Sanskrit document) involves a woman fumigating her vagina by crouching over a pot of stewed onions. In the early twentieth century Egyptian peasant women used to try to induce abortions by lying between railway tracks. The sensation of having a speeding train rush over you was meant to induce a miscarriage through mortal terror.

> ⚲ In Victorian England people advertised special houses where an unmarried woman could spend her pregnancy in secret.
>
> ⚲ It was said that the promiscuous Julia (daughter of the Roman emperor Augustus) "took passengers only when the boat was full," i.e., had lovers only when she was pregnant.

Many cultures have had strict laws against abortion. Some of the earliest were seen in Assyria, where a woman who had an abortion was impaled and left unburied. If the woman happened to die during the abortion, the same was done to her corpse.

The most extreme form of birth control is the killing of newborn babies. In ancient Greece this was a common practice with unwanted children or those who were obviously disabled. In some Native American tribes newborns were killed during migrations to prevent them from slowing down the group. In some cultures the children of dead fathers were killed, as their mothers would not be able to support them.

WHATEVER TURNS YOU ON

Sexual Perversions

In these liberated days of sexual laissez-faire, where erotic preference has become a badge of identity to be worn with pride, perversions are often referred to as *paraphilias*, derived from Greek words meaning "alongside of" and "love."

Common paraphilias include exhibitionism, fetishism (urges associated with nonliving objects), frottage (erotic rubbing), pedophilia, masochism, sadism, and voyeurism. It's thought that many of these conditions start with a mild childhood fixation that is gradually reinforced by repeated associations with pleasurable sexual activity.

Most noncriminal paraphilias are no longer treated as serious mental illnesses unless they cause "clinically significant distress" or impairment in "psychosocial functioning"; those that do are often treated with hormones that reduce testosterone levels and/or antidepressants. Nonchemical treatments

♂ In 1993 a man in Hereford, England, was given eighteen months for having sex with the pavement. Two years later he was put on three years' probation for simulating public sex with a bin liner.

♂ The eighteenth-century Scottish biographer James Boswell used to masturbate by rubbing himself against tree trunks in public places.

♀ In Japan *No Pan Kissa* are coffee shops with mirrored floors that let customers look up the waitresses' skirts.

might involve aversion therapy, counseling to improve social skills, and "orgasmic reconditioning," where the subject masturbates while fantasizing about their paraphilia, then switches to something less bizarre at the moment of orgasm.

👣 Frottage

Some of the best-known frottage fans are the "gropers" who infest Japan's rail network. Usually found on crowded commuter trains, they use the packed conditions to get close to their female victims and indulge in all sorts of uncommuterish behavior. This might range from smelling and rubbing to open masturbation. The problem is so bad that Musashi University

♀ A Belgian optician was arrested in 1995 for making female patients strip and dance to accordion music before fitting them with contact lenses.

♂ In 1992 a 44-year-old Pennsylvania judge promised to let criminals off if they let him shampoo their hair.

> **♀** *Acrotomophilia* is an erotic fixation with amputees. Adolf Frederick, king of Sweden (1751–71), had seven mistresses; two were one-armed, two were one-legged, two were one-eyed, and one had no arms at all.
>
> **♂** An *acrophiliac* is someone with an erotic fixation about heights.
>
> **♀** *Axilism* is sexual attraction to armpits.

holds groper-avoidance classes for female commuters. Some gropers have achieved fame through their activities. Samu Yamamoto, a Tokyo café owner, became a celebrity in 1994 when he published his autobiographical *Diary of a Groper*. At least one Tokyo sex club has a room equipped like a subway carriage where men can indulge groper fantasies.

👣 Scatology—*Doing the Dirty*

Many people have commented on the connection between sexuality and defecation. Freud suggested that children went through various stages in sexual development, one being a "sadistic" anal stage involving expulsion and destruction.

Some find defecation exciting. Phrases in Mozart's private correspondence suggest he had an interest in the scatological. In letters sent to his cousin Maria in 1777 he wrote, "I wish you a good night but first shit in your bed and make it burst," "Oh, my arse is burning like fire!—perhaps some muck wants to come out?" and "I kiss your hands, your face, your knees and your—in a word, wherever you permit me to kiss."

Many scatology fans combine their hobby with voyeurism. Some brothels have glass tables made for a girl to defecate over, enabling customers to watch from underneath. In the Victorian erotic journal *My Secret Life,* the author, "Walter," tells how he found a knothole in the wall of a ladies' toilet at a rural Swiss railway station. Walter settled in and spent an entire weekend watching female passengers squatting on the privy (only taking time out to diddle the stationmaster's wife).

Public toilets are often a favorite haunt of voyeurs. In 1991 a Connecticut man turned himself in to state park rangers admitting he'd been crawling under the ladies' outhouses, and in 1987 a plastic-wrapped man was found waist-deep in the cesspit under the ladies' lavatory in a California state park.

Other voyeurs have gone high tech. In 1996 a man was arrested for installing secret "toilet cams" in a number of ladies' restrooms, and many Internet sites claim they can offer a candid inside view of public toilet cubicles.

A specialist breed of fetishists are known as "toilet slaves," people who enjoy being defecated and urinated on (so-called "brown showers" and "golden showers"). At bondage parties a toilet slave might be chained to the john to keep it licked clean or to act as a human bidet. In extreme cases they might act as a complete sewage disposal system.

> ⚥ In 1992 a 20-year-old Englishman was treated for his sexual attraction to his Austin Metro.
>
> ⚥ A Los Angeles man was arrested in 1981 for sneaking under the tables at the university library and painting women's toenails.
>
> ♀ In 1990 an Englishwoman was taken to the hospital wearing only a coat of varnish and a dog collar.

To train a slave to eat feces (a practice known as *co-prophagy*), a dominant partner will often insert corned beef or chocolate mousse up their rectum to simulate a turd.

A few people really enjoy eating feces. One American enthusiast sabotaged the water supply in his local public toilets, making them impossible to flush. Once in a while he'd pop round with a bag and collect any deposits. Another sex offender, known as the Peanut Butter Kid, used to lick his own excrement off his victim's genitals.

According to one source, human feces has a "charred" flavor, but apart from that is very similar to the original food. Another described it as tasting of "rotten Hungarian peppers in a soft cream," another as strong and "sweetish." Most people who've tried it say it smells worse than it tastes. In the nineteenth century one eccentric European prince liked his mistress to defecate in his mouth. He got around the flavor problem by insisting she live on marzipan.

Water Sports—*Pee Is for Pleasure*

Known as *urolagnia* or *urophilia,* the term *water sports* describes sex play involving urine. Many people think urine is dirty, but assuming you have healthy kidneys, it's virtually sterile. Urine can smell foul, but enthusiasts avoid this by

An English flasher from the mid-1980s used to stick his erection through mailboxes.

In 1989 a doctor of traditional Chinese medicine was arrested for fondling his assistant's breasts. He claimed he was looking for acupuncture points.

> ♂ A 27-year-old Texas man was arrested in 2001 for an act of public lewdness. He was found crouching in the aisle of a convenience store inserting a can of hairspray up his rectum.
>
> ♂ In 2001 a Florida man was caught using a tiny lens in his shoe to videotape underneath women's skirts.
>
> ♂ A California man was turned on by swallowing shaved Barbie heads. After they passed through his bowels, they were washed and used again.

drinking plenty of diluting fluid and avoiding protein (which produces strong-smelling urine) and stinky foods like asparagus. Some go as far as drinking cologne to kill the taste.

Water sports fans entertain themselves in a variety of ways. The simplest sex game is known as a Golden Shower, where one partner pees over the other. Cataracts of the Nile requires the male to pee over his partner's clitoris, while Log in the Amazon requires the female to pee over the man's penis. The Fountain of Venus is an act of oral sex where the man licks the woman to orgasm, at which point she pees in his mouth. In the Spitting Snake the man pees in the woman's mouth. Peeing can be combined with normal penetration. If the woman pees while the man's penis is inserted in her vagina, it's known as Watering the Oak; if the man pees, it's called Flooding the Cave.

👣 Roman Showers

Apart from brown showers and golden showers, there are also Roman showers. Here the sex partners simply vomit over each other. It's as easy as that.

🐾 Sadomasochism—*Hanky Spanky*

S&M has been around a long time. The two-thousand-year-old *Kama Sutra* of India has a chapter devoted to people hitting each other, even describing the sound each blow should make. It also contains a warning about using implements such as the "wedge," scissors, pinchers, and piercing instruments. At least one Indian ruler killed his wife with scissors, and another blinded a dancing girl while indulging in rough-and-tumble.

For some reason the English have a longstanding reputation as fans of sadomasochism. Flagellation is often referred to as the "English vice," and many brothels have an "English room" equipped like a dungeon. However, sadomasochism and bondage are enjoyed the world over, and the terms *sadism* and *masochism* both have continental roots.

Most people have heard of the Marquis de Sade (1740–1814), but few know how he acquired his reputation. He started his career by abducting and torturing a young woman to test a healing balm he'd invented. Later escapades included serving chocolate pastilles laced with Spanish fly at a banquet, eloping with his wife's sister, and being charged with the abduction and rape of several virgin servant girls. He was sent to the Bastille and later a mental home, where he wrote his most famous work, *120 Days of Sodom*, containing

ALGOPHILIA, sexual arousal through pain, is surprisingly common. In 1953 the Kinsey report said that 50% of people were aroused after being bitten. One source has estimated that 17% of the U.S. population indulges in some form of sadomasochistic activity.

PEOPLE were sometimes beaten for medical reasons, as it was thought that a thrashing was good for you. Old folks were beaten to improve their eyesight, women were whipped to help them conceive, and many doctors thought a thrashing "cleansed" the body. In seventeenth- and eighteenth-century France it was even used to "cure" the mentally ill. Flagellation was also thought to be "improving"—horses were beaten to make them fatter, and in ancient Greece it was thought the regular spanking of a girl's bottom made it pleasantly plump.

accounts of more than six hundred perversions, many of them involving the dominatory sexual violence we now refer to as sadism.

The term *masochism* was first used by the Austrian scientist Richard von Krafft-Ebing in his 1886 work *Psychopathia Sexualis.* For his role model Krafft-Ebing chose the author, and fellow Austrian, Leopold von Sacher-Masoch (1836–95). Sacher-Masoch was a successful novelist who in 1870 started putting his own sexual fantasies into print. His first erotic work was *Venus in Furs*, which involved a fur-clad dominatrix putting her hapless male slaves through their paces. Sacher-Masoch insisted his wife act out these fantasies for him and she put up with it until he started demanding she have affairs with other men—he even advertised for candidates in the local paper. This was too much for Mrs. Sacher-Masoch (pregnant at the time), and she left him.

Professional Flagellators

Both the empress Catherine the Great and the English poet Algernon Swinburne enjoyed a good thrashing, and in

♂ In the late nineteenth century a U.S. inventor came up with an electric whipping chair. It had a rotary flogger positioned under a seatless chair.

♀ The "trap of Fronsac" (named after its French inventor) was a counterweighted chair that flipped back when a person sat in it and spread their arms and legs. The Chinese called similar devices "romantic chairs."

♂ The eighteenth-century engineer Chace Price attempted to make a machine that would flagellate forty people simultaneously.

Victorian times many books and pamphlets were published on the subject, including *The Merry Order of St. Bridget, The Romance of Chastisement,* and *An Experimental Lecture*, by Colonel Spanker.

The Victorian period saw many professional flagellators. Perhaps the most famous was Mrs. Theresa Berkley, a prostitute who kept house at 28 Charlotte Street in London. Mrs. Berkley was an expert who kept a variety of whipping appliances on hand. Rods were stored in water to keep the wood supple, and bunches of nettles were kept fresh in vases. Various whips, thongs, and scrubbing brushes were on hand, as well as cat-o'-nine-tails with needlepoints attached to the leather. Other whacking material included ox-hide straps studded with nails, and bunches of holly, gorse, and a prickly evergreen plant known as "butcher's bush."

Theresa also invented the "Berkley Horse," a contraption that positioned the victim in a good flogging position but still allowed easy access to their face and genitals. The Horse (or "Chevalet") earned Theresa a fortune—many clients paid through the nose to be ill treated. One gentleman had a sliding scale of payment. Once chained to the Horse, he would pay £1 for first blood, £2 for blood running down to his heels, £3 for his heels to be bathed in blood, £4 for a pool of blood on the floor, and £5 for unconsciousness.

School Punishment

It's been suggested that the popularity of flagellation in England was thanks to the beatings handed out in public schools. Reay Tannahill in her book *Sex in History* points out the flaw in this argument: children of all classes have been beaten all around the world. Having said this, it must be admitted that many British schoolmasters were prodigious floggers. In the eighteenth century Eton schoolboys had half a guinea added to their annual account to pay for birches.

This sort of treatment probably did leave an impression on some people, and in at least one school punishment day was distinctly erotic. In a letter dated 1859 one gentleman recalled that delinquent boys in his school were whipped bent over the back of a servant girl. The girl happened to have huge breasts and encouraged the boys to play with them while they were being beaten.

Corporal punishment was also seen in some girls' schools. At the end of the eighteenth century a London school called

AN early English deviant was a flagellant known as Whipping Tom, who lurked around Holborn, the Strand, and Fleet Street. Tom would accost lone women, lift their skirts, and beat their buttocks. As one contemporary writer put it, he'd "make their butt ends cry Spanko." Tom's reign of terror was confined to the year 1671, and he was never caught.

Regent House was run by a Miss Pomeroy who used two rods; one was made of birchwood, and the other (a fearsome weapon called "Soko") was made of whalebone bound in waxed threads. There were two grades of punishment at the school, private and public. In the latter the victim was stripped bare in front of the school, her feet were put into stocks, and she was bent over a desk for a beating.

A few people paid good money to watch these activities. Around 1792 a London banker came to an arrangement with the headmistresses of two girls' schools. In return for a suitable fee, he used to visit the premises in secret and watch the girls being caned through a peephole.

Many ladies enjoyed a good beating. In the eighteenth century the members of various lesbian clubs were said to flog each other with rose twigs. A female flagellation club met in London's Jermyn Street every Thursday, where members would pair off and take turns whipping and caning each other.

Autoasphyxiation

An extreme example of sadomasochism is autoerotic asphyxiation. Many people enjoy the sensation of being partially strangled or hung, though it is a risky business. Michael Hutchence's death in a Sydney hotel room was thought to have occurred in this way, the singer hanging himself with a belt. The practice has been popular for years, and some men find it difficult to get an erection in any other way. In 1793 a wealthy merchant from Bristol came to London to see if a bout of "suspension" could cure his impotence. He hired the services of a young prostitute in Charlotte Street, and a few minutes' hanging produced very gratifying results. However, the

ACCORDING to one source, Hong Kong prostitutes working from sampan boats would stick their heads in the water during sex and partially drown themselves. The vaginal spasms caused by their near-death experiences were apparently very stimulating for their customers. An infamous Japanese sex criminal called Kirita (executed in 1958) used to throttle his victims to death while raping them to achieve the same effect.

merchant suddenly took a turn for the worse, and the young woman ran into the street to seek help. Members of the Society for Reviving Drowned Persons (a kind of eighteenth-century EMT service) were called, and the merchant was saved.

It's not just men who enjoy asphyxiation. A U.S. police training manual cites a case in the 1980s where a woman was found crouched in her closet with a ligature around her neck and a vibrator up her vagina. Although foul play was suspected at first, subsequent investigation pointed to accidental self-asphyxiation during an elaborate masturbation ritual.

People practicing autoasphyxiation usually apply pressure to the noose around their neck by crouching and letting the rope slowly take their body weight. The danger is that pressure on the carotid arteries in the neck will interrupt the blood supply to the brain and cause unconsciousness. Once this happens, the victim slumps, and the pressure from the rope causes death by strangulation. In the United States around seven hundred men and women die each year from this type of sex game.

🔸 In 1992 it was reported that a U.S. man wearing a bulletproof vest used to shoot himself to get sexually aroused.

🔸 In 2001 a male Pasadena submissive died after being force-fed 2.5 lbs of peanut butter during a bondage game.

🔸 The French writer Jean-Jacques Rousseau (1712–78) used to expose himself to women in the hope they'd hit him.

 BDSM

BDSM stands for "Bondage and Discipline/Dominance and Submission/Sadomasochism" but the three groups can be referred to individually as B&D, D&S, and S&M. Another related acronym is SSC—"Safe, Sane, and Consensual."

Although a lot of people believe that BDSM consists only of bondage and beatings, there is also a psychological component in which a *sub* (also known as a *bottom*) is subjugated by a *dom* (also known as a *top*). Where this subjugation is extreme, the participants are known as *master* and *slave*. Sub/dom relationships may be purely psychological but are usually reinforced physically through bondage and discipline, the sub being a masochist and the dom having sadistic tendencies.

 Equipment

Binding materials used in BDSM include ropes, scarves, tape, and belts. Chains are popular, as they cannot tighten accidentally. Items called spreader bars can be made or bought that incorporate shackles that separate the legs and offer unhindered access to the genitals. Larger items of bondage furniture include padded boards, gymnastic horses, racks, crosses, benches, and stocks. Some firms even make "portable dungeons" that can be set up in a room within minutes. There are also inflatable beds and chairs on the market that incorporate cuffs and other restraints. Clamps are widely used, which may range from clothespins and crocodile clips to purpose-made nipple-clamps, breast crushers, and genital clamps. Other miscellaneous items of equipment include ball gags, face masks, genital harnesses, and internally spiked bras.

For chastisement, belts, riding crops, flails (resembling cat-o'-nine-tails), and rods are popular choices, though paddles are favored by many as they rarely break the skin. For the more technically advanced, a range of electrical stimulation machines are available that will deliver electric shocks of varying intensity.

Two specialized areas of BDSM activity involve the use of wax and ice. Many people enjoy having hot wax dripped on them. If it comes from a burning candle, the wax should not be hot enough to cause serious injury. Alternatively, ice can

SHIBARI (Japanese rope bondage) was invented in the medieval period as a torture, but it has now been developed into something of an art form. In *shibari* short lengths of rope are used to restrain the body in a very stylized way, the knots often being positioned over acupuncture points. *Shibari* bondage styles include *shinju* (breast bondage) and *karada*, in which the ropes are knotted in a diamond-shaped body harness.

⚥ In 1981 a Moroccan man was charged with sexually assaulting a pelican on the Greek island of Skyros.

⚥ A worker at the San Antonio zoo was fired in 1985 after it was discovered he'd had sex with a number of inmates, including a baboon, a gazelle, an oryx, a pig, a duck, and a goat.

⚥ A Thai man was recently sentenced to fifteen years in jail for having sex with an elephant. He claimed it was a reincarnation of his dead wife.

be used, either rubbed on the outside or inserted as rods in the anus or vagina.

Piercing is another popular BDSM activity. Some practitioners pierce the clitoris, labia, penis shaft, glans, and scrotum. In some cases piercing literally involves pushing a spike through the flesh. In other cases the piercing is long term and is used to display studs and rings. Some fetishists use rings in the lips, nipples, and genitals as methods of restraint. Labia rings are often used to hold open the vaginal lips during sex play.

One unusual male BDSM practice involving piercing is called ballooning. Here a hole is made in the scrotum, and air or water is pumped in until it inflates like a hairy beach ball.

👣 Animal Lovers

Sex with animals (sometimes known as *zoophilia*) has been condemned by most societies. In the Old Testament it says, "Neither shalt thou lie with any beast to defile thyself therewith: neither shall any woman stand before a beast to lie down thereto: it is confusion." The penalty for bestiality among the Hebrews was death, sometimes by burning. Death is still the penalty for bestiality under Islamic law.

ʕ•ᴥ•ʔ Cross-breeding

One of the main reasons for a mistrust of bestiality was the idea that cross-breeding between species could result in the creation of new animals. For example, in the second century A.D. the classical writer Aelianus described a foal that was the result of the "strange union" of a mare and a groom.

One of the most famous examples of supposed cross-breeding was the creation of the Minotaur, a creature that had the head of a bull and the body of a man. According to legend, Pasiphaë, wife of King Minos of Crete, fell in love with a sacred bull and asked the architect Daedalus to help her seduce it. Daedalus built a hollow fake cow, and once the queen was hidden inside, the contraption was trundled off to the bull's paddock. It's not recorded if the queen enjoyed the encounter, but the bull must have, for Pasiphaë gave birth to a bull-headed boy she named Asterius (aka the Minotaur).

The belief in cross-breeding persisted until relatively recent times. In New England in 1646 the unfortunately named

♂ In 1991 a 38-year-old Englishman was prosecuted for performing a sex act with Freddie, a 12–foot bottlenose dolphin.

♂ A Denver cowboy applied for a license in 1992 to marry his horse. (He was refused.)

♂ In 1989 a drunken London Transport worker was prosecuted for attempting to have sex with a cat on an underground train.

Thomas Hogg was accused of fathering a piglet. It was said the young piggy resembled Mr. Hogg because it, like he, had a "wall-eye." To try to prove this accusation, Mr. Hogg was ordered to fondle the piglet's mother, then do the same to another sow. Apparently Mom became visibly excited by Mr. Hogg's caresses, while the second sow rebuffed his advances. Despite this compelling evidence, it was decided to convict him of the lesser charges of filthiness, lying, and pilfering, and he was whipped and sent to prison.

In some cases a man accused of bestiality could get a lesser sentence if he could prove he hadn't ejaculated and risked inseminating his victim. One such was a fifteenth-century French craftsman called Simon, who was caught having sex with a goat. Simon claimed he was unable to ejaculate and was examined by surgeons, who were inclined to believe him. Two expert witnesses—prostitutes—then had a

In 1998 a San Francisco man was charged with operating a whips-and-chains sex dungeon, where you could also have sex with eels, an anteater, and a water buffalo.

The *Sunday Sport* reported in 1991 the case of a 55-year-old Turkish man who was having an affair with his donkey. His wife was granted a divorce after the man refused to sell the animal.

The English poet Algernon Swinburne (1837–1909) was rumored to have sex with a pet monkey he dressed as a woman.

Theodora, empress of Byzantium (508–548), started life as an erotic performer; one of her acts involved sprinkling grains of wheat over her vagina and having geese peck them off.

♂ In 1993 a Kenyan man was arrested (for the fifth time) on a charge of having sex with a sheep. He said he did it to avoid VD as he could no longer afford the medication to treat it.

♂ A 41-year-old Arizona man was arrested in 1994 for trying to solicit oral sex from a horse.

♂ In 1994 a 59-year-old Englishman sat down to watch a wedding video with friends. Unfortunately the wrong tape was chosen, and his guests watched their host having sex with the neighbor's dog.

look and did all they could to disprove his claim. They couldn't, and Simon escaped death but was branded, given a thrashing, and had his right hand cut off.

One gruesome example of supposed cross-breeding comes from seventeenth-century England, recorded by a man called William Turner. In 1674 he wrote, "At Birdham near Chichester in Sussex, about twenty-three years ago, there was a monster found upon the common, having the form and figure of a man in the fore-part, having two arms and hands, and a human visage, with only one eye in the middle of his forehead: the hinder part was like a lamb.... This young monster was nailed up in the church porch of the said parish, and exposed to public view a long time, as a monument of divine judgement."

👣 Bestiality B.C.

Some ancient societies weren't that worried by bestiality. A code of law laid down by the Hittites in 1400 B.C. stated that sex with a cow, sheep, or pig was an evil to be punished, but those having sex with a horse or mule faced no penalty. There were also rules for animals attempting to have sex with their master. If an ox attempted to mount a man, it was killed, but a pig trying the same thing got off scot-free. Perhaps a bull or ox trying to mount a man would have been regarded as a case of attempted murder. The fact that sex with horses and mules was not punished suggests it was an ingrained habit that the authorities would find hard to break. Records suggest that many nomadic horsemen made use of their steeds as sex partners.

The ancient Egyptians were relatively blasé about sex with animals. One Egyptian sect indulged in temple orgies with goats as part of a fertility rite, and Herodotus records that some Egyptians had sex with crocodiles. In this case Egyptian men would surprise a couple of crocodiles having sex, chase away the male, and rape the female. This wasn't inspired by lust; having sex with a female crocodile was meant to make you lucky. In a similar way some Arab fishermen thought that having sex with a dead female dugong

IN addition to dogs, horses, and bulls, fowl such as hens and ducks have also fallen prey to zoophiles; sex with birds is known as *avisodomy*. One case from nineteenth-century France involved a landlord who kept finding his chickens dead in their coop. He grew suspicious of one of his tenants and caught him in the act, covered in blood and feathers. One unpleasant poultry perversion was practiced in imperial China. Here the head of a goose was pulled off or shut in a doorway at the moment of climax, the muscular contractions of the bird's death throes adding to the pleasure. It's said that geese were provided for this purpose in some European brothels.

👫 DEATH was often the fate of an animal caught in a compromising position with a human. In 1642 a New England colonist called Thomas Granger was found guilty of sexual relations with a mare, a cow, two goats, five sheep, two calves, and a turkey. Thomas was condemned to death, as were all his victims except the sheep. No one could tell the abused sheep apart from the rest of the flock, so they were all reprieved.

There was a similar case in eighteenth-century France. Here one Jacques Feron of Vanvres was sentenced to death for having sex with a she-ass. Both were taken to the gallows, but at the last minute the ass was reprieved after the townspeople and the local priest signed a petition testifying to her good character.

prevented you from drowning. Dugongs (sometimes called sea cows) often drowned when caught in fishing nets, and having sex with the corpse was meant to stop its relatives from dragging you under in revenge.

In America, bestiality was considered normal among tribes such as the Hopi and the Kupfer Inuit, and in ancient Peru acts of bestiality were often depicted on pottery decorations. In East Africa the men of many pastoral tribes had sex with livestock; many Masai youths used donkeys for sex rather than risk tampering with the village virgins. During the 1950s sex with animals was part of the initiation rites of the Mau Mau terrorists, and more recently the AIDS crisis has resulted in a number of African men turning to livestock to avoid infection.

In India some Hindu sects considered it an act of piety to have sex with sacred animals such as cows and monkeys.

Some temples even sold the sexual services of sacred animals.

 ## Europe

Some Western countries have been tolerant of bestiality. In seventh-century Ireland, Church law equated bestiality with masturbation, both sins requiring only two years' penance. In thirteenth-century Sweden sex with animals was outlawed, but previously a perpetrator was liable to a fine only if the animal's owner sued for damages.

In time penalties got tougher, and bestiality laws were often passed alongside those dealing with homosexual sex. For example, in Denmark in 1683 it was decided that both acts were punishable by burning. Under English law bestiality carried the death penalty after the Reformation and continued to do so till the nineteenth century, but only if it could be proved that a man had ejaculated inside an animal. These harsh sentences don't appear to have put many people off, however. During the seventeenth century the Catholic Church tried to ban male herdsmen, a measure that suggests bestiality was a common vice. This law is similar to one enacted by the ancient Incas, who required that all male llama drivers be chaperoned.

Women and Animals

Most classical stories of bestiality involved women and animals. One of the most famous examples in literature is taken from *The Golden Ass,* a work written around A.D. 160 by the Roman author Lucius Apuleius. The story describes the adventures of a man who finds himself turned into a donkey, and toward the end of the book he's hired for a night of sex by an insatiable Roman matron.

Another example of bestiality in literature is Emile Zola's *The Land,* a story of French country folk. This nineteenth-century novel was considered so shocking, the book's publishers were prosecuted for obscenity. One passage reads, "[S]he grasped the bull's penis firmly in her hand and lifted it up. And when the bull felt that he was near the edge, he gathered his strength and, with one single thrust of his loins, pushed his penis right in. Then it came out again."

Brothels have sometimes put on animal sex shows. Usually the woman is a willing partner, but this wasn't always the case. Sex between women and animals was a common entertainment in the Roman circus. Often the woman was a condemned convict who was ravished (often to death) by a bull, jackass, or large dog. At other times female slaves had to suffer the attentions of a variety of beasts, including giraffes, lions, zebras, cheetahs, leopards, and wild boars, all of which were especially trained for the job. It's not certain how these animals were encouraged to mate with humans, but in the past the makers of stag movies featuring bestiality used to collect secretions of female animals in heat and smear them over the genitals of their starlets. No doubt similar methods were used by the Roman *bestiarii* in charge of the Colosseum animals.

Women zoophiles only occasionally crop up in historic criminal records, one example being a Toulouse woman in the Middle Ages who was burned for having sex with a dog. Part of the reason must be that a woman's choice of animal sex partners is more limited than a man's, and smaller animals like dogs and goats are easier to secrete indoors away from prying eyes. In contrast many men convicted of sex with animals were caught out in the open. In 1641 William Hackett, an American colonist, was caught buggering a cow in a field. It was a Sunday, and William had assumed everyone would be at prayer, but he was spotted by a woman too sick to go to church. Another example comes from an English court deposition of 1670: "as he (Thomas Rigg) and Elizabeth his wife were going through Gillimore town field...they espied one Christopher Sunley of Gillimore aforesaid being upon a mare with his arms clasped about her loins, and jumping at her with his body, in a beastly and unseemly manner for the time they were going about twenty yards."

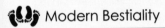 ## Modern Bestiality

In 1892 a French surveyor of roads known as "N" was accused of having sex with a farmer's dog while he was meant to be supervising some roadwork. The case is unusual in that the man, not the dog, was on the receiving end. Once he realized he'd been spotted, N tried to set the dog on the witness, but the pooch was apparently too tired for further exertion. Later N denied he and the dog had copulated, claiming he'd dropped his trousers so the dog could lick him and help relieve his chafed thighs. Many doubted it was possible for a dog to have anal sex with a man, so a doctor got a volunteer to simulate sex with the same animal to see what would happen. The dog reacted with complete uninterest.

It's probably a coincidence, but there seem to be a number of instances of Frenchmen having sex with dogs in public places. In 1880 a seventy-four-year-old man was found in a public urinal in the Rue Publa. The old gent had his penis lodged in the jaws of a Newfoundland dog, which he was masturbating. (He got four months in jail and a sixteen-franc fine.) Around the same time a man was discovered kneeling with a dog between his thighs in a urinal on the Boulevard Voltaire (six months and sixteen francs).

Unlike the case of the road surveyor, another French bestiality case of 1865 definitely did involve penetration. In this sorry tale a farmer's wife came home to find her husband at death's door after being buggered by a bull. As the farmer told it, he'd dropped his trousers to relieve himself in the yard when he heard a commotion from the bull's stall. Thinking the bull was in danger, he rushed into the barn with his trousers at half-mast. The bull then knocked him over and had anal sex with him. A doctor was called, but the farmer died of a perforated rectum eight hours later.

Many European countries have now decriminalized bestiality, the act being covered by general indecency laws and those preventing cruelty to animals. The first U.S. state to drop its bestiality laws was Illinois in 1962. Today bestiality is not legislated against in twenty-six states. One example is Missouri, where laws against gay sex and bestiality were dropped after a court ruling. Gay sex was later recriminalized, but the lawyers never got around to animal sex. One famous, now deceased, proponent of animal sex was Missouri resi-

ACCORDING to a 1948 survey, 8% of adult U.S. males had had sexual contact with animals. In cities this figure was 4%, in the countryside, 17%. These sex acts consisted mainly of vaginal intercourse, the masturbation of animals, and some oral sex, mostly with dogs and calves. For females the overall figure was 36%, with an even split between the city and country. In these cases most acts were oral, involving cats and dogs.

A PLUSHIE is a soft toy, and plushies (short for *plushophiles*) are the people who love them. Most plushies simply have "a thing" for fuzzy toys, but some try to emulate them by dressing up in fur suits. Some plushies combine toys and suits by stuffing a suit with toys and using it as a life-size sex doll. Sex with a soft toy might only involve rubbing, but if penetration is required, male plushies will create an SPH (strategically placed hole) while females will add an SPA (strategically placed appendage). Plushophiles have developed their own glossary, including terms such as *cuddlick* (a cross between a cuddle and a lick), *floof* (to roughly fluff out fur), *furplay* (plushie foreplay), *furson* (a plushophile person), *huggle* (a cross between hug and snuggle), *nuzzlick* (a cross between a nuzzle and a lick), *snugglick* (a cross between a snuggle and a lick), and *yiff* (the act of plushie sex).

dent George Willard, who lived with his pony, Pixel, in a trailer. George became famous through various television appearances (though his interview on *The Jerry Springer Show* was never broadcast), and he even wrote a book about the joy of sex with animals. In contrast there are now a number of organizations (among them PETA and ASAIRS) that actively campaign against all forms of bestiality.

Necrophilia— Diddling the Dearly Departed

Necrophilia usually refers to the act of sex with a corpse, but it can also mean an erotic fascination with death. An example of the latter was the French actress Sarah Bernhardt (1845–1923), who often slept in a rosewood coffin and is said to have entertained many lovers in it.

⚥ In the New Testament Apocrypha a girl called Drusiana dies of shame after being propositioned by a man called Andronicus. Not to be thwarted, he tries to break into her tomb and rape her corpse.

⚥ Some brothels keep a death chamber, complete with funeral parlor furnishings and coffins.

♂ The French revolutionary Danton (1759–94) discovered his wife had died while he'd been on a trip, so had her dug up to kiss her good-bye.

⚥ The ancient Greek hero Achilles had sex with the corpse of the Amazon Queen after he killed her.

Necrophilia is usually practiced by people with ready access to corpses. According to Herodotus, the ancient Egyptians used to prevent embalmers from tampering with bodies by keeping them in the house till they started to decay. Undertakers have always had a bad reputation in this respect, and it's been suggested that the chastity belts of the Middle Ages were locked onto dead women as often as live ones.

According to an American survey of 1989, of 122 people who'd admitted to necrophilic tendencies, just under 60 percent had jobs that involved handling corpses. But other professions have their quota of necrophiles. In 1894 a Greek medical student visiting an Athens morgue came across the body of a local beauty and proceeded to have sex with it, while the Thai police recently arrested a Buddhist monk for having sex with a forty-year-old dead woman left in his care.

Surprisingly, this gruesome activity can have a positive outcome. In 1992 a mortuary attendant in Bucharest was having sex with the body of an eighteen-year-old girl when she suddenly "came to life." It seems his molestation had snapped her out of a coma. The girl's parents were so delighted, they refused to press charges.

Many countries don't have laws that cover necrophilia. In the example of the Thai monk mentioned above, the police discovered they could not prosecute him for defiling a corpse and had to charge him with damaging the coffin. Few U.S. states have necrophilia laws. In 1995 Florida police charged a man with killing his mother but were astonished to learn they couldn't prosecute the man's friend for having sex with the corpse. A similar case occurred in Washington in 1993. Police apprehended a man who twice entered funeral homes to have sex with the inmates but discovered there was nothing technically illegal about it.

 ## Famous Necrophiliacs

FRANÇOIS BERTRAND: Born in 1822, Bertrand became a sergeant in the French Army and, around 1847, started making regular visits to the Père-Lachaise paupers' cemetery near Paris. Bertrand had sex with the bodies he unearthed and often slashed his dead lovers, pulling out their entrails and mutilating their sexual organs. Those who came across his handiwork claimed some of the corpses had been "gnawed" at, but Bertrand always denied he was a cannibal. Most of his victims were young females, and although he preferred his bodies fresh, even advanced decomposition didn't put him off. Bertrand's career ended in 1849 when he was shot and captured. He was sentenced to one year in prison and later vanished.

COUNT KARL TANZLER VON COSEL: A German veteran of the First World War, the count moved to the United States around

1930 and found work in a Florida hospital. Here he fell in love with a young Cuban women called Elena. Sadly, Elena died soon afterward, but the count rescued her corpse from the mausoleum and took her home. Details of what happened next are sketchy, but the count used whatever medical expertise he had to rebuild Elena's body, including her sex organs. Ten years later the police (acting on a tip) raided the count's home, recovered Elena's preserved body, and cremated it.

HENRI BLOT: Henri's hunting ground was the Saint-Ouen graveyard in France. In 1886 he was discovered by the cemetery groundskeeper fast asleep by the open grave of his most recent victim, a young ballerina. Henri is most famous for a brazen statement he made in court. When defending his actions, he told the judge, "How would you have it? Every man to his own tastes. Mine is for corpses!"

VICTOR ARDISSON: Victor was born in France in 1872 and began exhuming bodies at the age of nineteen. He became the mortician in a small town and in his career may have violated over a hundred corpses. Victor's activities came to light in 1900, when suspicious neighbors informed the police. His home was raided, and the authorities discovered the decaying body of a 3½-year-old-girl. According to Victor, he'd regularly had oral sex with the dead child and fully expected that it would result in her resurrection. Also found in his house was an object that Victor called his "little bride," the severed head of a thirteen-year-old girl. The head had been in Victor's possession for years, and he regularly slept with it.

KAREN GREENLEE: Karen is a California woman arrested for stealing a male corpse in 1979. An apprentice embalmer in Sacramento, she should have driven the corpse to the cemetery but instead drove off into the countryside for a two-day sex session. California law could not prosecute Karen for necrophilia (it not being officially illegal), but she was convicted of the lesser charges of interfering with a legal burial and the illegal use of a hearse. Later Karen

MORE BIZARRE PARAPHILIAS:

Dentrophilia—sex with trees

Gerontophilia—sex with an elderly person

Hodophilia—sex in strange places

Ochlophilia—sex in crowds

Somnophilia—sex with a sleeping partner

Xenophilia—sex with strangers

Endytophilia—sex while remaining clothed

Lactaphilia—sex with a breast-feeding mother

Mysophilia—arousal by body odor

Harpaxophilia—arousal by paying for sex

Agrexophilia—arousal by being caught or seen

Amurophilia—sex with the blind or blindfolded

Other recognized sources of particular sexual arousal include: ants, bees, burial, cars, dolls, ears, feet, food, ghosts, hair, heights, the outdoors, rape, religious artifacts, shoes, snakes, stealing, strangulation, tears, teeth, uniforms, vomit, water, and wealth.

confessed to abusing up to forty male corpses during her career, having sex by rubbing herself against their genitals and faces. Karen was also attracted to the blood the freshly embalmed corpses "purged" out of their mouths when she lay on them.

BARE NAKED LADIES (AND GENTS)

A Short History of Pornography

It is hard to define pornography. Originally the word meant to "write about prostitutes," but these days anything designed to sexually arouse is generally regarded as pornographic. Pornography was popular in ancient Rome, and walls were often decorated with erotic friezes showing bacchanalian orgies. In Pompeii images were painted outside brothels to advertise the services inside, and the streets were decorated with phalluses pointing the way to the nearest house of ill repute.

Few Romans could afford the expense of handcrafted friezes or parchments, so most ancient pornography was for the select few. In fifteenth-century Europe this situation changed with the introduction of printing, but since the output of most early presses was strictly monitored, there was little mass production of obscene writing and imagery. It was also difficult to create detailed pictures using crude wood-blocks, so visual porn had to wait for the more advanced engraving techniques of the sixteenth century.

The most famous pornographic work of the sixteenth century was *Aretino's Postures*, named after the Italian satirist Pietro Aretino. Pietro wrote sonnets celebrating sixteen sexual positions (the *Sonetti lussuriosi*), illustrated by the artist Giulio Romano. The *Postures* (aka *I Modi*, "The Ways") was published in 1525 and was a great success. It's thought the engravings were originally commissioned by the pleasure-loving Pope Leo X, but his uptight successor Clement VII destroyed all the copies he could find. But copies of Romano's copperplates were smuggled into France, where extra positions were added and the collection eventually grew to a total of thirty-six "venereal motions." Copperplates could be duplicated relatively easily, and *Aretino's Postures* spread all over Europe. In 1674 copies reached Oxford University, where the students of All Souls started mass-producing prints until their thriving porno press was discovered by the dean.

In successive centuries most pornography consisted of erotic literature containing the occasional illustration. Famous examples from this period are: *L'Ecole des filles* (The Girls' School) published in 1655, and *Fanny Hill: Memoirs of a Woman of Pleasure*, written by John Cleland around 1749.

Some were humorous and had a satirical bent, for example: *A Full and True Account of a Dreadful Fire that Lately Broke Out in the Pope's Breeches*, written in 1713. Many lurid titles were penned in the eighteenth and nineteenth centuries, including: *Little Merlin's Cave, As It Was Lately Discover'd, by a Gentleman's Gardener, in Maidenhead-Thicket; A Midnight Ramble, or the Adventures of Two Noble Females; The Secrets of the Black Nunnery Revealed; The Lustful Turk;*

The Pleasure of the Rod; Lascivious Scenes in the Convent; Confession of a Washington Belle; and *Sweet Seventeen: The True Story of a Daughter's Awful Whipping and Its Delightful If Direful Consequence.*

Many of these books seem to reveal an obsession with nuns and noblewomen. These fixations seem to have been universal—the Chinese and Japanese penned works such as *The Confessions of Lady Nijo* and *The Ocean of Iniquities of Monks and Nuns*.

The first porn magazines also came into existence at this time. One of the most famous was *The Pearl—A Journal of Facetiae and Voluptuous Reading*. This was a monthly magazine published in London between 1879 and 1886 containing obscene lithographs and serialized pornographic novels.

Some visual porn appeared as colored prints. To pay off his gambling debts, the famous English caricaturist Thomas Rowlandson (1756–1827) produced large numbers of colored illustrations with titles such as "The Wanton Frolic," "The Toss Off," and "The Country Squire Newly Mounted." But this material was too expensive for most people, and much literary pornography was littered with classical allusions and foreign phrases that could only be understood by the educated. Porn for the masses had to wait until the arrival of photography.

The first porn boom began with the explosion of the dirty postcard market in the 1880s. Photographic postcards were cheap to buy and there was little control of their sale and distribution. In 1909 around 800 million were sold in England alone, and a good proportion of them were of a sexual nature. After a police raid one London vendor was found to have 6,000 cards in stock, of which 2,287 were judged to be obscene. Many cards were soft porn, consisting of "educational" illustrations of naked tribeswomen, or re-creations of famous artworks using nudes. Other cards were far stronger, some illustrating subjects like bestiality and scatology.

IN France an act called "Le Coucher d'Yvette" was performed onstage in 1895 and featured a girl partially stripping off while she looked for a flea in her clothing. The first completely nude girl to appear on the stage was a performer in the Parisian Folies-Bergère in 1912. It caused a huge scandal, but afterward every show in town had one. In America the origins of the classic striptease are found in the burlesque shows of the nineteenth century, which were inspired by a popular vaudeville revue of 1868 called *Lydia Thompson and Her British Blondes*. The Blondes performed parodies (burlesques) of straight theater, in which girls played the male roles wearing short tunics and tights, much like the principal boys of traditional British pantomime. By the 1870s there were numerous female musical troupes touring the country supported by male comics. Burlesque shows (often pronounced "burleycue") mixed dances, such as the can-can and the hootchy-kootchy, with songs, drama, and comedy. According to legend, the first show to feature a striptease did so by accident: a tap dancer called Hinda Wassau lost part of her costume while performing in Chicago's Haymarket Theater around 1930. Another story has it that a dancer at Minsky's Burlesque "accidentally" stripped in 1917 (a story told in the 1968 film *The Night They Raided Minsky's*, starring Britt Ekland). It's more likely that striptease came into being gradually, as promoters paid girls more to wear less. Public censure caused these burlesque theaters to close in the 1940s, but the strippers simply relocated to nightclubs, which became the topless bars and lap-dancing clubs of today.

TEMPEST Storm (aka the Torso) is an American stripper who still makes a living at the age of 75.

Moving Pictures

The first moving photographic images were created by the English photographer Eadweard Muybridge, who invented the "zoopraxiscope" in 1879. His device used a revolving plate with incremental photos pasted around the rim. Of the 733 photosets Muybridge created, 454 were of nude, or nearly nude, men and women. These displays were designed to be anatomical studies, but many bought them for more prurient reasons. A later development was the What the Butler Saw Machine, or "mutoscope." These machines contained a drum of around 850 incremental photographs that revolved when you cranked a handle. Saucy mutoscope shows had names like "How Girls Undress," "The X-Ray Gown," "Ladies Night in a Turkish Bath," "Girl Climbing Apple Tree," "The Pretty Stenographer," and "How Bridget Served the Salad Undressed." One New York mutoscope show of 1905 was called "The Flatiron Building on a Windy Day" and showed ladies' skirts being whipped up by the wind.

The mutoscope represented a parting of the ways for porn. The market for printed pornography was still going strong, but with the development of film many mutoscope classics were transformed into movie releases that helped found the cinematic porn industry.

CLASSIC MAGAZINE TITLES PAST AND PRESENT

A-Cup Honeys, All Natural D-Cups, Anal Action, Asian Babes, Bachelor Party, Bad Babes!, Bare Are They Now?, Bare Assets, Barely Legal, Bazooms, Beach Girls, Beaver Hunt, Best Porn Action, Big & Black, Big & Fat, Big Bust Amateur, Big Butt, Black Nylons, Black Pleasure International, Blondes in Action, Boob Cruise, Boob Tube Busters, Boobs & Buns, Boobs & Butts, Buf Swinger, Bunnies, Bustin' Loose, Butt Lust, Cad, Candy Girls, Cheap Thrills, Cheeks, Clean Shaven, Co-Ed Babes, Co-Ed Virgins, College Girls, Come of Age, Couples In Heat, Derriere, Dirty, Double-D Fever, Exotic Blondes of Scandinavia, Eyeful, Fabulous Femmes, Feminine Form, Femme, Femme Fatales, Fifty +, Finally Legal, First Time Ever, Flashers, Fling, Forty & Foxy, Foxiest Females, Full Frontal Assault, Furry Females, Gals Galore, Giant Boobs, Girl Crazy, Girls on Girls, Girls Who Cheat, Going Bust, Golden Globes, Good Sports!, Gorgeous Groups, Hairy Girls, Hardcore Housewives, Hefty, Here She Is!, High Heels, Hometown Honeys, Hometown Nymphos, Honey Cups, Honeybuns, Hook Up, Hooker, Hooters, Horny Babes, Horny Housewives, Hot Babes, Hot Bodies, Hot Buns, Hot Chocolate, Hot Couples, Hot Denim Daze, Hot Encounters, Hot Flashers!, Hot Housewives, Hot Shots, Hot Spot, Hot Swinging Couples, Island Girls, Jiggle, Jock Magazine, Juggs, Jumbo Hooters, Just Singin' in the Nude, Kinky Clobber, Kinky Couples, Knockers, Latin Ladies, Leg Heaven, Leg Lust, Leg Parade, Leg Passion, Leg Scene, Legal & Tender, Lesbo Action, Lewd Chicks, Lifestyles of the Rich & Shameless, Like Mother—Like Daughter, Little Annie Fanny, Locker Room Fantasies, Lonesome Gals, Man's Favourite Pastime, Mature Nymphos, Mature Pink, Mega Mams, Midnight, Mink, Modern Sunbathing, Monster Tits, Nasty, Nasty Nymphos, Nasty Photos, Nasty Women, National Screw, Naughty Amateurs, Naughty Neighbors, Network Nudes, Nylon Jungle, Older 'n' Bolder, One-Handed Reader, Oral Addicts!, Orgy Girls, Oriental Dolls, Outdoor Girls, Panty Girls, Party Chicks, Plump & Pink, Posh Wives!,

Pussycat, Quickie, Readers' Wives, Real Wives 100 percent, Rear Action, Rear View, Red Hot Amateurs, Sex Gazette, Sexy Girls Next Door, Shaved Smooth, Shaven Havens, Smokin' Strippers, Spanky, Sporting Women, Stacked, Stacked & Packed, Stars in Heat, Supermamas, Swingers, Thigh High, Thrills Nude Wives, Top Heavy, Treasured Chests, Uniform Special, Up the Skirt, Video Vixens, Wet and Wild, Woman 2 Woman, Women in Heat, Women in Uniform, Young & Stacked.

Magazines

Before the Second World War those looking for pictures of nude men and women had to visit art galleries, buy photography magazines, or subscribe to a naturist publication like *Health & Efficiency* (established in 1900). A number of mild "cheesecake" pulp magazines sprang up after the First World War, imitating the spicy publications soldiers brought home from France, but in the interwar years printed hardcore pornography was hard to find. During the Second World War patriotic pin-up girls softened the public attitude to girlie magazines, and there was a boom in "tits and ass" titles. The first mainstream softcore men's magazine was *Playboy,* first published in 1953, with Marilyn Monroe as its first centerfold. The first issue sold 50,000 copies, and by its second anniversary its circulation had risen to 400,000. Initially *Playboy* restricted itself to breasts and bottoms, but it went full frontal when its competitor, *Penthouse,* first exposed pubic hair in its April 1970 issue. These titles lagged behind Scandinavia, however; the world's first full-color hardcore sex magazine, *Private,* was published in Sweden in 1965. It wasn't until

THE 1970s saw the first openly gay porn magazines appear on newsstands, though discreet gay porn was first produced back in the 1950s. One of the first of these early titles was a New York publication called *After Dark*, specializing in tasteful pictures of young male dancers and actors. Its West Coast rival, *Physique Pictorial*, was for bodybuilder fans and concentrated on athletic beach-bum beefcake.

Hustler magazine published the first "pink shot" in 1974 that American readers got a gynecological view of the female sex organs. Porn for women also hit the shelves at this time—the first issue of *Playgirl* appeared in 1973.

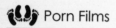 ## Porn Films

Hardcore porn films or "stag movies" have been made since the 1910s. One of the first was an Argentinian film called *Sartorio*, made in 1907, featuring a man in a devil costume having oral and vaginal sex with a woman. In one of the first U.S. porn films, *The Free Ride* (1915), a motorist has sex with two female hitchhikers. Another movie involved a man having sex with three women through a hole in a fence, the joke being that the girls substitute themselves with a goat. These films were made for private viewings, porn vendors travelling the country with a projector and visiting brothels and private clubs.

Before 1924 softcore nudity was also seen in some mainstream Hollywood films. This relaxed attitude changed after two prominent sex scandals of the early 1920s (the most famous involving Fatty Arbuckle, a dead starlet, and a bottle). To clean up its image Hollywood created the Hays Office for the self-censorship of studio productions.

To fill the softcore gap created by the Hays Office, a group of showmen known as The Forty Thieves took to touring the American "Sucker Belt" (the South and Midwest). Their traveling cinema shows featured mildly titillating films purporting to warn of the perils of loose living. These films had suggestive titles like *Secrets of a Model*, *Sex Madness*, and *Damaged Goods* and illustrated the degradation of young people who embraced a life of sin. The films were advertised as being extremely raunchy but were, in fact, very tame and often a disappointment to paying customers. Many projectionists had a "square-up reel" of stronger material to play in case duped audiences started to riot.

In the 1950s it was decided that nudity in a film was permissible as long as it was not sexual, and films started to

MANY porn movies have punning titles or are spoofs of famous mainstream films and TV shows. For example: *Jurassic Pork, I Dream of Queenie, The Beverly She-Billies, Dead Men Don't Wear Rubbers, The Texas Dildo Masquerade, Penetrator II, Anal-ize This, The Bare Bitch Project, Remembering Times Gone Bi, Forrest Hump, Sheepless in Montana, You've Got Male!, Muffy the Vampire Layer, PocaHotAss, E3: The Extra-Testicle, Queer and Pleasant Stranger, Shaving Ryan's Privates, G*A*S*H, Bright Lights Big Titties, Let Me Count the Lays, Whore of the Worlds,* and *Tittanic.* The names of many porn stars are equally memorable: Dave Hardman, Wilde Oscar, Vince Voyeur, Seymore Butts, Dick Witte, Rod Majors, Bunny Luv, Chi Chi LaRue, Jewel De'Nyle, Misty Rain, Luzy Purl, Holli Woods, Gail Force, and Christy Canyon.

A parlor game has been devised to let you make your own "porn star" name. It's easy—simply combine the name of your first pet with the name of the street you live on.

appear extolling the virtues of nudist camps. In the U.S. the first of these films was called *Garden of Eden* (1954), while one of the first U.K. offerings was *Naked as Nature Intended* (1961). To make sure viewers had something worth watching, the filmmakers cast their own nudists, often magazine models or strippers. In 1959 the first nonnudist nudie film, *The Immoral Mr. Teas*, was made by Russ Meyer. The film was tame by modern standards, but unlike other nudie films of the time, it was stylish and well made and did a lot to increase the respectability of these offerings.

During the 1950s and '60s there was a gradual relaxation of U.S. antiporn laws—the right to view porn was treated as a civil liberties issue. The number of porn cinemas rose from twenty in 1960 to more than 750 in 1970, but rather than screen full-length features, they showed short hardcore "loops," cheap Super-8 films that ran on a continuous reel.

Hardcore reached mainstream audiences in 1972 with the release of *Deep Throat,* starring Linda Lovelace and Harry Reams. *Deep Throat* was the first full-length porn feature with a story, and it made its Mafia backers a fortune, raking in over $4,500 for every dollar invested. In America the controversy surrounding *Deep Throat*'s popularity led to a 1973 Supreme Court ruling that local communities could decide for them-

THE X rating for films was dropped after the X-rated *Midnight Cowboy* won the Oscar for best movie in 1969. For many years an X-rating indicated an explicit, often sleazy sexual content, but once mainstream films like *Midnight Cowboy* started appearing, the censors had to create a new distinction between "pornographic" and "adult." The result was the G, PG, R, etc. ratings we have today.

PORN star Annabelle Chong was once featured in a video where she had sex with 251 men. In 1996 Jasmin St. Clair broke this record with a claim of 300, while in 2000 Spantaneeus Xtasty smashed the 500 barrier with a 551 score. Within a few weeks a porn newcomer called Houston topped this with a claim of 621 men in less than eight hours.

A NURSING home in Copenhagen regularly shows pornography to its inmates. It relaxes the patients as effectively as drugs but at a fraction of the price.

selves what was obscene. This led to America becoming a legal patchwork, with some areas having very liberal pornography laws and other communities banning it altogether. Despite these changes the porn film industry thrived, thanks first to the development of the VCR and later to cable and satellite channels that let people view porn in the privacy of their own homes.

Today the United States produces an estimated eight to ten thousand new porn titles a year. One estimate puts annual VCR/DVD sales at 700 million units. Most of these films are cheaply made (the most expensive costs around $200,000), and most only sell between a thousand and three thousand copies, an occasional blockbuster (like *Uncut*, starring John Wayne Bobbit) may sell more than fifty thousand copies. Today the total U.S. porn industry, including books, magazines, videos, live sex acts, and the Internet, is worth in excess of $10 billion a year.

THE equivalent of the porn Oscars are held every year. There are more than seventy-five categories, some of the most distinctive ones being Best Anal-Themed Series, Best Specialty Spanking Tape, Best Group Sex Scene, Best Oral-Themed Feature, Best Transsexual Tape, Best Solo Sex Scene, and Most Outrageous Sex Scene. The trophies handed out at the Erotic Gay Video Awards are known as Dickies.

Cybersex

The development of personal computers in the 1970s and '80s led to the creation of another porn outlet—the Internet, which allowed techno-perverts to copy pornographic images and swap them on computer billboards. In 1989 the newly created user-friendly World Wide Web proved to be ideal for viewing and selling porn. These days you can even use the Web to buy the real thing—many escort agencies and prostitutes use it to advertise their wares. According to a recent survey, 60 percent of Internet searches are about sex, and one-third of all Internet commerce is porn-related. An idea of the breadth of the Internet porn scene can be gauged by the names of some recently created sites—Kink for Yourself, Londonfetishscene, Pissing Porn, Hotty Twatty Phone Sex, Face Smothering Pics, Nobscan, Mistress Domina BBW, Big Blonde Jugs, Voyeur Visions, Your Neighbor's Wife, Tit-Tastic Teen Tits and Ass, All For Fetish, Wet & Wild Amateurs, China Doll Massage & Acupressure, and Venus Envy. Incredibly, the Internet has been doubling in size every hundred days, so we can expect a lot more of the same.

Mainstream Film Porn Awards

Apart from hardcore pornography, many mainstream films have included a significant sexual content. The following awards celebrate some of the more infamous ones.

The award for Most Erotic Use of a Dairy Product goes to... *Last Tango in Paris* (1972), in which Marlon Brando plays an American widower apartment-hunting in Paris. He meets a beautiful local girl, and lots of amorous activity ensues. The most famous scene involves a bout of rough anal sex using a stick of butter as a makeshift lubricant.

The award for Raunchiest Religious Epic goes to... Cecil B. DeMille's *The Sign of the Cross* (1932). This remarkable film includes episodes of sadism, lesbianism, erotic bathing scenes, the bared boobs of tormented Christian martyrs, and orgies. This (and similar films) were sold on the grounds that, being biblical and historical, they were uplifting and educational. The censorship of the Hays Office soon stamped them out.

The award for First Screen Kiss goes to... May Irwin and John C. Rice in *The Kiss* (1896). This one-minute film made for the Edison kinetoscope features a fully clothed middle-aged couple having a kiss. Oddly enough it was a remake, a re-creation of a kissing scene in a famous Broadway play of the same name. At the time it was denounced as pornographic, and the Catholic Church called for a ban.

The award for Most Painful Simulated Orgasm goes to... Hedy Lamarr in the Czech film *Ecstasy* (1933). Hedy (then known as Hedwig Kiesler) plays an adulterous woman

A BOOK AT BEDTIME

Recommendations from the Literary Canon's Top Shelf:

Fanny Hill (1749), John Cleland
The rise to respectability of a naïve prostitute in bawdy eighteenth-century London. Banned in the U.S. until 1966.

120 Days of Sodom (1784), Marquis de Sade
From the mind of the man who gave his name to sadism, the story of four men who act out their sick, abusive, criminal fantasies.

Venus in Furs (1870), Leopold von Sacher-Masoch
A fictional exploration of Masoch's (the man who gave masochism its name) sexual peccadilloes, where a man craves sexual enslavement by a dominatrix.

Amorous Exploits of a Young Rakehell (1902), Guillaume Apollinaire
A young man's wild and explicit reminiscences of his sexual corruption at the hands of his aunt, his sister, and their friends—from the pen of the great surrealist poet.

Lady Chatterley's Lover (1928), D. H. Lawrence
Perhaps the most famous "dirty book" ever—Lawrence's novel of an adulterous affair between a sexually unfulfilled upper-class married woman and a gamekeeper.

The Story of the Eye (1928), Georges Bataille
Surrealist erotica that aimed to revolt and horrify the bourgeoisie. It slays as many sacred cows as possible with endless, brutal violations, up to and including murder.

Tropic of Cancer (1934), Henry Miller
Autobiographical tales of the prestigious sexual exploits of an American in Paris. Banned in the U.S. until 1961.

Helen and Desire (1954), Alexander Trocchi
Written in a week and one of the founding books of the erotic Olympia
Press, it is the story of Helen Seferis, who runs away from home in
Australia and ends up going all over the world as a prostitute and slave.

Story of O (1954), Pauline Réage
Domination and willing debasement are acted out in a Parisian S&M love
affair.

Delta of Venus (1969), Anaïs Nin
Literary erotica with that feminine touch from Henry Miller's onetime
lover.

called Eva who spends a lot of her time naked, entertaining her lover in the woods. Legend has it that the director livened up her on-screen portrayal of an orgasm by sticking a pin in her backside at the crucial moment.

The award for Raunchiest British Film of the 1940s goes to . . . *The Wicked Lady* (1945). This was the first UK film to be censored for its U.S. release by the Hays Office, mainly due to Margaret Lockwood's plunging neckline. Trivia fans may be interested to learn that the actress playing the bare-breasted horsewhipped wench in the 1986 remake was Marina Sirtis, who went on to play Counselor Troy in *Star Trek: The Next Generation*.

The award for Best Supported Breasts goes to . . . Jane Russell in *The Outlaw* (1943). Production Code complaints about Jane Russell's revealing clothing and pneumatic chest kept the film out of the theaters for three years. Part of the problem was the specially designed brassiere that producer Howard Hughes made for Ms.

Russell, an item of clothing that literally thrust her mammaries into the spotlight.

The award for Most Celebrated Cinematic Pedophile goes to ... James Mason in *Lolita* (1962), who lusts after a 14-year-old nymphet played by Sue Lyon. Mason gives a marvelously sweaty performance as an obsessed professor, but the film isn't actually that explicit. The film was remade in 1997 with Jeremy Irons as the professor and Dominique Swain in the title role.

The award for First Mainstream Pubic Exposure goes to ... *Blowup* (1966), in which London photographer David Hemmings spends an extended scene cavorting with two teenage girls. All three lose their clothing in the process, and there are brief but unmistakable glimpses of pubic hair.

The award for Most Infamous Homoerotic Wrestling Match goes to ... Alan Bates and Oliver Reed, who grappled naked by the fireside in *Women in Love* (1969). Rumor has it that Oliver Reed was a little embarrassed by the size of his organ compared to Mr. Bates's. To compensate, he used to retreat behind a screen at intervals and increase his dimensions with a little manipulation.

SEX FOR ONE

Masturbation and Other Hobbies

Most of us are wankers. According to one survey, 95 percent of men and 75 percent of women masturbate or have masturbated. One Christian website has estimated that around 150,000 U.S. citizens are masturbating at any one time, and that Americans masturbating in the workplace costs the country $3.14 billion a month in lost productivity. Another source has calculated that at any one time, 2,040,816 women are masturbating worldwide.

 Ancient DIY

Masturbation has a long history. In ancient Egypt the god Osiris was said to have created all living things through an act of masturbation, and public masturbation became part of some religious ceremonies. Even the pharaoh did it, masturbating during his enthronement ritual. In ancient Greece it was known as *thrypsis,* the "rubbing," while the Romans called it *masturatus* and believed the habit was the invention of Hermes, messenger of the gods, who was often represented as a phallic deity.

In India masturbation also had religious links. Lord Shiva was masturbated by a deity called Agnee, who then created the war god Kartikeh from his semen. Krishna, known for his self-contemplation, became a sort of patron god of masturbation, an act known as *hautrus* (manual orgasm) or *panimathana* (hand churning).

In the Middle East it had many names. In Arabic it was called *jeng* (jerking), *jelq* (flipping), *jerk* (juggling), and *mushtzeni* (fist-beating). The Turks called it *istimney-bilyet* (the practice of self-control of the stalk) while the Persians knew it as *maulish-e-zubb* (shampooing the cord).

For and Against

Some cultures have encouraged masturbation. One old Arabic text called *On the Lengthening and Thickening of the Rod* recommended the rubbing and constant handling of the penis to increase its size. Other races have frowned on "self-abuse." For much of Jewish history it was punishable by death. Many Jews and Christians have taken the biblical story of Onan as proof that God is antimasturbation. In the Book of Genesis Onan was commanded to impregnate his dead brother's wife but pulled out before climax to "cast his seed upon the ground" and was promptly struck dead by God. Masturbation is often called *onanism* in memory of this crime, despite the fact that he was not actually masturbating at all.

Another reason for an antimasturbation policy was the belief that every ejaculation was a proto–human being possessing a soul. In this case each masturbatory act could be considered an abortion. This theory was formulated in classical times and persisted until the nineteenth century.

Masturbation was also regarded as weakening by some: the Taoists of China believed that each ejaculation depleted a man's yang energy, and until recent times, many physicians (including Sigmund Freud) thought that masturbation caused physical injury—its supposedly detrimental effects including madness, hairy palms, drooling, depression, lassitude, forgetfulness, and bad eyesight.

Over the centuries a number of methods have been employed to discourage masturbation. One coach at the ancient Olympic Games (776 B.C. to A.D. 394) made his athletes wear leaden penis sheaths to suppress erections. The idea that sex weakens an athlete is still prevalent, especially in boxing circles—champions like Sugar Ray Robinson and Jake LaMotta used to abstain for six weeks before a fight.

In Victorian times a change of diet was recommended as an antimasturbation measure. Hot, spicy foods were thought

🔗 In 2001 an Oklahoma couple was charged with tying their son to his bed to stop him from masturbating.

🔗 A New York man working for the department of social services was arrested in 2002 for masturbating into colleagues' coffee cups.

🔗 To intensify the sensations of masturbation, a New York man recently injected cocaine into his penis. He developed a three-day erection and numerous blood clots. His gangrenous penis eventually fell off in the bath.

MANY animals masturbate. Chimps and monkeys have been observed fondling themselves and even giving themselves oral sex. Elephants have been known to use their trunks. Dolphins also like rubbing themselves against things, and keepers often make sure suitably rough objects are left in their tank for this purpose. Other animals also use tools. On one occasion a porcupine was observed masturbating with a stick held in its paws. Male red deer have a curious masturbatory habit: at certain times of the year their antlers become very sensitive, and repeatedly rubbing the tips against foliage stimulates an ejaculation.

to encourage lustful behavior, and female masturbators were given away by their love of mustard, spices, and vinegar. To solve the problem of spicy food, Dr. Kellogg, a lifelong campaigner against the "solitary vice," designed his cereals to be as bland as possible. He also recommended more drastic measures: male masturbators could be discouraged by threading silver wire through their foreskin to close it up, while drops of carbolic acid on the clitoris were thought to deaden desire in girls. The doctor even sanctioned clitoridectomies, and performed one on a ten-year-old girl. In a separate case of 1897 a man had his penis cut off as a cure for masturbation, presumably at his own request. Some believe that fondness for circumcision started during this period, not for hygienic reasons but as a preventative measure against self-abuse.

Victorian and Edwardian inventors came up with many inventions to stop masturbation. For example, "sleeping rings" with internal spikes to discourage erections, electrical belts that triggered an alarm if the penis became stiff, and chastity belts that securely covered the genitals survived as antimasturbation devices well into the 1930s.

👣 Sisters Are Doing It for Themselves

A wide variety of objects have been used by women as aids to masturbation. In 1743 a Parisian doctor recorded how he'd rescued a perfume bottle from the vagina of a nun, while another French doctor of 1897 wrote of his experiences with corks, thimbles, wine flasks, shot glasses, and even a compass. It's more usual to find broom and hairbrush handles being used as masturbatory aids, though according to one twentieth-century sex survey, candles are the number-one favorite. Water is also very popular; jets from showers and whirlpool baths apparently produce very satisfactory results. Frottage (erotic rubbing) is another favorite—many women describe techniques that involve grinding against pillows, cushions, or stuffed toys held between the legs. Others lie face-down and rub against the floor. Another technique is called "riding the seam," where squeezing the thighs rubs the vagina against the stitched gusset in a pair of jeans.

Another rubbing technique is called *mulierre*, where a woman rubs a strip of fabric, a bathrobe belt, a pair of tights, a string of beads, or a pearl necklace between her legs. To do this hands-free, some women straddle a cord tied between two chairs. Feathers and makeup brushes can also be used to masturbate, while others find cold sensations erotic and masturbate with a popsicle inserted in the vagina or anus. There's a record of one woman using a long frozen water-filled balloon as a giant icy dildo.

As a final thought, one must not forget the edible sex aids, including cucumbers, zucchini, bananas, plantains, salamis, and—popular with at least one lady—Polish sausages.

 ## Dildos

The use of dildos seems to have started back in prehistoric times. Suspicious-looking "batons" carved from bone and wood found at some Paleolithic sites would have made excellent dildos. In the Gorge d'Enfer region in France, archaeologists have found a double baton that could have been used by two women at the same time; it even has holes for harness straps. Many archaeologists tend to be reluctant to admit these might be sex objects and refer to them as arrow- or spear-straighteners.

Dildolike objects from 4000 B.C. have been found in the ruins of the Indian Harappa civilization. The ladies of ancient Egypt used them—dildos have even been found in the tombs of Egyptian queens. The ancient Greeks made good use of these objects, though they knew them as *olisbos* (meaning "slippers," presumably on account of the olive oil used to lubricate them). A Greek play written in the third century B.C. involves a woman who goes to a friend's to borrow her dildo, only to discover it has already been lent out to a third party. It's suggested she buy her own, and she is recommended the dildos made by a cobbler called Cerdon. Most ancient dildos were made of stuffed leather, and the leatherworkers of the Greek city of Miletus (in modern Turkey) had a reputation for craftsmanship of the highest standard.

In China expensive dildos were often made from ivory. Chinese harems did not have restrictions against phallic objects—unlike those of the Middle East, where even the cucumbers were served chopped—and harem girls often tied

ONE of the largest off-the-shelf dildos you can buy is the Jumbo Giant Dong. This monster (including balls) is 16 inches long and 3 inches wide. One of the smallest dildos is the 3-inch Mini Dong.

dildos to their groins and used them on each other. Another technique known as the "live limb" involved a woman strapping a dildo to her ankle and using it on herself. Some sixteenth-century texts refer to a "Cantonese groin"—part of a "sprouting plant" that swelled up in hot water to make an excellent dildo. Unfortunately for modern gardeners, the identity of this plant seems to be a mystery. Another unusual Oriental dildo was a Japanese face mask with a large penis-shaped nose. These masks were used by actors in ribald comedies and were very popular off-stage too.

In Renaissance Europe the Italians were famous dildo manufacturers. In fact the name *dildo* is thought to be derived from the Italian *diletto*, meaning "delight," though the modern Italian name for these objects is *passatiempo* (pass the time). An alternative origin for the term *dildo* might be the old English term *dill-doll*. In this case *dill* is derived from the Norse word *dilla,* meaning "to soothe."

Some of these early dildos were made of unusual materials like velvet and glass. A few sophisticated models included a bag of hot milk or water, to mimic an ejaculation.

Many dildos were sold by milliners, who made them as a sideline, but there were a few shops that specialized in dildos and other marital aids. A famous nineteenth-century example in London was Mrs. Philips's discreet establishment, just off Leicester Square.

The advent of India rubber saw the end of stitched dildos;

THERE'S a town called Dildo on the eastern shore of Trinity Bay, Newfoundland. Despite its obvious rudeness, the townsfolk are proud of their town's name and have refused to change it. Some believe the name has obscure Portuguese or Spanish roots, others that it's from the Indian name for a local tree. Most are content with the idea that English sailors named the bay after the penis-shaped headland that forms the town's harbor.

the first rubber models appeared around 1840. Rubber was ideal for the job, and it wasn't long before the Victorians were churning out a huge variety, everything from double-ended models to those incorporating a chinstrap.

Today there's a huge variety of dildos for sale. Some are modeled on the organs of famous porn stars, others are shaped like vegetables, and some are made in the shape of the penises of animals, such as dogs, dolphins, bears, and horses. One manufacturer makes inflatable balls with dildos sticking out of them; you insert the shaft and bounce around on the floor as if it were an erotic Space Hopper.

Vibrators

Vibrators have been around for longer than you might think. Cleopatra is said to have kept a small container of buzzing bees by her bedside for use as a primitive vibrating device. Flies were also used in a similar way, though in this case the exposed vagina was smeared with honey to encourage them to scuttle over it, the pitter-patter of tiny feet having a stimulating effect.

The modern vibrator was invented as a health aid. In the

late nineteenth century many doctors treated female "hysteria," "pelvic heaviness," and "excessive lubrication" by manually massaging a patient's privates until she had a "paroxysm." To supplement this hands-on treatment, water jets and steam-powered vibrating devices were also used. One of the first of these was the coal-fired "Manipulator," invented by Dr. George Taylor in 1869, and in 1883 the first electric model was developed by Mortimer Granville.

These electric vibrators were soon available to the public through mail-order ads in ladies' magazines and catalogues like Sears, Roebuck. The devices came in a wide range of shapes and sizes and were touted as massage cures for a range of ailments, from backache to piles, though the obviously phallic ones were often reserved for the use of doctors. Vibrators were considered respectable devices until the 1920s, when they started making appearances in pornographic literature and stag movies. Thereafter they were shunned by polite society.

Today vibrators are very popular; a recent survey suggests that one in five women between eighteen and thirty-five

♂ After running short of cash, a Russian rubber factory in Volgograd had to pay its workers in dildos.

♂ In 1995 a 16-year-old boy electrocuted himself after trying to make a masturbatory device by connecting a cow's heart to the fusebox.

♀ One magazine ad of 1921 advised husbands to buy their wives vibrators to keep them "young and pretty."

♂ "Diesel Dick" is an involuntary erection caused by engine vibration. It's often suffered by long-distance truck drivers.

IN a crowded market sex toy manufacturers have to use a lot of imagination when naming vibrators and dildos. A few examples: Flexible Double Dong, Rabbit Pearl Vibe, Double Dick, Microwavable Cock, Bully Boy, Lil Hotty Vibe, Ez-Rider, Mighty Thor, Thriller Dong, Deep Stroker, Magic Cock, Ballsy Dong, Pink Prober, Cyber Cock, Monster Cock, Jelly Flexible, Tower of Love, Hard On, Super Cock, Super Hot Pink, Pleasure Tree, Jumbo Jack, Super Duper Dong, Manhandler, Veined Double Dong.

has used one. However, another source suggests that less than 5 percent of women actually use penetrative objects during masturbation and that most dildos and vibrators are bought by men.

Vibrators are not the only things that buzz, and many household appliances can be used as makeshift devices. The automatic washing machine on spin cycle is a popular choice, as are electric toothbrushes. Another favorite is the electric razor (after the cutting head has been covered by band-aids). Some women even use the vibration produced by hi-fi speakers.

Specialist Sex Aids

Butt Plugs: Some vibrators are designed for anal use and are called *butt plugs*. These plugs are generally shorter than vaginal sex toys and incorporate a T-bar to prevent them from disappearing up the anus.

Anal Beads: Also known as Thai Love Beads, these are pea- or marble-sized spheroids attached to a cord. Inserting the beads in the anus and pulling them out rapidly is meant to produce titillating effects. Anal beads resemble a string of pearls; in the past pearl necklaces were often used in exactly the same way.

Clitoral Stimulators: These are small vibrating pads that excite the clitoris. Some come with a harness enabling them to be worn during sex.

Duo-Balls: Also known as Ben-Wa Balls, Rin-No-Tama Bells, Burmese Bells, or Love Eggs, these are an Oriental invention popular in the West since the eighteenth century. The simplest balls (or bells) consisted of a small hollow metal sphere containing a loose metal pellet or a blob of mercury. When inserted in the vagina, any motion caused the loose material to move within the sphere in a stimulating way. Many Chinese ladies apparently enjoyed their balls while on a swing or in a hammock. These days the (often vibrating) balls are made of plastic, and two or three might be joined together on a cord.

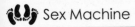 Sex Machine

Dildos and vibrators have now been combined with pump-action machinery that mimics the thrusting action of real sex. These gadgets rejoice in names like The Intruder, The Monster, The Fucksall, The Crane, The Trespasser, The Probe, The Hammer, The Drilldo, and The Goat Milker. In some the dildo is attached to a pneumatic pumping arm;

> THE Roman empress Messalina sometimes ordered men to be continually masturbated till they were impotent or dead. In India the female worshipers of Kali sometimes did the same to their male sacrificial victims.

others achieve a thrusting motion with a wheel and driving rod arrangement working like a locomotive transmission in reverse.

Another type of bonking machine is The Sybian, which looks like a cylinder or saddle with a vibrating post sticking out of the top. The user inserts the post in the vagina or anus, and the whole device then vibrates. The post is set to jiggle up and down, back to front, or from side to side as required.

Gentlemen's Relish

Most men masturbate with the hand (in Latin *cum digito*). In the 1960s a Japanese survey discovered that 54 percent of males masturbated manually, 28 percent used "devil's tongue plant," 17.5 percent rubbed against bedding, 14 percent used the openings of bottles, and 10.5 percent rubbed themselves between their thighs. As well as this, some made holes in gourds, others masturbated with banana peels, rubber tubing, vibrators, rubber bands, condoms, and chickens (though technically this would be bestiality), and a few by "climbing trees."

For those wondering what devil's tongue plant is, its Latin name is *Amorphophallus konjac*, and it's widely cultivated in the East for its edible tubers. When boiled the tubers make a stiff gelatinlike substance called *cone-yuk* that resembles tofu. Apparently a hole bored in a block of *cone-yuk* simulates a vagina very nicely.

Fake Vaginas

It's hard to create a device that mimics the interior of the vagina, but many have tried. In ancient China artificial vaginas

> ⚥ 64% of adolescent males can reach an orgasm in less than 10 seconds.
>
> ⚥ One in every 1,250 men can ejaculate through mental stimulation alone.
>
> ⚥ According to a survey, 3 out of 4 men fantasize while masturbating, while only 1 in 12 women do.

called "bachelor masturbation pillows" were made from leather stuffed with cotton. These heart-shaped creations had a slit in them and were tied to the backs of chairs, enabling gentlemen to use them in a standing position.

These days materials like latex and silicone make it easier to simulate the texture of a vagina. Most of these fakes are in the form of an internally ribbed, open-ended sleeve. Some are manually operated while others include a vibrating component. Some models are closed at one end and incorporate a tube and air bulb that can be pumped to create a sucking sensation. More expensive varieties are electric, fully automatic models with hands-free action. To avoid accidental discovery by a loved one, one commercially available fake vagina is disguised as a flashlight.

Some fake vaginas are incorporated into life-size sex dolls that also feature penetrable mouths and anuses. These dolls can range from the basic to the advanced. Some models offer vibration, suction, and self-lubricating orifices. Some sex dolls are cut-down versions that simply consist of a pair of buttocks with a vagina and anus. For those after something different, the Hustler Company manufactures a pair of vibrating rubber breasts called the Double Scoops Titty Fuck.

USING purpose-made sex toys is much safer than relying on household objects. A Parisian doctor of 1743 recalled a case where a young man got his erect penis caught in his wedding ring, and another who became trapped in the loop of a large key. More recently an Englishman was taken to the hospital in 1995 when his penis became caught in a wine bottle, a situation marginally less embarrassing than the Florida man whose organ became trapped in the suction filter of a public swimming pool in 1994. Added to these are the numerous stories of penises being caught in vacuum cleaners.

Those reluctant to spend money on fake vaginas can make their own using a slit length of foam rubber and a condom. Alternatively, handy household masturbatory aids include inflated water wings, the grooves in an air mattress, and socks or stockings.

Fruit 'n' Veg

Some male masturbators use fruit and vegetables. A centuries-old Mediterranean method involves boring a hole in a warm melon, or large orange. As the Turkish saying has it, "A woman for duty, a boy for pleasure, but a melon for ecstasy." A more modern technique uses a partially hollowed-out cucumber (or zucchini, banana, plantain, or papaya) wrapped in tape. The cucumber is put in a microwave to warm and soften it and then lubricated with oil. A small hole has to be made in the "closed" end, but when in use it can be covered with a finger to create a sucking sensation. Alternatively the cucumber can be rolled between the hands to create a "spinning vagina." Another masturbatory food is

ONE specialist area of male masturbation is solo oral sex, or *au-tofellatio*. It's estimated that around three men in a thousand are able to pull off this trick. In a case from 1908 one American doctor had this feat demonstrated to him by a young mental patient. The boy sat on the doctor's couch, curled himself into a ball, and transformed into a rolling, gasping, and writhing bundle of autoerotic pleasure. The doctor had him committed to a sanatorium. Today porn stars who can perform the act include Al Eingang, Grant Fagan, and Scott O'Hara. A similar feat is *autopederasty*, where those with a long, flexible penis can stick it up their own anus.

pasta—if enough is boiled into a gluey mass, it can be used like the *cone-yuk* described earlier. Another source recommends placing the penis between warmed slices of luncheon meat.

Fun with Your Urethra—"*Sounding*"

"Sounding" is a unisex method of masturbation involving the sensitive tissue of the urethra, the channel that carries urine from the bladder. Some people masturbate by probing the urethral opening, but this often results in objects slipping into the bladder. One of the first recorded instances of this habit was in 1621, when a doctor was called out to retrieve a bone needle that had disappeared up the urethra of a woman. The habit seems quite widespread; one nineteenth-century German gynecologist recalled being called out to forty-seven such cases in his career. The number of objects that can be used in this way is limited only by the imagination, but they include pieces of wood, rope, screws, pipe cleaners, latex fishing worms, ball bearings, pens, balloons, condoms, soldering wire, plastic tubing, even bullets. Those committed to the practice buy purpose-made dilators and catheters from medical suppliers.

Up the Bum

Many people have great fun sticking household objects up their bottoms. For some reason the habit is most common among middle-aged men. Things often go awry, however, and practitioners have to seek medical help to recover lost objects. In 1986 a survey of medical literature on the subject discovered items as diverse as an apple, an artillery shell, a frozen pig's tail, a pool cue, a pepper pot (inscribed "A Present from Margate"), an ice pick, a turnip, a wire spring, a salami, an ax handle, and a parsnip. The most popular objects were bottles and jars, with vibrators coming a close second, and dildos taking bronze.

One grisly rectal find was a collection of burnt match ends; these had been inserted en masse and ignited in a murder case. In 1955 another man did something similar in a suicide attempt—he inserted a cardboard tube in his bottom and used it as a funnel to drop a firecracker inside.

Another painful anal adventure involved a man sticking a frozen fish up his backside. After two or three strokes the fish started to thaw, and its dorsal fin popped up like a hook, preventing its removal.

When retrieving these items, forceps and vaginal retractors are used to "deliver" objects as if they were babies. One of the most bizarre cases of this sort was a concrete enema poured into a man's rectum by his boyfriend. The man used a funnel to introduce the concrete mix, then popped in a Ping-

Pong ball to prevent it from squirting out again. Predictably the concrete mass soon became uncomfortable, and its owner waddled to the hospital to have it removed. The lump (a perfect copy of the rectal cavity) was delivered and found to weigh almost ten ounces.

In many cases it proves impossible to pull the object out, and an abdominal incision is made so the object can be pushed out from the inside. As a last resort a large incision is made in the colon, and the object is retrieved through the hole.

Only slightly less bizarre than the objects found up bottoms are the excuses as to how they got there. A common story involves accidentally "sitting" on an object while in the nude. One man claimed he'd got a screwdriver jammed up his bottom after sitting on it while he was undressing for a shower. Another man reported that he was washing his dog in the shower when he slipped backward and landed awkwardly on a glass jar.

Pet Shop Shenanigans

One bottom activity that appears to be an urban myth is *animal stuffing*, where a small rodent like a gerbil, mouse, or hamster is inserted up the anus and allowed to run around. According to some, the animal is introduced inside a plastic bag to prevent it from doing too much damage. Although many rumors have circulated about this practice, there's no proof it has ever taken place.

Enemas

Although primarily used for medical reasons, some people find enemas very stimulating and enjoy the sensation of flooding their rectum with liquid. (*Colonic irrigation* involves flooding both the rectum and the colon.) Although some enema fans have been known to experiment with liquids like wine, soft drinks, or spiced fluids, it's not wise to use anything but warm water or milk. There's also a danger in bloating your insides with too much fluid; one source recommends 10.1 fluid ounces as a maximum. Be warned, there are considerable dangers in enema play, not least being diarrhea, dizziness, fainting, nausea, weight loss, fatigue, and belly cramps.

YOU'RE THE ONE THAT I WANT

Sex and Marriage

In many early cultures people didn't bother getting married—mating was haphazard within the tribe, and any children were raised in common. A Roman traveler in A.D. 155 reported that the Caledonians (in present-day Scotland) shared their womenfolk, girls having sex in the open with the best of the tribe's warriors. A similar system was observed by the ancient Etruscans of Italy, where all women were shared by law.

In other societies powerful men have disdained a share-and-share-alike attitude and tried to keep more than one woman to themselves. The practice of taking on more than one spouse is known as *polygamy*. In the case of one man with many wives, it is known as *polygyny*. Where one woman takes multiple husbands, it's called *polyandry*.

The Harem
(The Teapot Must Have Many Cups)

The most famous example of polygyny was the harem of the Ottoman sultan, though technically most harem girls weren't wives in the legal sense. The harem was founded as an official institution by Muhammad II in 1454, and it survived till 1909. In this system the sultan usually remained unmarried but fathered sons on an inexhaustible supply of slave girls.

Contrary to popular belief, harem girls did not lie around in gauzy clothing sipping drinks all day. In fact, it seems to have had similarities to a boarding school: girls lived in dormitories and were looked after by matrons (one to every ten girls), only moving to private quarters if they bore a son.

Most of the time harem girls did useful tasks like embroidery, making coffee, and bookkeeping, but when it was time for the sultan to choose a bed partner, they competed fiercely. According to an account of 1668, when the sultan approached the harem, warning bells rang and the area was cleared of prying eyes. The girls then gathered in the harem garden in skimpy outfits and attempted to entice the sultan by singing, dancing, or performing "lewd acts."

At any one time there might be between 300 and 1,200

In 1922 an Englishwoman called Mrs. Theresa Vaughan admitted marrying sixty-one husbands. Throughout her career as a bigamist she averaged one marriage a month.

Between 1949 and 1981 an American called Giovanni Vigliotto contracted 104 marriages in fourteen countries. In 1983 he got twenty-eight years for fraud.

women in the harem, and some never got to sleep with the sultan at all. Those who didn't were pensioned off to live with the defunct harem of the previous sultan in the Old Seraglio. If chosen, a girl was bathed, stripped of any body hair, and perfumed. She was then taken to the sultan's quarters and, after a night of passion, was entitled to keep all the money or jewels she could find in the sultan's pockets.

One of the more eccentric sultans was Ibrahim, who ruled in the mid-seventeenth century. He had a virgin every Friday and on one occasion had his entire harem (then numbering three hundred) drowned in the Bosporus on a mad whim. The walls of his boudoir were covered in mirrors, and his floors were carpeted with sable, as he liked the friction it produced on his knees. (He must have also built up a considerable charge of static electricity.) Ibrahim had a horse fetish and would often assemble his girls in the garden, where he would pretend to be a stallion and run about in the nude ravishing them. Cows, too, also caught his fancy. After seeing the private parts of a cow, he sent agents throughout the empire carrying golden models of the creature's vagina to find a girl

---

IN some societies polygyny was encouraged by local customs that gave a man sexual access to his wife's sisters. In China when a man took a wife, he often took on her sisters as secondary wives. Not only that, he also took on the handmaidens of his bride and her sisters as concubines. Something similar was seen in some South American tribes, where a husband was allowed intercourse with his wife's sisters; the wife often had the same access to her husband's brothers. In North America a man of the Hidatsa tribe was allowed to have sex with his sisters-in-law in the final stages of his wife's pregnancy.

who was similarly equipped (a story that has curious parallels with Cinderella). Eventually a "gigantic" Armenian woman was found who fit the bill.

Most Chinese emperors had harems (as an old saying went, "The teapot must have many cups"). The number of wives and concubines was often dictated by numerology. Apparently the ideal combination was one queen, three consorts, nine second-rank wives, twenty-seven third-rank wives, and eighty-one concubines. The queen only had sex once a month, for the purpose of procreation; the emperor harvested life-giving yin essence from his lesser wives in the meantime. There was a strict rotation system, ensuring everyone got what they were entitled to. In the eighth century Chinese harem girls who had slept with the emperor were stamped on the hand with indelible ink to prevent them from queue-jumping.

👣 Polygyny in the West

In the West polygyny was never widely practiced, though in the Middle Ages local bigamy laws were sometimes relaxed in areas where warfare had thinned out the male population. In seventeenth-century Germany the Thirty Years' War killed so many men that the Diet of Franconia decreed that all single men under sixty should take on two wives. A similar situation was seen in Paraguay in the 1870s, where warfare resulted in a sex ratio of seven women to one man.

In England some returning travelers are said to have imported the harem habit from abroad. The eighteenth-century Lord Baltimore became so fond of his oriental harem that, on his return, he recruited a new one, building a huge West London home to accommodate them. Another gentleman re-

> ♂ Accompanied by the pope, Francis I of France sat by the bed of his 14-year-old son Henri and his bride Catherine de Médicis on their wedding night to make sure the marriage was consummated.
>
> ♂ Ethelred the Unready (978–1016) spent his wedding night with his wife and his mother-in-law.
>
> ♂ In 1096 Pope Urban II said that knights wishing to go on the Crusades should first get the permission of their wives.

turning from India did the same on a smaller scale. He recruited six "harem girls" (apparently with the full approval of his wife); the whole extended family lived in a house in Soho Square.

The most famous example of Western polygyny is the variety practiced by the Mormon Church. The early Mormons took their cue from the Old Testament, arguing that if it was good enough for the ancient Hebrews, it was good enough for them. In its nineteenth-century heyday the average Mormon family consisted of 2.4 wives and 16 children.

The nineteenth-century Mormon leader Brigham Young had twenty-seven wives and managed to father fifty-seven children. He used to inform a wife of an impending visit by marking her bedroom door with chalk.

Today the Mormon Church has officially banned the custom, but there are still Mormon diehards who take on more than one wife. According to practitioners, three wives is said to be the ideal number—two women fight, and four or more don't get enough individual attention.

👣 Polyandry

There are few recorded instances of queens and empresses having male harems, though Kahina, queen of the Berbers (650–702), is said to have had a harem of four hundred willing studs. A more common situation is polyandry, where one woman takes on more than one husband, a custom that has been practiced in many parts of the world and is still popular in parts of India and Tibet. Ancient Indian texts mention men, usually brothers, marrying the same woman. In one case Virkshi, the daughter of a Hindu saint, was spliced to no less than ten brothers. The custom seems to have originated in areas where poor arable land prevented the subdivision of farms. In these cases a father's land would be divided between his sons, but only his eldest son would take a wife. All the brothers then shared the one wife (sexual favors being allocated on an "oldest first" basis) and farmed their land communally. Any children produced were automatically attributed to the eldest brother.

Polyandry has also been popular for other reasons. In areas where custom demanded a man pay for a bride, sharing your brother's was a good way of saving money.

Polyandry is still common in some areas. In 1994 a Chinese newspaper reported on a small Tibetan village where 8 percent of the population were living in polyandrous marriages. Thirty-seven families consisted of one wife and two husbands, while three consisted of one wife and three husbands. This was despite the fact that of the village's 1,710 inhabitants, 874 were women and 836 men.

Until relatively recently, a variation on this custom was seen in the Nayar tribe of India, where it was customary for a woman to take many lovers. In this case a husband could never be sure if his wife's children were his own, so he would live with his sister and help raise his nieces and nephews.

 Child Brides

In some cultures girls used to be married at a very young age to try to secure their future; the custom was also a (virtually) foolproof way of ensuring the bride was a virgin. In ancient Egypt girls might be married as young as six, and throughout much of European history the age of consent was twelve for girls and fourteen for boys. In Britain these were the legal ages of consent till 1885.

Most cultures recognized the dangers of exposing young girls to the rigors of a marriage bed and took precautions. In cases where a marriage contract was with a prepubescent girl, the bride would normally return to her parents after the

---

♀ In China men and women are sometimes married after death to give them a companion in the afterlife.

♂ In parts of India a bridegroom was expected to deflower his bride if she died before the wedding; otherwise she could not be cremated. The act had to be witnessed by the village priest.

♀ In Kenya the Luhya tribe practice wife inheritance, in which a widow marries another member of her old husband's family. If the widow refuses to remarry, the family waits until she dies, then pays a man to have sex with her corpse so that she can be posthumously "inherited."

♂ In ancient China a cockerel often stood in for the groom at a wedding if he was too sick to attend.

> ♀ In Greece tradition demanded that widows not remarry. However, they were granted "honorary male status" and allowed to visit traditional male domains such as coffeehouses.
>
> ♀ In India some Hindus married trees to "cheat" astrological predictions that warned of the death of a first spouse.

wedding and stay with them until she reached child-bearing age.

The practice of marrying children was common in the Middle Ages, especially in royal circles, where weddings were often a matter of diplomacy. For example, Marguerite, the daughter of John the Fearless, duke of Burgundy, was born in 1393 and betrothed to the French crown prince at just eleven months. When the prince died in 1401, she was betrothed to his younger brother. The two were married in 1404 when she was eleven, the marriage finally being consummated in 1409.

👣 Age of Consent

Today the age of consent around the world differs widely. In countries like Malta, the Philippines, Mexico, and the Netherlands, sex with a minor is considered statutory rape only if the victim is under twelve. Above this age prosecution can follow only if the victim or their parents make a complaint. Some exceptions are made to these laws to discourage child prostitution. For example, in the Philippines the police can prosecute even where no complaint has been made, if it can be shown that the child was paid or coerced.

In countries like Guyana, Nigeria, Japan, and Korea, the age of consent is thirteen, but again provisions are made against minors participating in prostitution.

In Europe the age of consent varies between fourteen (e.g., Italy, Liechtenstein, and Austria) and seventeen (Ireland), but the law is often confusing. In Germany the age of consent is technically sixteen, but sex between the ages of fourteen and sixteen is allowed if the other person is under twenty-one, and as long as no money or gifts are exchanged. If you're twenty-one or over, it is illegal to have sex with anyone under sixteen. In Iceland the age of consent is fourteen, but there are "antiseduction" laws that prohibit sex under the age of sixteen if the act is encouraged with gifts or false promises.

A similar situation exists in the United States, where state laws peg the age of consent from anywhere between fourteen (e.g., Hawaii) and eighteen (Arizona). Some state laws are confusing as they consist of many layers of often contradictory legislation. For example, according to one source, it is

IN ancient Rome citizens sometimes had a legal duty to get married. Worried by the falling birth rate, Emperor Augustus declared that any widow must remarry within two years, and divorcées had to remarry within eighteen months. He also made it impossible for bachelors to receive legacies left to them in wills; childless couples were only allowed half a legacy. Former slaves were also encouraged to have children. If a freeman had one child, he had to leave half his possessions to his former owner; if he had two children, the proportion dropped to one-third; and three children left the former owner with nothing.

> ♀ In 1717 a French engineer in Egypt reported that some local women put their menstrual discharges in their unfaithful husbands' food, thinking it was a poison. The effects of "menstrual poisoning" were meant to be similar to scurvy; the hair and beard fell out, and the teeth became loose.
>
> ♂ In North Africa a Tuareg wife who has been offended by her husband starts to strip in public until he apologizes.

technically legal to have sex with twelve-year-olds in Iowa, but to do so you have to be married to them, a state of affairs that is no longer possible. Otherwise the age of consent is sixteen, unless the partners are less than five years apart in age, in which case consent can be granted at fourteen.

The highest age of consent on record is twenty-one, a situation found in Madagascar and Trinidad and Tobago. Some countries don't bother with an age of consent. In Turkey any sex outside of marriage is illegal, the youngest marriageable age being fifteen.

👣 Marriage Customs

Unlike modern weddings, the guests at a medieval ceremony might also be invited to the wedding night, a custom known in Scandinavia as "bedding." Nonconsummation was one of the few ways in which a marriage could be annulled, so the wedding party often escorted the bride and groom to their bedchamber to make sure they got off to a good start. Sometimes the priest would come along too and bless the bed. Some wedding guests would go so far as to strip the bride and groom naked, but as time went on, this was replaced by the bride throwing a garter to the wedding crowd

♂ Among the Choctaw Indians, the marriage ceremony started with a footrace between the bride and groom. The bride was given a head start, and if she wanted the marriage to go ahead, she'd slow down to let the groom catch her.

♀ In Tibet there's a courting custom called *t'lao mao hui*. A man steals the hat of a woman he fancies, and if she likes him, she visits him to get it back.

♂ As part of the pygmy marriage ritual, a wife carves her name on her husband's forehead.

as a symbolic striptease. Later even this display of underwear was considered too raunchy, and the bride took to throwing her bouquet instead. In some cases the wedding party revisited the happy couple the next morning. This might be to check that they were still in the same bed or to examine

WIFE selling, though not common, has been a feature of English life for centuries and seems to have been treated as a "quickie divorce." The first recorded example occurred in 1533, and since then there have been 387 documented cases. In 1796 a wife was advertised for sale for 5 shillings, the advertisement describing her as "damned hard mouthed and headstrong," but adding that "all body clothes will be given with her."

In a case of 1823 a drover called John Nash auctioned his wife in a Bristol market, selling her to a young man for sixpence. The wife was happy to go but the buyer immediately sold her to another man for ninepence. The wife was not pleased with this development and went off with her mother.

ACCORDING to a survey by the condom manufacturer Durex, the global average for annual married sexual encounters is 109. Childless married couples came in at 103 times a year, while couples with children scored 115 times. According to a U.S. survey, the sex rate for married couples diminishes over time, so couples in the 18–29 range have sex nine times a week, 30–39 seven times a week, 40–49 six times, 50–59 four times, and 60–69 three times. Others might prefer to follow the guidelines of an ancient Jewish law—here laborers were advised to have intercourse with their wives twice a week, ass drivers once a week, and the unemployed every day.

the sheets for virginal blood. Couples probably started going away on honeymoon holidays to avoid this sort of interference.

Some early marriages were violent kidnappings: a groom took a "best man" to help him steal a bride from a neighboring tribe or village. Forced marriages were common in medieval Italy, where an unscrupulous man might marry into a rich family simply by kidnapping and raping one of the daughters. A similar situation was seen in eighteenth-century England. Daniel Defoe wrote a book called *Conjugal Lewdness* in 1727, in which he spoke against the scandal of young heiresses being kidnapped and married against their will. Once married, their new husbands would strip them of their wealth and leave them in poverty.

YOU CAN'T DO THAT!

Sex Laws from Around the World

Because of a legal system where individual states, counties, and even towns can pass their own laws, the United States has acquired more than its fair share of weird legal pronouncements. The following is a short selection of the stranger sex-related laws; reading them, we can only assume that most were passed hurriedly, in response to local scandals. It's not certain how many are still current.

- In Bozeman, Montana, a law bans sexual activity between members of the opposite sex in the front garden of a home after sunset if they're nude.
- During lunch breaks in Carlsbad, New Mexico, couples should not engage in sexual acts while parked in their vehicle, unless the vehicle has curtains.
- In Cleveland, Ohio, women are not allowed to wear

patent-leather shoes. This is in case their highly polished surfaces offer a reflected view under their skirts.

- Clinton, Oklahoma, has a law against a person masturbating while watching two people having sex in their car.
- In Norfolk, Virginia, it is illegal to have sex in a motorcycle sidecar.
- In Ashland, Kentucky, "No person shall keep or knowingly harbor at his house, or her house, within the city any women of ill repute, lewd character or common prostitute—other than wife, mother or sister."
- Married couples in Cattle Creek, Colorado, cannot make love while bathing in lakes, rivers, or streams.
- In Connorsville, Wisconsin, it is illegal for a man to shoot a gun while his female partner is having a sexual orgasm.
- In Detroit, couples are not allowed to make love in an automobile unless the vehicle is parked on the couple's property.
- In Harrisburg, Pennsylvania, it is illegal for a female toll collector to have sex with a truck driver inside her booth.
- In Helena, Montana, a woman can't dance on a table in a saloon or bar unless she's wearing at least 3lb 2oz of clothing.
- If they are in Newcastle, Wyoming, couples should not have sex while standing inside a store's walk-in meat freezer.
- In Oxford, Ohio, it's illegal for a woman to strip while standing in front of a man's picture.
- It is illegal for a man to surf naked with a sock over his genitals in Margate City, New Jersey.

It's not just the United States that has eccentric laws. The following is a selection of unusual sex-related legislation from around the world.

- In Lebanon men are allowed to have sex with female animals. Having sexual relations with a male animal is punishable by death.
- As an antibestiality measure, unmarried Peruvian men are not allowed to keep a llama.
- In Bahrain a male doctor may legally examine a woman's genitals but is prohibited from looking directly at them during the examination. He may, however, look at their reflection in a mirror.
- Islamic law prohibits the viewing of a corpse's genitals, a ban that also applies to undertakers. The sex organs of the deceased have to be covered at all times.
- The penalty for masturbation in Indonesia is decapitation.
- In Tropea, Italy, only young women "capable of exalting the beauty of the female body" are allowed to sunbathe nude in public.
- In Sverdlovsk, Russia, couples cannot have sex on a tombstone within fifty feet of any road or pathway.
- In Georgetown, Guyana, the penalty for having sex while bathing in the nude is for the couple to be covered in a coat of paint, attached to a donkey, and taken on a tour of the nearest village.
- In Budapest, Hungary, there is a ban on having sex in a room with the lights on.
- In Santa Cruz, Bolivia, it is illegal for a man to have sex with a woman and her daughter at the same time.
- In Riga, Latvia, it is illegal for couples to quarrel while having sex.
- Spicy foods with "aphrodisiac qualities" are banned from Peruvian prisons.

THE MISSIONARY POSITION

Sex and Religion

Sex has long played an important part in many religions. In ancient cultures the principal deities were fertility gods and goddesses whose worship would ensure a plentiful harvest and good hunting. Over time cultures developed more sophisticated theologies, but the worship of fertility gods remained popular. One of the most obvious fertility symbols is the penis, and phallic worship has been practiced all over the world. In Corsica six- to ten-foot-high penis-shaped idols have been found dating back to 4000 B.C. The earliest Chinese religions involved worship of the sexual organs; many jade and pottery phalluses were manufactured in the region around 2000 B.C.

Several gods have been represented as penises. For example, Chimata-No-Kami, the Japanese god of crossroads and paths, was represented by phalluses placed at cross-

DURING the colonial period Javanese peasants started worshiping a Dutch cannon in the belief it was a phallic symbol.

roads, as was Hermes, the Greek god of travelers, whose roadside phallic statues were known as herms. Phallic gods were often connected with highways and roads as they were considered lucky, and travelers frequently needed all the luck they could get. The tradition is still alive today; Saint Christopher, the patron saint of travelers, is a Christianized version of Hercules, yet another phallic deity.

Phallic worship was common in the Middle East, and the "sacred pillars" mentioned in many early texts are believed to have been phallic. Indeed, the pillars at the gates of Solomon's temple are thought to have been penis-shaped. Baal, the chief god of the Phoenicians, was worshiped as a phallus, as was Asher, the supreme god of the Assyrians. (Asher's two "assistant gods" were testicles: Anu on the right, and Hea on the left.) Numerous other gods were phallic entities—such as Bacchus, Priapus, and Osiris—many of whom were depicted sporting huge erections. Other common phallic representations were clubs, bulls, rams, goats, serpents, torches, and fire. Even the eternal flame tended by the Vestal Virgins of Rome has been interpreted as a phallic symbol.

Phallic Crosses

The *ankh* or "Egyptian cross" is a sexual symbol representing eternal life. Here the cross represents the penis and testicles, while the oval above it is a vagina. Another supposed phallic cross is the T-shaped Hebrew Tau. In the Old Testament the

> **MANY** people believe that "giving the finger" is an invitation to "sit on it," but "the finger" is probably an old Roman phallic gesture designed to avert the evil eye. Alternatively Sir Richard Burton suggested that the gesture (the *digitus impudicus* or *digitus infamis*) was a secret hand signal used by Roman homosexuals.

prophet Ezekiel decries "whoredom" being committed "with the images of men," and it's thought this passage refers to a golden Tau being used as a dildo. Sometimes crosses and phalli have been combined—in Italy Etruscan tombs have been found decorated with crosses made of four penises.

 ## Romans

In Rome the penis was regarded as a good luck symbol, in the same way we think of horseshoes today. Many Roman women wore penis-shaped amulets to ward off evil, and Roman houses often had a penis carved by the doorway together with the motto "Happiness dwells here." Statues of phallic gods like Hermes (mentioned above) were erected at crossroads, and passing women touched their—often multiple—erections for good luck. Oil lamps were made in the shape of penises to scare off night demons, and penises were often carved on the handles of workmen's tools to encourage prosperity.

> **IN** Rome Venus was worshiped by married women on the first of April and by prostitutes (male and female) on the twenty-third.

👣 Priapus—"King Dong" of the Gods

One famous Roman phallic god was Priapus (son of Aphrodite and Dionysus), who was often shown with an erection larger than his entire body. Today the medical term *priapism* refers to a state of permanent erection—apparently not as fun as it sounds. Apart from being a fertility god, Priapus was also the guardian of gardens, and his statues were placed in orchards to deter thieves. Some statues were accompanied by threatening ditties, for example:

> Steal once, I'll give it to you in the rear.
> Try it again, I'll overflow your mouth.
> And if you steal a third time,
> you'll suffer both punishments at once
> Mouth and rear packed beyond the limit.

Another example reads:

> When you get the urge for a fig
> and are about to reach out to steal one
> stare long and hard at me
> and try to guess what shitting
> a twenty-pound, two-foot-long turd would feel like.

They're certainly more effective than the modern "polite notice." Priapus was represented as a dwarfish figure, and some believe his statues have survived into modern times as garden gnomes. The traditional conical red cap of the garden gnome is a clue—this headgear is identical to the "Phrygian cap," a well-known phallic symbol.

Maypoles and Bread Rolls

Many Greek and Roman festivals were held to honor fertility deities. In April the Festival of Venus was celebrated by parading a giant flower-strewn phallus on a cart while the local prostitutes gathered naked at her temple.

A modern remnant of these festivals is the maypole, a relic of phallic worship. Philip Stubbs, an Elizabethan Puritan, made the following observations about the May Day festivities: "Every parish, town and village assemble themselves together . . . they go to the woods and groves, some to one place, some to another, where they spend all night in pleasant pastymes. But the cheerest jewel they bring home from thence is their Maie pole which they bring home with great veneration . . . and then fall they to banquet and feast, to leape and daunce about it."

Many other pagan practices survived into Christian times. In pagan Europe Easter cakes and loaves were made in the shape of penises and offered in sacrifice. This practice was adopted into the Christian faith, though the shape of the cakes was changed, and they were marked with a cross to emphasize their new Christian status—hence the hot cross bun. In France this custom is said to have survived into the nineteenth century. In the town of Saintes, the Fête des Pinnes ("Feast of the Privy Members") was held every Palm Sunday; the townsfolk paraded through the streets with bread phalluses. Apart from its fertility aspect, the erect penises in these cases might have been regarded as potent symbols of resurrection.

 SOME Japanese Shinto festivals are surprisingly earthy. In March a festival called *Honen Matsuri* is celebrated near Nagoya. Here an eight-foot wooden phallus is paraded through the streets while people eat penis-shaped sweets and suck on phallic lollipops. A similar vagina festival is held a week later. In April a festival called *Kanamara Matsuri* is held in Kawasaki to celebrate the vanquishing of a demon who lived in a woman's vagina. The demon used to bite off any penis that entered the vagina, until a local craftsman made a steel dildo that broke the demon's teeth. As well as eating the usual penis-shaped foods, people wear fancy-dress costumes embellished with huge erections.

Saintly Studs

In the early Christian Church some saints took on the roles of pagan gods like Priapus and were represented with huge erections. Many churches had a saint's penis as a relic over which wine might be poured as part of a fertility prayer. A church in the French town of Embrun claimed to have the dried penis of Saint Foutin, supposedly the first bishop of Lyons. Foutin had a huge following in France and Italy till the eighteenth century. His statues sported huge erections, and wax models of his penis were often used in worship, thousands being manufactured so the faithful could buy one and take it to church. Some churches had so many, they had to be hung in the rafters, where they rattled like wind chimes. How Foutin got his phallic reputation is not certain, but some think he was a Christianized phallic deity. Other "phallic saints" include Saint Guerlichon, Saint Ters of Belgium, Saint

Giles of Brittany, and Saint Rini (or René) of Anjou. Most of these saints were represented with an erect phallus, but one of them, Saint Arnaud, was a little more discreet—he wore an apron over his privates that was lifted only for barren women.

Vagina Worship

Like the penis, the vagina has also been worshiped, and it was often represented by a doorway, sacred pool, or "holey" stone. An example of the latter was seen at the temple of Aphrodite at Paphos, in Cyprus. Here perforated stones were used to cure barrenness in women and increase virility in men. Local peasants were still carrying out fertility rites in the temple ruins as late as 1896. Some say the Hebrew Ark of the Covenant represented the female sex organs. The ark was copied from the Egyptians, and in their case there is no doubt

MANY churches built from 1000 to 1200 were decorated with obscene imagery. In Spain the pilgrim route to the tomb of St. James of Compostela was dotted with churches displaying sexual images, including a couple having sex upside down and a man sucking his own penis. In one French church carvings show a woman having sex with a snake, and a woman doing 69 with a toad. These illustrations were probably meant as warnings against immoral acts but would have also served as lurid attractions to draw in pilgrims. In the British Isles some medieval churches are decorated with *sheela-na-gigs*—stone carvings of women with huge vaginas and men with giant erections, thought to be Celtic fertility symbols. A sheela-na-gig in St. Michael's Church, Oxford, is now kept in a box, though whether this is to preserve it or hide it is not certain.

A BIBLICAL euphemism for the sex organs was "feet." Pubic hairs were known as the "hairs of the feet."

it represented the vagina. More evidence is seen in the objects carried inside the ark, such as the Rod of Aaron and the Tablets of the Law, which some have interpreted as phallic symbols. Another supposed vaginal symbol was the Hebrew Tabernacle, a large ritual tent thought to have been copied from the Babylonians. The tent was unusual in that it consisted of layers of red-dyed skins covered with hairy pelts and had a tall slitlike opening through which priests forced a passage during festivals. The ancient Hebrews seem to have worshiped both sets of sexual organs. (The altar of Jacob at Bethel was a pillar that some think was a stone phallus.) At least one scholar has suggested that the long-running feud between the Hebrew states of Judah and Israel was a religious war between penis and vagina worshipers. The latter were probably followers of Asherah, the Hebrew goddess of fertility who was often worshiped alongside Jehovah.

Some vaginal symbolism is said to have survived in Christianity. One theory has it that the *tonsure* (first worn by the Egyptian priests of Isis) mimics the vagina, and others believe the *chasuble*, the sleeveless vestment worn by priests, does the same.

 ## Christian Sex

Christian churches have traditionally disapproved of sex unless done for the purposes of procreation. The Church Fathers particularly disapproved of priests having sex, an attitude shared by many religions. In the early Church priests could marry, but the rules were changed so bachelor priests could not marry after being ordained. In 386 Pope Siricius tried to ban married priests from having sex with their wives, and in 1074 Pope Gregory VII excommunicated all married priests, a measure backed up by the first Lateran Council of 1123, which made celibacy compulsory for clerics.

This ban affected a huge number of men. In thirteenth-century England one in twelve adult males was a cleric. Unsurprisingly, the laws against clerical sex were widely ignored and few people expected the minor clergy to take them seriously. The senior clergy had to be more circumspect, however. Thomas Cranmer, archbishop of Canterbury from 1533 to 1556, was rumored to keep his wife hidden in a box while they were traveling.

Monks and nuns were expected to be celibate, though many early religious communities in the Celtic church were not segregated unisex establishments. One such English community, founded in 1148, was called the Gilbertine, after its founder; seven hundred monks and a hundred nuns shared thirteen cloisters, and rumor had it that nearly every single nun fell pregnant. Mixed houses like these provoked much ribald poetry, for example: "Tho some are barren. Does yet others/By fryars help prove teeming mothers." Saint Brigitte of Sweden criticized some nunneries for keeping their doors open "night and day" and said such establishments were little better than brothels.

 THE bishop of Liège managed to father 65 illegitimate children before he was deposed in 1274.

Celibacy proved hard for some, and there are many examples of outbreaks of sexual hysteria in nunneries. Nuns and monks often claimed they were visited by lascivious night-demons (incubi and succubi). In one famous medieval example, a nun's incubus was found cornered under her bed. On being dragged out it was found the demon had taken on the form of the local bishop.

Popes and cardinals were as prone to temptation as anyone else. Although most popes may have been pious men, we tend to remember the grubbier ones. Pope Boniface VIII (1294–1303) kept two nieces as concubines and fathered their children, and Innocent VIII (1484–92) is sometimes called "the Honest" because he acknowledged his illegitimate children. The children of popes were usually passed off as nephews and often given high-powered jobs; hence the term *nepotism,* from the Italian for nephew, *nipote.*

Two of the most notorious popes were John XII (955–64) and Cardinal Rodrigo Borgia, who became Alexander VI (1492–1503). According to one contemporary, Pope John's debaucheries "exceeded all bounds"—his catalog of sins included the keeping of concubines, incest, and sodomy. Short of cash, he once turned the Basilica of St. John Lateran into a brothel. As to his death, some say he was poisoned by a relative of one of

🜨 In the 1980s Pope John Paul II declared there was no sex in heaven.

🜨 It's said that Pope Leo VIII died of a stroke while committing adultery.

🜨 The sixteenth-century satirist Pietro Aretino once wrote a joke will for an elephant belonging to Pope Leo X. In it the animal left his genitals to a notoriously randy cardinal.

♂♀ IT'S not just Christian clerics who have had a bad reputation. Stories of priestly misbehavior are common all over the world. In Singapore Buddhist nuns had the nickname *moh tow foo,* meaning "priests' pillows." As a mark of their faith, Buddhist nuns are shaved bald, but some so-called "Playgirl nuns" were known to put on a wig and slip out to spend shrine funds for a night on the town.

his conquests, others that he was hit on the head with a hammer by a man who caught him in bed with his wife.

Pope Alexander was cast from the same mold. It's rumored he slept with his daughter Lucrezia, and when he was fifty-seven, he took on a fifteen-year-old blond mistress jokingly nicknamed "the Bride of Christ." In 1501 he famously hired fifty prostitutes for an orgy; his guests competed to see who could have sex with the most.

Many communities seemed to think it perfectly normal that their priests had sex. An insight into the life of one French rural priest was provided by the Inquisition around 1320. Apparently the priest deflowered the village maidens when they came of age and often continued having sex with them after they were married.

Randy priests were not confined to France. In 1643 John Wilson, the vicar of Arlington, was accused of acts of sodomy with eighteen members of his congregation and of having sex with his horse. In his defense the vicar said he took to bestiality and buggery because he did not wish to breed bastards.

In the early Church hearing confession could sometimes lead to lustful behavior. In the old days confessions were heard privately in a room where one thing often led to another. There were so many cases of confessors and priests

 ACCORDING to one medieval philosopher, women weren't worth the trouble. As he put it, "A good woman is but like one eel put in a bagge amongst 500 snakes, and if a man should have the luck to grope out that one eel from all the snakes, yet he hath, at best, but a wet eel by the taile."

losing control of themselves that the semipublic confessional box was made compulsory in 1614.

Some priests even tried to use their influence with God to help them get laid. In a report of 1592 a Spanish priest in Rome was denounced after making prayers asking God to make four nuns yield to his lusts. As well as saying them himself, the priest had been bribing monks to repeat these prayers during mass. In the seventeenth century an abbot called Davot, working at Nôtre-Dame de Bonne-Nouvelle, took money to place love charms written on slips of paper under the communion cloth.

This sort of behavior was nothing new. In A.D. 200 a priest of Saturn called Tyrannus used to tell the husbands of beautiful women that the god required the presence of their wives. These women would retire for a night of contemplation in the temple, and once the woman was locked in, Tyrannus would sneak in the back, climb into a hollow bronze statue of the god, and command the woman to sleep with him. This ruse went on for ages, until eventually one of the women recognized Tyrannus's voice in the dark.

Celibacy

Many clerics took their vows of celibacy seriously, and some early Christian figures tested their resolve in enterprising ways. One such was Saint Scuthin, a sixth-century Irish monk who slept between two "round-breasted virgins" to test his willpower. Saint Brendan heard of this practice and decided to try it himself. Brendan managed to resist temptation but found it impossible to sleep between the two young women. They suggested he jump into a tub of cold water if it got to be too much for him. More recently Indian holy men have tested their resistance in the same way—even Gandhi slept beside naked girls to test his willpower.

Many religious folk have gone to great lengths to avoid temptation. Saint Uncumber, a Christian princess engaged to a pagan, prayed for ugliness and was given a beard. The good-looking Saint Christopher of Cyprus did the same and was given a dog's head. Today the monks of the Greek monasteries of Mount Athos avoid temptation by banning women entirely. Even female animals are prohibited.

Married Sex

Although the Church has encouraged matrimony, it has tried to impose limits on "married love."

Some theologians said that no sexual congress should take place on Thursdays (the day of Christ's arrest), on Fridays (the day of his death), and Sundays (the day of resurrection). Mondays, Wednesdays, and Saturdays were also considered holy by some, so theoretically sex could be limited to Tuesday evenings (all daytime sex was banned). However, there were also blanket bans on sex for forty days before Easter, Pentecost, and Christmas, and on the seventh, fifth, and third day before Communion.

In the Puritan settlements of America even kissing was not allowed on Sundays, and since a child was thought to be born on the same day it was conceived, any child born on a Sunday might be refused baptism.

Various sexual positions were also frowned on, and married couples were often asked to tell their priest how they had sex so he could offer advice. Sex in the missionary position was considered blameless, the next best was from the side, then sitting or standing. Sex from behind (*retro canino*) was the worst and might carry a seven-year penance.

In 1012 the German bishop Burchard of Worms detailed 194 different sexual sins and described the penalties for each.

Sex on a Sunday was punished with four days on bread and water. Sex with your mother earned you penance on holy days for fifteen years. Habitual sodomy with your wife was twelve years' penance on holy days; and with your brother, fifteen years. Sex with a horse, cow, or donkey earned you forty days on bread and water once a year for seven years if you were unmarried, but those with wives had to suffer for ten years if it was only done occasionally; married men who habitually had sex with livestock were punished for fifteen years. Those practicing lesbian sex with any sort of strap-on device had five years' penance, while sex with a stepdaughter earned you penance until the day you died. One curious

THE early Church had a number of theories regarding the impregnation of the Virgin Mary. One carving shows God blowing sperm through a long tube snaking up Mary's skirt. Others believed that Mary was made pregnant through her ear, which, according to some, is why nuns wear wimples to cover them up. Another theory had it that God's sperm was carried to Mary in the beak of a dove.

sin involved a man having sex with a hollowed-out piece of wood. It's not certain how common this practice was in eleventh-century Germany, but it would earn you twenty days on bread and water. Punishments imposed on the clergy were stricter than those for ordinary people. One authority recommended thirty days of fasting for any monk guilty of masturbation, and fifty days for any bishop doing the same.

👣 Christian Sects

There have been many Christian sects, each with its own attitudes to sex. The medieval Cathars believed all sex was bad and discouraged even married couples from indulging. The Shakers of the New World were equally prudish and didn't even keep household pets in case they saw them mating. Taking things to extremes, the third-century Valerians of the Middle East and nineteenth-century Russian Skoptzy both believed in castration to keep you on the straight and narrow (see Chapter 5).

Other sects were more promiscuous. The Mormons believed in polygamy, and the religion's founder, Joseph Smith (1805–44), had around fifty wives, including five sets of sisters and one mother-and-daughter pair. A lesser-known sect was the Perfectionist movement established in New York in the mid-nineteenth century. The sect's founder, John Humphrey Noyes, believed in sex without procreation and advised men to withhold from orgasm when having sex. The sect's Lake Oneida community had about three hundred members, and individuals had to get the permission of a central committee before having sex with each other.

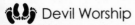 Sinister Sects

In some sects ideas toward sex and procreation developed on more worrying lines. The Chislenikzy of Russia preached that to be saved from sin, man must first commit sin, and the more sinful you were, the better. The second-century Carpocratian sect of Alexandria believed all men were in the grip of demons and the best way to conciliate them was to live a life of dissipation and lechery. The Lothardi believed men should be moral aboveground, but underground they could do what they liked and so indulged in subterranean orgies. This sect might be similar to one described around 1114 in France near Soissons. Here heretics would gather in vaults and cellars, where candles would be lit while the female members stripped. The candles were then snuffed out, and everyone had sex with whoever they came across first. Any baby that was born as a result of an orgy was killed by throwing it repeatedly through the flames of a fire. The corpse was then reduced to ashes and baked into bread to be eaten by the cult's members (in all other respects the cult was strictly vegetarian). Other cults like the Euchites also used sex as part of their rituals and killed any babies born to their members, draining them of blood before burning the body. Many of these groups believed that God was in fact the Devil (and vice versa) and that to have children was to present the "evil one" with more souls.

Devil Worship

Not surprisingly, orthodox Christians regarded members of the more gruesome cults as devil-worshipers, and when tried, witches were accused of all sorts of licentious behavior.

IN the past religious relics were big business for the Church—pilgrims often traveled hundreds of miles to worship them. The more prestigious the relic, the more visitors, and the more money a church acquired through donations. Not surprisingly, the relics associated with Jesus—splinters of the "True Cross," for example—were the most venerated, but his body having ascended to heaven, the only part of Jesus to be physically left behind would have been his circumcised foreskin. The possession of the foreskin was like money in the bank, and at one point in the twelfth century, there were eight churches claiming to own it. Pope Innocent III (1198–1216) regarded all these relics as suspicious and refused to declare any of them authentic, but Clement VII (1523–34) came out in favor of the foreskin held at the church of Charroux. In 1900 the Vatican took a firm line on foreskins and declared they were all "irreverent."

These accusations may have been accurate in some cases—the testimony of witches was often taken under torture, so it's hard to know how much to believe—but many men and women seem to have taken part in midnight orgies with a figure they believed was Satan. In 1595 an English witch said she'd had sex with the Devil and described his penis as huge and rigid with no testes or scrotum. In 1612 one French witch said the Devil's penis was half a yard long, of medium thickness but crooked, very rough, and almost pointy. A Scottish witch of 1662 said the Devil's member was "exceedingly great and long like a stud horse amongst mares," his semen being as cold as spring water. Another described a forked penis that entered the anus and vagina at the same time. It's possible that in many cases women attended orgies where the Devil was represented by a man, or woman, wearing some sort of strap-on device. Alternatively these orgies might have been drug-induced masturbation fantasies. It's been suggested that the traditional image of a witch riding on a broomstick is a bowdlerized version of the true state of affairs. The theory is that a witch would smear hallucinogenic substances on the end of her stick and use it as a wooden dildo. The drugs would be absorbed though the vaginal membrane, and the combination of chemical and sexual stimulation would result in all sorts of weird fantasies and perhaps a "flying" sensation. The theory was tested in 1992 by the German folklorist Dr. Will-Erich Peukert, who re-created one of these psychoactive salves and applied it to his armpits. The doctor is said to have had a wild time that fully confirmed this hypothesis.

THE OLDEST PROFESSION

Sex for Sale

Modern prostitution has many faces, from the glamorous call girl to the rent boy offering a quick bout of cheap "hand relief" in a dark alley. All these modern professionals might be surprised to learn that some of their earliest forebears are best described as "erotic nuns" who carried on their trade from places of worship.

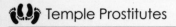 Temple Prostitutes

Temple prostitution probably started in the Middle East, the earliest record of it being in Mesopotamia around 2300 B.C. Temple prostitutes acted as part-time priestesses, assisting in the worship of fertility gods and goddesses and giving part, or all, of their earnings to the temple they served.

In Babylon there were three classes of prostitute, the semisecular *harimtu*, the more sacred *qadishtu*, and at the top the *ishtaritu*, who were dedicated to Ishtar, the goddess of love. The holier the prostitute, the more you paid.

In Egypt the revenue earned by temple prostitutes helped pay for many public works. The pharaoh Cheops used this money to help finance his Great Pyramid, and some say he even forced his own daughter into the trade. The Old Testament records that harlots were to be found in the temples of the Canaanites, and Solomon is believed to have allowed the male and female prostitute worshipers of Baal and Moloch into the temple at Jerusalem. Most Jewish kings did the same—only a few "righteous rulers" like Hezekiah and Josiah tried to stop the practice.

Ancient Greece had temple prostitutes. According to Strabo, the Temple of Aphrodite Porne (literally "Aphrodite the Whore") at Corinth had a thousand girls working for it. In times of peace the girls concentrated on making money; in times of war or famine they would offer up prayers and make sacrifices.

The practice was also common in the Orient, where prostitute priestesses worshiped the phallic and vaginal deities of the Shintoists and Buddhists.

In India there were many Hindu sacred prostitutes. It's been suggested that the erotic carvings found on the outside of many Hindu temples acted, in part, as advertisements for the activities inside. The Temple of Juggernaut at Pooree, for example, contained a huge brothel with a thousand devotees. Girls working in the temples came from varied backgrounds. One of the few options for a high-caste woman escaping an unhappy marriage was to seek the sanctuary of a temple and become a prostitute. Indian temple prostitution continued until 1947, when the government cracked down on the practice.

In some cultures ordinary women were also required to prostitute themselves in the name of religion. In the fifth century B.C. Babylonian women had to sell themselves at least once outside the Temple of Mylitta, sitting in the dust until someone gave them a silver coin. The attractive ones didn't sit for very long, while the ugly or afflicted sometimes had to wait years. This sort of prostitution survived into fairly recent times. In the Egyptian city of Tanta (halfway between Cairo and Alexandria) the annual feast of Ahmed al-Bedawi was celebrated by married women and girls, who set up their tents and had sex with the first man to ask. The custom continued into the nineteenth century.

Ancient Greece

Like the Babylonians, the Greeks also recognized different ranks of prostitutes. The lowest were the *dicteriads,* usually slaves, and above them were the *aleutridae,* professional musicians, acrobats, and dancers who often performed in the nude. At the top were the intelligent and witty *hetaerae,* who were graced in all the social arts. Some became very famous—the hetaera Aspasia ran one of the most influential literary and political salons in Athens, and Thais of Athens (mistress of Alexander the Great) eventually married Ptolemy I and became queen of Egypt.

The hetaerae were notorious for their love of money (a slang term for prostitute was *lupta,* meaning "she-wolf"), and many became very wealthy. One famous prostitute had the nickname "Clepsydra" because she timed her clients with a

TEMPLE prostitution has never been part of the Christian tradition, but the Church has owned a few brothels over the years. In the fourteenth century Pope Clement VI acquired a brothel in Avignon nicknamed "the Abbey." When not servicing clients, the girls spent their time performing religious duties. Pope Julius II was so impressed by the Abbey's income that he built one like it in Rome. Other popes had a more saintly attitude. In 1198 Pope Innocent II recommended all good Christian men marry prostitutes to save them from sin, and set up a number of Magdalen Homes for reformed working girls.

water clock, a *klepsudra*. Prostitutes paid taxes on their earnings, and a successful prostitute was such a money-spinner, she often had to get a special license in order to leave the country.

The Greeks were responsible for what might have been one of Europe's first secular brothels. In 549 B.C. the Greek lawmaker Solon established a large brothel, or *dicterion,* which he staffed with slaves and female convicts. The brothel workers attracted trade by standing outside bare-breasted or in thin gauzy clothing. One writer described the choices available: "anybody can pick out a favorite: skinny or fat; curvy, lanky, or bent over; young or old; firm or lush."

Another way of attracting trade was to wear special shoes. Many street girls had the words "Follow Me" inscribed in reverse on the soles of their shoes so they'd leave an unambiguous message as they walked down the dusty pavements.

The "Lays" of Rome

Like the Greeks, the Romans also thought of prostitutes as "wolves," and brothels were known as *lupanaria* from the Latin for wolves, *lupae*. Roman prostitutes would use wolf calls to attract their customers. Some establishments were very luxurious, even employing professional beauticians (*ancillae ormatries*) to help primp the girls. Lower-class brothels were known as *fornixes*, a term related to the modern word *fornication*. *Fornix* means "archway," and many cheaper street girls serviced their clients under bridges and the archways of the local circus. *Fornixes* were often small, shabby buildings. One that survived in Pompeii consists of a number of small windowless booths. Outside each cubicle a girl's name would be written by her curtained door, together with her price and the services on offer. Some establishments specialized in very perverse activities, offering animals and "unweaned babies" for oral sex. The emperor Domitian outlawed the prostitution of babies in A.D. 84 when he set the lower age limit for prostitutes at seven.

Some tavern girls hired themselves out to supplement their regular wages. These women were known as *assellae* after the *as*, the smallest coin in circulation. The very cheapest prostitutes were the *quadrantariae*, who worked for a quarter of an *as*. Other classes of prostitutes were the *putae* or common whores (from *puteus*, meaning "well" or "tank"); the *gallinae*, who combined prostitution with robbery; the part-time prostitutes called the *prostibulae*; and "party girls" known as *delicatae*.

Street girls (sometimes called *meretrices*, from the Latin *merere*, "to earn") were required to dress differently from respectable women and often favored brightly colored transparent clothing. They were allowed only sandals on their feet, and their hair could not be worn in a fillet, the mark of a virgin. Most prostitutes dyed their hair blond or red to distinguish them from respectable Roman brunettes, but as time went on blond hair became fashionable, and to the confusion of many, Roman women started dyeing theirs with saffron. Some married women even posed as prostitutes for fun. Messalina (the wife of the emperor Claudius) used to don a blond wig, gild her bared nipples, and sell herself under the name Lycisca.

Any woman could become an amateur prostitute, but there were advantages to being officially recognized as you could take complaints about customers to the authorities. To become a registered prostitute, you had to report to an official called the *aedile,* who would record your professional name, your age, and the price you intended to charge. Once registered, a prostitute received a license, the *licentia stupri,* in return for which she had her earnings taxed. The *aedides* saw a sudden upsurge in business around A.D. 19 when new laws against adultery were introduced. The law stated that any married man with a mistress who was not a registered prostitute could be prosecuted for unnatural vice. To get around this, many respectable women asked to be added to the prostitute list to protect their married lovers.

👣 British Brothels

The first British brothels were probably those founded in London to service the Roman garrisons. A Roman "red-light" district sprang up in the northwest of the city, but in time the center of vice transferred south of the Thames to the area now known as Southwark. This region was outside the

BATHHOUSES (or *bagnios*) that operated much like modern saunas became popular after the Crusades, and many turned into brothels known as *stews* or *stewes*. The laws regulating stews were strict. In 1161 King Henry II decreed that no stewholder could keep a girl against her will, let her live on the premises, or charge more than 14 pence a week for the rent on her room. No married women, nuns, or sick women were allowed to be employed, and once paid, a girl had to entertain her client all night. Girls could advertise themselves by sitting at windows but were not allowed to importune passersby or "chide or throw stones" to get their attention.

jurisdiction of the City of London, and it gradually became a criminal boomtown. Ironically this land was owned by the Church, the area coming into the hands of the bishop of Winchester in 1107. For many years Southwark was known as "the Bishop of Winchester's Liberty," and "to be bitten by the Winchester Goose" was a euphemism for contracting VD. Although some bishops were tempted to close down the area, most were pragmatic and recognized that a red-light district had its uses. As Thomas Aquinas said, "If you take away the prostitutes, you fill the world with sodomy."

In the medieval period many large brothels sprang up on the south bank of the Thames. There were about eighteen in all, a number that remained constant over the years. The brothels were painted white with their names in big letters on the side; the signs were large enough to be read from the north bank. Brothel names were often like those of taverns— The Blue Maiden, The Crane, The Cross Keys. A certain amount of innuendo was attached to names like The Unicorn, The Gun, and The Elephant, and names like The Cardinal's

Cap and The Phrygian Cap were euphemisms for an erect penis. Other Southwark street names testify to the unwholesome activities that went on there. A document of 1549 recorded names like Lowsie Mead, Sluts Well, Whores Nest, Durty Lane, Deadmans Place, Naked Boy Alley, and Theeves Lane.

Although Southwark was the center of London vice, prostitution was found everywhere. West Smithfield once boasted a "Cock's Lane" (originally Cokkeslane) that had nothing to do with poultry, and "Bordhaew" or "Brothel Lane" (built on land leased from St. Paul's Cathedral) sprang up near the Guildhall. Many brothels disguised themselves as legitimate enterprises. In 1385 one Elizabeth Moring was prosecuted for running a "call girl" business, her girls masquerading as

ONE seventeenth-century Southwark brothel was very famous. Around 1603 the Manor House of Paris Gardens in Southwark was opened as a brothel by Donna Britannica Hollandia. This was the pseudonym of an English madam called Elizabeth, who chose the name Hollandia as Flemish women were reckoned the best brothel keepers. The Manor House (an abandoned gambling den) was a fortified structure surrounded by a moat, and Elizabeth hired pikemen to guard the premises. Apart from being secure, it was also very near the Globe, Swan, and Hope theaters, ensuring a good supply of customers. An attempt to close the brothel failed in 1631, when a band of officials approached the house and were lured onto the drawbridge. The drawbridge was rigged to collapse, and the party ended up in the muddy moat while Elizabeth's girls threw chamberpots at them. Further assaults were repulsed, and the house became known as Holland's Leaguer (later Hollands Leger). Today the site is covered by Hopton Street, just by the Tate Modern.

> In 1392 any convicted London prostitute was fined her clothes. She had to give all her upper clothing to the Guildhall and all her lower clothing to the arresting officer.

> In nineteenth-century Britain some prostitutes had "England expects every man to do his duty" tattooed on their inner thighs.

apprentice embroiderers. Many women operated on the streets—so many, in fact, that the City had to build a separate prison for "Nyghtwalkeres" in 1296.

To separate working girls from ordinary townswomen, prostitutes had to wear a uniform or badge. In 1345 the law stated that whores had to wear a red rose or ribbon, but in 1351 this was changed to a hood or headscarf of striped cloth (usually red and white). In 1437 the uniform was a red hood and a white wand held in the hand.

In 1546 Henry VIII ordered the Southwark stews to be closed to try to halt the spread of syphilis, but they were officially reopened in 1549 by Henry's son, Edward VI. Over the next hundred years or so the laws against prostitution were gradually relaxed. In 1641 unlicensed prostitution ceased to be a crime at all unless it caused a public nuisance.

Restoration Romps

The Puritan Roundheads attempted to stamp out London vice after the English Civil War but didn't do a very good job. In 1660, the first year of the reign of King Charles II, a broadsheet publication called *The Wandering Whore* listed a hundred brothels, the names of two hundred independent prostitutes (one known as Fair Rosamund Sugar-Cunt), and

ONE enterprising eighteenth-century Londoner published a regular newsletter called *The Fashionable Cypriad,* listing the famous prostitutes who operated in the bars of Covent Garden theaters. Another famous publication called *Harris's List of Covent Garden Ladies* was published by a Drury Lane tavern-keeper. Copies were published annually from 1760 to 1793, the print run sometimes reaching 8,000 copies.

Extracts from *Harris's List of Covent Garden Ladies* (for the year 1788):

Miss Sims—No. 82 Queen Ann's Street East.
"Tall as a grenadier yet not withstanding her size we hear her Low Countries are far from being capacious but, like a well-made boot is drawn on the leg with some difficulty and fits so close as to give great pleasures to the wearer."

Mrs. Dodd—No. 6 Hind Court, Fleet Street.
"She is, indeed, turned of forty, rather fat and short, yet she looks well . . . if you are not soon disposed for the attack she will shew you such a set of pictures that very seldom fails to alarm the sleeping member . . . She is the perfect mistress in the art of restoring life and performs the tender friction with a hand as soft as turtles down. . . . After giving you a whole night's entertainment is perfectly satisfied, and will give you a comfortable cup of tea in the morning, for one pound one."

Mrs. Chinsherline—No. 36 Titchfield Street.
"She is the daughter of a banker in the City and might have remained with her first undoer for many years longer had not her itch for variety and the brandy bottle got the better of [her] . . . Of a very warm temper especially when tempered by her favourite liquor of which she loves to take large and copious libations, ever desirous of seeing the bottom."

Miss Johnston—No. 6 Church Court, St. Martins Lane.

"Would make a monk disregard his vow of celibacy or a mahometan think that he had got one of the daughters of paradise . . . [She is] so very careful of her health, that before she receives her guinea, she must examine everyone of her partner's legs."

Miss Cowper at a China Shop, Russell Court.

"This humble girl is thankful for a crown . . . She has lately been to visit her parents in Derbyshire and is now returned a tolerable fresh piece again."

Mrs. Howard—No. 14 Moor's Place, Lambeth.

"[She has] contracted such a habit of intimacy with the gin bottle that, unless a person is particularly partial to it, it is almost intolerable to approach her . . . The grove below is well thatched and ample enough in size to take in any guest, but still she has learnt the knack of contracting it and a small made gentleman may feel the tender friction."

Miss Corbet—No. 16 Goodge Street.

"In regards to price she has one fixed rule, she always measures a gentleman's may-pole by a standard of nine-inches and expects a guinea for every full inch it is short of full measure."

Madam Dafloz—No. 46 Frith Street, Soho.

"She has one qualification which many English girls want which is a certain cleanliness in the Netherlands . . . She constantly mounts her bidet and with a large sponge laves the whole extent of the parish of the Mother of all Saints."

Miss Emma Elliot—No. 8 Acton Street, Gray's Inn Lane.

"This truly lovely women is about twenty and whilst she remains in a state of silence commands every attracting charm the heart of man can wish ... [She has] a very pretty mouth when her tongue is inactive but when once she gives loose to that unruly member she pours forth such a torrent of blackguardianism that shall destroy every attractive feature."

the details of fifty pimps. Many similar publications were in circulation. Most posed as antivice tracts, but their real purpose was to advertise the services of working girls (known in Restoration parlance as "punks," "trugs," and "tweaks").

The Strand was a popular venue for prostitutes, as this was the main thoroughfare connecting Parliament and the City. The theater district of Drury Lane and Covent Garden also became centers of prostitution during the Restoration; some smaller theaters like Goodman's Fields were entirely surrounded by brothels. The first women appeared onstage at this time, and many actresses were recruited from local brothels, some theater managers even visiting whorehouses to scout for talent. Nell Gwyn came from such a background,

SPECIAL mention is given to a Miss Kilpin, who frequented the bottom of Ludgate Hill around sunset. She is described as "a beautiful woman about twenty, tall and finely shaped with fine black eyes and hair of the same hue that floats in curls down her back and worn without powder." Miss Kilpin was unique in that she never went into a house with a man, only a hackney coach, and never accepted payment. Harris supposed she was the wife of a local dignitary who wasn't being satisfied at home. As to her fondness for coaches, Harris wrote, "We have been told that the undulating motions of the coach with the pretty little occasional jolts contribute greatly to enhance the pleasure of the critical moment if all matters are rightly placed."

moving from a life of vice to the stage—and then to King Charles II's bedchamber. The theater saloon bars became notorious pick-up joints, thronging with outrageously dressed prostitutes carrying calling cards in their cleavages.

Many men went to the theater just to meet girls. It got so bad that productions were disturbed by huge crowds of gentry gathering backstage to make dates with the actresses. Eventually Queen Anne had to ban any person of quality from the backstage area and stopped the wearing of masks by females—a measure meant to curb the activities of masked prostitutes, who prowled the stalls looking for clients.

Also popular in the seventeenth century were pleasure gardens like Bagnigge Wells, the Apollo Garden, and later Vauxhall and Chelsea's Ranelagh Gardens. The gardens started as respectable entertainments for genteel society, but many became notorious as the haunts of prostitutes and, like the theaters, men started to go just for the girls. Pepys visited one of these gardens in 1668 and reported that customers "go into the arbours where there is no man and ravish the women there." Apparently the prostitutes and their clients made an uproar like "Cavalcanti's Bloodhounds."

Another respectable diversion that turned bad was a showboat moored on the Thames called *The Folly,* which was built in the shape of a castle with turrets on its four corners. The boat contained several saloons and a large deck for

SOME early nineteenth-century London prostitutes had bizarre names. For example: Elephant Bet, Finnikin Fan, the Yarmouth Bloater, Flabby Poll, Fair Eliza, and the Black Mott.

promenading. It was a perfect pick-up joint and became notorious for its prostitutes and their sword-wielding pimps. Also popular at this time were the "night houses," the forerunners of the modern nightclubs, dens of sin that opened when the theaters and other entertainments closed.

In the reign of George III the number of London brothels stood at 2,000, and by 1840 this number had either dropped to 1,500 or risen to 5,000, depending on whom you listen to. There was a huge demand for fresh girls, and brothel-owners (then known as "bawds") would often employ procurers to seek out new recruits. Popular hunting grounds were the London mail-coach stops, dropping-off points for young people coming to London to seek their fortune. Other procurers would deliberately lure girls into the metropolis by placing newspaper advertisements that promised lucrative careers in service. Many took to the roads themselves and enticed young women with tales of the gaiety of London life. Some men even went so far as to pose as vicars and fortune-tellers to win a girl's trust.

♀ In the eighteenth century prostitutes called "posture girls" would pose to show off their bottoms. For an extra charge you could spank or cane them.

♀ Visitors to a seventeenth-century London brothel could try their hand at the "half-crown chuck," an early version of tiddlywinks. In this game a girl stood on her head with her legs apart, and gentlemen competed to see how many half-crowns they could flip into her vagina.

♀ One eighteenth-century London prostitute was called "Clarice la Claterballock."

THE first "modern" English brothel was opened in 1750 by Mrs. Goatby in Berwick Street, Soho; it was based on brothels she'd seen in Paris. Parisian brothels used to employ *essayeurs,* men who were paid to chat up and fondle the girls to encourage timid clients. In Paris state-regulated brothels known as *maisons de tolérance* were in existence until 1946.

In Victorian times young girls were even imported from the Continent, shipped over from France, Germany, and Switzerland. The biggest exporter was Belgium, where the outward-bound girls were known as "English parcels."

Some sex workers came from outposts of the empire—a celebrated brothel-keeper of the eighteenth century was Miss Harriot, a Jamaican slave who was brought to London and freed on the death of her master.

Girls from poor families probably looked on prostitution as easy money compared to the life of drudgery they'd face otherwise. In 1793 it was estimated that 40 percent of London prostitutes were former factory workers, while 6 percent were ex-servants. Apart from the professional prostitutes there were also part-timers, sometimes known as "dolly-mops" (in France they were called *midinettes*), who worked as shop-girls, seamstresses, milliners, or nursemaids during the day and made extra pocket money in the evening.

In the nineteenth century the center of London prostitution moved away from Covent Garden and Drury Lane to Haymarket and Regent Street. Brothels were now less open in their activities, and many operated as massage parlors or manicurists. Others invented fanciful names for themselves and advertised treatments for rheumatism, gout, and neuralgia. One well-known flagellation brothel called itself the Balneopathic Institute, where "nervous disorders" were treated with a dose of the whip and birch.

Rent Boys, Gigolos, and Lesbians

Ancient Babylon had male homosexual prostitutes, and they were also found in ancient Greece, though some citizens found their makeup and effeminate clothing scandalous. One writer bewailed the appearance of these youths parading in the streets, saying it would be easier to "hide five elephants in

---

IN the past, areas connected with the sex industry were given unambiguous names. Some, such as London's Maiden Lane and Love Lane (now the site of a large city police station), are inoffensive. However, the more graphic Gropecuntlane was a name found in a number of English towns and cities, but as time went on, became sanitized: in London the name Gropecuntlane appears in the records as late as 1276, but by 1349 it had changed to Grape Street, and later into Grub Street. Other names went through a similar metamorphosis. Slut's Hole became Sluts' Well, Codpiece Lane became Coppice Lane, and Whores Lie Down became Horsleydown. Meanings often become forgotten over time; for example Drury Lane is derived from the word *druerie* or *drowerie*, which used to refer to "sexual love." Even Threadneedle Street, home to the Bank of England, might be a sexual euphemism.

Similar sanitation was found on the Continent. In Paris the Rue de Pélécan (Pelican Street) is derived from Rue du Poil au Con (Cunt Hair Street), the haunt of prostitutes who defied a rule that prostitutes must shave their pubic hair. In many parts of Europe prostitutes were known as Roses, and probably inspired street names such as Rosengarten and Rosenstrasse.

ST. MARGARET of Cortona, St. Mary Magdalene, St. Mary of Egypt, St. Lawrence, St. Vitalis, and St. Nicolas have all been patron saints of prostitution. The Christmas gifts given by St. Nicolas to young women were often meant to provide them with a dowry and so save them from a life of vice.

one's armpit" than ignore their presence. The majority of these prostitutes would have been slaves, criminals, or prisoners of war.

Male streetwalkers were also found in ancient Rome. Many would do their business under the arches of the Coliseum, displaying their wares by hoisting their tunics above their buttocks.

In the city of Alexandria around A.D. 200 an early Christian writer complained of brothels where "the men play the part of women and the women that of men," and this sort of vice seems to have been popular in the Middle East. In Turkey a class of male prostitute used to exist called *jinq* or *ginq* (meaning "jerker" in Arabic), who only performed fellatio. In Morocco there was another class of male prostitute called *maricónes,* who were usually of mixed Moorish and Spanish extraction. *Maricónes* would only practice their arts on circumcised men. Some advertised themselves as "kosher," meaning they only serviced Jews.

The Victorian explorer Sir Richard Burton observed male prostitution in various forms during his travels. In 1845 he reported on homosexual male brothels in Karachi, and described male prostitutes in West Africa, where the king of Dahomey kept a corps of virile men for the use of his Amazon bodyguard.

Some Western brothel keepers provided both men and women for wealthy ladies. In 1889 it was estimated that there were forty establishments in Paris that provided girls for bisexual or lesbian ladies; these brothels often had separate entrances for their male and female customers.

Mary Wilson, a nineteenth-century London brothel keeper, once planned to open an establishment for ladies called The Eleusinian Institute. This brothel would have been staffed by "vigorous men" kept "in a state of great exaltation produced by good living and inertia" and viewed prior to selection through a darkened window. To maintain discretion, access to the brothel would have been through a shop that sold ladies' goods.

 ## Continental Prostitution

For much of British history prostitution was officially illegal but widely tolerated, and it flourished like the speakeasies of Prohibition America. On the Continent, however, most prostitution was under strict control, either from the central government or local civic authorities—the benefit of legally sanctioning prostitution was that the profits of vice could be taxed.

In Renaissance Italy prostitutes played an important part in the life of a town. Like other tradespeople, the girls usually

IN 1260 the Spanish authorities recognized five types of pimp: those who lived in brothels or on brothel earnings; those who recruited girls; wholesale dealers in white slaves; husbands who prostituted their own wives; and landlords who leased temporary accommodation.

A GERMAN contribution to the sex trade was the mobile brothel. First used in the First World War, these brothels operated near the front and were used to provide relief for the fighting men. There were two grades of brothel, red-light brothels for privates and NCOs and blue-light brothels for officers. Apparently the girls averaged ten customers a day between 4 and 9 P.M., with clients allowed only ten minutes at peak hours.

belonged to a guild, had their own patron saint, and took part in a town's festivals. In one city the annual footrace between the local working girls was said to be a bigger draw than either the "jew's race" or "old man's race."

Relations between a town and its brothel weren't always civil, however. In the early eighteenth century Toulouse had a brothel called the Grande Abbaye whose profits were divided equally by the city and the local university. The Abbaye prostitutes had to wear a white scarf or ribbon to distinguish them from ordinary townswomen, but they petitioned Charles VI to be allowed to get rid of them. The king agreed, but the townsfolk were outraged and many prostitutes were assaulted. The prostitutes went on strike and later moved to a new larger out-of-town brothel called the Château Vert.

Another French monarch with a soft spot for prostitutes was Louis XI, who, in 1474, presented the Federation of Parisian Courtesans with their own flag and a drum-and-fife band for use in public processions.

SIXTEENTH-century Rome had a complement of 6,800 registered prostitutes to service a population of 90,000 (one working girl for every 6.5 males). The popes were varied in their attitudes to prostitution. Pope Sixtus IV (1471–84) taxed them. Pope Alexander VI (1492–1503) rented out buildings as bordellos, and Pope Julius II (1503–13) created a special prostitutes' quarter in Rome. Pope Pius V (1566–72) tried to contain prostitution, literally—by building a wall around the red-light district in 1569.

 ## China

In ancient China visiting a prostitute was thought to be a vitalizing activity for men, as prostitutes accumulated a lot of valuable "yin" energy through their work. This yin energy compensated for the male "yang" lost through ejaculation, so theoretically sex with a prostitute was more beneficial than sex with your wife.

Historically, the brothels of China were divided into three classes. The cheapest were staffed with slaves and the wives of condemned criminals. The middle-rank brothels served food and drink and had upper rooms equipped with beds. A high-class premises might be known as a House of Singing Girls, a Sing Song House, or a Tea House, in which the principal activity was musical entertainment. Rich men would book a room in a Sing Song House, entertain their friends and business associates, then go home and have sex with their wives or concubines. It was only men too poor to afford a harem who would visit a sex-only brothel.

Chinese brothels were often decorated in a distinctive

♀ In China prostitutes used to be called "fallen flowers" because they could be picked up by anyone.

♂ In 1993 two 78-year-old Taiwanese grandmothers were arrested as prostitutes.

♂ In China gigolos used to be known as *thor hai fan,* meaning "men of the slippered-feet existence."

way. Those made of green lacquered wood were known as Green Bowers, while blue-painted establishments were called Blue Chambers. Some brothels were government-run. During the Sung Dynasty (960–1279) the Imperial Board of Revenue set up a number of special "wine houses" that operated as brothels. To identify them, these houses had a red lantern in an upper window, a custom that eventually spread to the West with the influx of Chinese workers during the American gold rush.

Other government brothels were the "barrack brothels" of the Great Wall, which appeared during the Ming dynasty (1368–1644). These were created to provide sexual services for the troops manning the wall and were staffed by paid recruits or by criminals and the wives of dissidents. These prostitutes were so numerous, they were sometimes used as auxiliary troops to help beat back attacks by nomads. Originally the barrack brothels were very rough and ready, but the service proved so popular that luxury versions started appearing for the benefit of civil servants.

Canton was famous for its floating brothels called "flower boats" (one famous example was named the Gate of the Flowery Frontage). These brothels were floating restaurants with small sex cubicles on the lower decks. Boats were usually booked for parties, the owner supplying the food, drink, music, and women. The girls were virtually slaves and weren't allowed to keep any of the money they earned. As time went on and they lost their looks, they were sold to a lower and lower grade of boat, until they were reduced to a life of manual labor.

Perhaps the Chinese city with the most lurid reputation was the port of Shanghai, which before the Second World War was described as the sex capital of the world. At its peak it boasted two hundred dance halls and three thousand brothels. An English journalist who lived in the city in the 1930s described bars where patrons (mostly foreign sailors) could sit with a girl and be masturbated under the table. Apparently the flood of slippery sperm on the floor was a major hazard, and one bar owner solved the problem by having his girls masturbate customers into paper bags. Another enterprising local combined prostitution with a taxi service. These cabs had a girl in the back to provide oral sex during a ride around town. A similar arrangement could be found in Hong Kong, where a girl and a sampan boat could be rented by the hour. All Chinese brothels were officially closed down by the Communist government in 1949, and prostitution is now a crime punishable by death.

THE largest red-light district in the world used to be Kramat Tunggak in North Jakarta. Its twenty-eight acres contained more than 220 brothels employing 1,000 to 2,000 girls. It was closed in 1999.

Japan

The Japanese had a highly organized prostitution industry confined to a city's red-light area, which was called the *yoshiwara*. The *yoshiwara* system was invented by a civil servant in 1612 and survived till 1958, when all these brothel quarters were closed down. The *yoshiwara* of Edo, the old capital, was virtually a self-contained town and known as "The Nightless City."

An unusual aspect of Japanese prostitution was the cage system where girls, dressed and undressed, were displayed in caged rooms open to the street. The cages were designed to protect the girls while allowing patrons an opportunity to inspect the merchandise. The higher-class brothels had cages with bars six or seven feet high that allowed the girls to sit and stand in comfort. The lower-class girls had much smaller cages. In some cases the girls were so cheap, and the cages so tiny, the girls had to lie down to get in them. Girls displayed in this way entered the cages in the evening and, unless they attracted a customer, were only released in the morning.

India

In India there were a number of grades of prostitutes, ranging from the highest, the *roopajeebhee* (ravishing nymphs), to the lowest, *ghautveyshyan* (harlots of the bathing places), who serviced pilgrims visiting the holy rivers.

Another group of high-class courtesans were known as *lingum-naree* (women of the celestial penis), who were distinguished by special markings tattooed on their breasts and thighs. The best courtesans were skilled in sixty-four arts covering all aspects of erotic, social, and intellectual activity. The Indians took this sort of training very seriously, and traveling instructors were often brought in by brothel-owners to raise standards.

Courtesans in Indian towns and cities were known as *vesya* or *ganika* and were usually organized into guilds. In return for operating freely, prostitutes were taxed the equivalent of two days' wages a month.

India also had caged prostitutes (the practice was imported from Japan in the nineteenth century), but most women sat in doorways while slave girls went into the streets to importune passersby on their behalf. According to a traveler of 1840, these girls were well educated, good singers, and had all their body hair plucked.

Many Indian prostitutes were widows (often child brides) cast out by their families on the death of their husbands. Other brothels operated as family businesses—each generation bred fresh boys and girls for the trade. If times were hard, a girl might be sold to a local brothel by her family, and in some cases a father would sell a daughter into prostitution to raise money for her sisters' dowries.

New World Prostitution

Prostitution has had a long history in the Americas. In northern Mexico tribes used to consecrate their new prostitutes in a special ceremony. The girl would sleep with all the local chiefs, and thereafter she was unable to refuse a man if he paid her price, even if she later got married.

One North American city that became famous for its

IN nineteenth-century San Francisco prostitutes worked in large four-story buildings called "cow yards." In 1898 the Twinkling Star Corporation built a huge 450-room cow yard called the "Nymphia." The doors of the rooms were equipped with shutters that closed when you dropped a coin in a slot. When your time was up, the shutters shot up, exposing you to view.

IN 1992 the police of Des Moines, Washington, discovered they could not prosecute prostitutes caught in sting operations unless they had sex with them. Since they weren't allowed to have sex themselves, they hired a convicted rapist to do it for them.

red-light district was New Orleans. Some say the city's sex industry took off in the 1770s when a call for white female settlers was answered by an influx of deported French prostitutes.

Prostitution in New Orleans took many forms—some girls worked from single rooms called "cribs," others from so-called "houses of assignation" that acted as centers for call-girl rings. Most prostitutes worked from two-story brothels that had a bar downstairs and bedrooms above; these houses usually had the name of their madam painted on the outside. The most exclusive brothels were luxurious mansions sometimes known as "sporting houses." One famous madam named Nell Kimball spent $20,000 on a three-story house in 1880 and opened two more before she retired. The working conditions in these houses were generally good; the girls kept a third of everything they earned and got one day off a week. Before the Civil War many New Orleans prostitutes were black slaves. Lighter-skinned slaves attracted high prices; some brothels paid as much as $5,000 for a new girl. A popular annual event was the Quadroon Ball, where girls were auctioned off for the night to the highest bidder.

Prostitution Today

In modern Britain prostitution is legal, but soliciting for customers in public is not, and it is illegal to have two girls working from the same premises. In most of America it is illegal to sell sexual services for money, though some Nevada counties have licensed brothels. In some states you don't even have to have sex for money to break the law; the agreement in itself is a crime.

Modern prostitution takes many forms. Old-fashioned bordellos are rare, as technically the girls have to live on the premises for it to be called a brothel. Massage parlors are more common, as are escort agencies that operate rings of call girls. Many people assume call girls are so called because you call them on the phone, but the term predates the telephone; it actually refers to the fact that the girl calls on you.

Many women work independently, either walking the street (regarded as the bottom rung of the profession) or using ads placed in newspapers, the Internet, shop windows, or phone booths.

> HOSPITAL authorities in Sydney, Australia, recently arranged a visit with a prostitute for a terminally ill boy who didn't want to die a virgin. It was done without the parents' consent.

TODAY most people would describe Bangkok as the sex capital of the world, but the trade was officially banned in Thailand in 1960. Despite this, prostitution is a national institution—most towns and cities have a multitude of establishments. Some sources estimate that 95% of Thai men have visited one. In the 1960s the international sex tourism industry started to take off when Thai brothel-keepers built Westernized bars and clubs to cater to foreign servicemen. Some of these establishments are now four-story buildings employing more than a hundred girls at a time. Today the sex industry employs hundreds of thousands of girls and is estimated to be worth around $4 billion. In the poorer northern region of the country roughly 28% of an average household's income is generated by one or more absent daughters, many of them working in the sex trade.

A specialized branch of prostitution is the professional dominatrix. This trade is particularly tough, as the job requires skill and personality. Additional drawbacks are the cost of the necessary equipment (one estimate puts the start-up cost at over $20,000) and the fact that most submissives are very loyal to their master or mistress. A new dominatrix might have to spend years building up a clientele.

As to earnings, a good rule of thumb is to look at the hourly rate of local lawyers. Apparently a good prostitute will earn the same. At the time of writing this rate was $100/hour in Springfield, Missouri, and $250/hour in San Francisco. Presumably the same rule of thumb is applicable in most cities around the world.

SEXUALLY TRANSMITTED DISEASES

The existence of venereal diseases—those primarily passed on through sexual contact—has been known since Roman times. Most diseases were lumped together as "leprosy," but a few were known as *morbus indecens aie cunnientis* (filthy diseases of the cunt).

Syphilis may have been one of these ancient diseases; although its origins are often blamed on fifteenth-century Spaniards bringing it back from the New World, no one is actually sure where it came from. It's just as likely to have been a virulent mutant of an existing form of syphilis that was spread by the mercenary armies criss-crossing Europe at the time. The confusion as to where it came from is obvious when you look at the names it was given: the Russians called it the "Polish sickness," the Poles called it the "German sickness," the Germans and English called it the "French sickness" (in Elizabethan parlance the "French welcome"), and the French blamed it on the Italians. The name "syphilis" comes from a Greek peasant who appeared in a poem written in 1521, in which the unfortunate Syphilis angers Apollo and is inflicted with body ulcers. The ulcers are then cured by Mercury—a pun in this case, as mercury had been used to treat skin complaints since the fourteenth century. To treat syphilitic sores, mercury was taken orally or applied as an ointment or as a vapor bath.

The mercury cure was only effective in the first stage of syphilis, which is manifested as skin lesions. These sores disappear after two or three months, and the sufferer then enters the second stage of flu-like symptoms, rash, and hair loss. If not treated, these symptoms disappear after three to six months, and the patient enters the latent stage, during which syphilis spreads throughout the body. Some victims never progress beyond this stage, while others experience a final tertiary stage years later that usually results in madness and a painful death.

In Victorian times the disease was extremely widespread. One source estimated that in Berlin in 1900 over a third of men between fifteen and fifty had syphilis. A number of effective treatments were eventually developed, including potassium iodide and salvarsan (the original "magic bullet"), an arsenic compound invented in 1910. Some religious groups were opposed to the manufacture of salvarsan, their argument being that a cure for syphilis simply led to more immoral behavior. Today the disease responds well to antibiotics. Syphilis is still common in Africa and Asia, but despite outbreaks following the Second World War and in the "free love" era of the 1960s, it is in decline in the West.

👣 Gonorrhea

One of the oldest sexually transmitted diseases is gonorrhea, a name coined by the Greek physician Galen in A.D. 200. The name comes from the Greek words *gonos* and *rhoila,* meaning "seed" and "flowing" on account of the unpleasant discharges it can produce. Gonorrhea is also commonly called "the clap," a slang term derived from the Old French *clapoir,* meaning "buboe" or boil. Although gonorrhea can be painful and result in long-term complications in women, many people have it but don't suffer any symptoms at all. The bacteria that cause gonorrhea live in the urethra. In the past the cure for men involved squirting a dilute solution of borax, zinc sulfate, and wood naphtha down the penis. The urethra might also be scraped clean by poking a small umbrellalike device down the head of the penis, opening the umbrella, and pulling it out again. Thankfully, the modern cure utilizes antibiotics.

👣 Herpes

Genital herpes is a chronic, lifelong viral infection. Symptoms include a burning sensation while urinating and the growth of painful crusty blisters, though as with gonorrhea, many people have it but don't suffer symptoms. There's no cure, but the symptoms can be treated and a suppressive therapy is available for sufferers who have regular outbreaks.

Oral herpes is a close cousin of genital herpes. It's been suggested that attempts to ban kissing in the past might have been measures to try and contain outbreaks of oral herpes. For example, the Roman emperor Tiberius once tried to ban kissing, and in England the practice was temporarily banned in 1439.

Pubic Lice

Pinhead-sized pubic lice (*Phthirus pubis*) infect hairy parts of the body, especially the groin and the underarms. They are sometimes spread sexually, but you can also pick them up by using contaminated bed linen. Some people infected with pubic lice have no symptoms, but most itch like crazy. In the past an eye-watering swab of pure alcohol was dabbed over the shaved privates to kill lice, but today there are a number of kinder shampoos and creams to do the job.

Hepatitis

Hepatitis is a viral infection of the liver. It is the only sexually transmitted disease that can be effectively prevented by a vaccine. It's a hundred times more infectious than HIV, but in the case of hepatitis B, 95 percent of victims recover. Left untreated, it can have serious consequences. Around half of all babies born to mothers with hepatitis B later die from liver cancer. There are five forms of hepatitis (A, B, C, D, and E), but A and B are the most common.

Genital Warts

These are caused by the human papillomavirus (HPV), the most common sexually transmitted viral infection. Like other conditions, you can be a carrier of this virus without suffering any symptoms at all. Between twenty-four and forty million people are thought to be carriers in the United States, and 20 percent of all sexually transmitted diseases in the UK are cases of genital warts.

👣 Trichomoniasis

"Trich" is a common sexually transmitted disease caused by a flagellated protozoan, *Trichomonas vaginalis*. Male sufferers don't usually have symptoms, but women experience painful urination, unusual discharges, and abdominal pain. Treatment consists of a single dose of antibiotics.

👣 Chlamydia

Chlamydia is the most common bacterial sexually transmitted disease in the United States and UK. Most people with the disease have no symptoms; those who do experience a discharge from the penis or vagina and a burning sensation when urinating. Treatment is with antibiotics.

👣 HIV/AIDS

AIDS stands for acquired immunodeficiency syndrome and represents the final stage of infection for those with human immunodeficiency virus (HIV). There are two viruses, HIV-2, found mainly in Africa, and HIV-1, found in the rest of the world.

AIDS was first identified in 1981 in the United States, but researchers have detected HIV in specimens collected in 1959 in central Africa. It acts by destroying white blood cells that play a key role in the immune system, so leaving the body open to infection by a variety of diseases. In the United States AIDS is the main killer of men in the twenty-five-to-forty-four age range and the fourth-biggest killer of women in this group. On average, it takes about seven to nine years for symptoms to develop. There's no cure, though drugs like AZT, DDI, DDC, and D4T can prolong life.

FUCK, ETC.

A Short Glossary of Sex Words

The rudest words in the English language are *cunt* and *fuck*—both are the only standard English words to have been routinely omitted from general and etymological dictionaries since the eighteenth century. Outside of official reports, neither could be printed in full anywhere within the British Commonwealth until the 1960s. The Oxford English Dictionary included the words for the first time in 1972.

 Cunt

The word *cunt* might have the same roots as the Latin *cunnus,* meaning "vulva." *Cunnus* has a long history. For example, it was used by the Roman satirist Horace (65–8 B.C.) when he wrote about the Trojan conflict: "*ante Helenum cun-*

nus teatorerrima belli causa" (before Helen's cunt caused the war).

No one is quite sure where *cunt* came from, though it might be a prehistoric German term as it appears as *kunta* in Old Norse and in Middle Dutch as *kunte*. In English, *cunt* first appears as a street name, a Gropecunt Lane being recorded in Oxfordshire in 1230 (see Chapter 17). In English literature one of its first sightings is in a proverb of 1325 that seems to warn against premarital sex: "geve thi cunt to cunning and crave affetir wedding." *Cunt* was not considered rude at this time and often appeared as a medical term. Even Chaucer (c.1340–1400) used it, spelling the word *queynte*. After 1400 the word seems to have lost its respectability, though Shakespeare does make a sly allusion to it in *Hamlet* when the hero asks if he can put his head in Ophelia's lap and says, "Do you think I meant country matters?" Recently the word has started to come out of the woodwork; in 1993 a Seattle grunge band called the Anal Cunts released their first single, and in the UK it was first spoken on T.V. in a 1998 drama about Oswald Mosley. *Cunt* is also the title of a 1999 novel by Stewart Home.

 ## Fuck

Although this word has traditionally been known as an "Anglo-Saxon expletive," it was largely unknown in English before the sixteenth century, though there are records of a man called John le Fucker in 1278. It's possible the word was considered too rude to write down. Most early examples of the word come from Scotland, which some have taken to mean that the word is Scandinavian in origin. It is probably related to the Norwegian dialect word *fukka* and the Swedish dialect word *focka*, both meaning "to copulate," all being derived from the German *ficken* or *fucken*. *Fuck* seems to have become respectable by 1598, when it appeared in an early English dictionary, *A World of Words* by John Florio, but by the eighteenth century it was out of favor again. Copies of D. H. Lawrence's *Lady Chatterley's Lover* (written in 1928) were not allowed to contain the word printed in full till 1963. Two years later the word had its first T.V. outing on a late-night satirical show in Britain.

Some have suggested that *fuck* ultimately derives from the Latin *fornix*, meaning "archway" or "vault"—the places where Roman streetwalkers did most of their business. This derivation is unlikely, but has given us the word *fornicate*.

Whore

The Old English spelling of *whore* was *haga*, later *hawe*. Its spelling reflected its Scandinavian roots, as in the Swedish *hora* and the Danish *hore*. It's also related to the German *hure* and Dutch *hoer*. Ultimately the word is thought to derive from an ancient Indo-European word meaning "lover." The words acquired a *w* due to an error made by medieval monks; many Old English words started with *hw*, but these were transposed to *wh* by scribes to bring them in line with Norman French (unfortunately this led some confused monks to indiscriminately add a *w* to any word starting with *h*).

In Latin countries words for *whore* are derived from the Latin *puteus,* meaning "well" or "tank"—thus streetwalkers might be called *putains* in France and *putas* in Spain.

Prick

This word probably derived from the Old English *prica*, meaning "point." It started to be used as a term for *penis* in the sixteenth century. Oddly enough, it was used by women in the sixteenth and seventeenth centuries as a term of endearment, an immodest maiden referring to her lover as "my Prick."

 Pussy

Some believe the word *pussy* as a slang term for the female organs has something to do with cats being warm and furry, but the sexual term probably has nothing to do with felines at all. It's more likely that the erotic *pussy* comes from the Old Norse word *puss*, meaning "pocket" or "pouch." In this case *pussy* would be related to *purse*.

 Vagina

This word is from the Latin for "sheath," and according to one source, it originally came from a euphemism for the female reproductive passage. The word *vagina* later gave rise to *vaina*, also meaning "sheath," the diminutive form of which is *vainilla* (or *vanilla*). This word was used to describe vanilla pods because of their sheathlike shape.

 Penis

This word is from the Latin for "tail," though the word wasn't adopted in English to describe the male sex organ until the seventeenth century. The diminutive of penis is *peniculus*, which in turn gives us *penicillus*, Latin for "paintbrush," the word that the Old French *pincel* is derived from. This in turn is the ancestor of the modern *pencil*, so etymologically speaking, *pencil* actually means "little penis," which is something to bear in mind next time you chew on one. The word is also related to *penicillin*, so called because of the brushlike shape of the mold's spore-bearing structures.

 ## Cock

It's thought that the slang word *cock* for "penis" is taken from the word *cock* as in "male chicken." Since the cock-chicken is masculine, upright, and randy, it's not hard to see how the connection was made. The origin of the name is believed to be onomatopoeic and derived from the bird's familiar wake-up call. The word *cockerel* is of fifteenth-century origin and was originally a diminutive meaning "small cock." In the 1770s the Puritans, embarrassed by the earthy-sounding *cock*, started calling cocks "roosters," a name derived from the term *roost cock*.

Sex Slang

There are innumerable slang terms, and a fair proportion of them deal with the subject of sex—one source has estimated that there are more than a thousand slang terms for the vagina. It's not only modern English that is slang-rich; according to Sir Richard Burton, sixteenth-century France had "four hundred names for the parts genital and three hundred for their use in coition," while the Greeks had nearly a hundred terms for pederasty. The following is only a small sample of English slang currently in use.

FEMALE MASTURBATION—Air the Orchid, Audition the Finger Puppets, Beat the Beaver, Club the Clam, Part the Red Sea, Tickle the Taco, Type the Gusset, Jill Off, Shuffle the Kit Kat.

MALE MASTURBATION—Articulate the Archdeacon, Backstroke Roulette, Bash the Bishop, Be an Owner-Operator, Beat the Meat, Do the Bologna Hop, Do the Five-Finger Shuffle, Choke the Chicken, Court Madame Knuckle, Dance with the Captain, Duel with the Pink Darth Vader, Dust the Duvet, Flog the Log, Get into Sixth Gear, Give Ronaldo a Rubdown, Glaze a Knuckle, Grapple with the Sausage, Have a Hand Shandy, Go Hand Solo, Go White-Water Wristing, Hitch to Heaven, Jack Off, Jack the Beanstalk, Jerk Off, Jerk the Gherkin, Knob Shiner, Knock One Out, Court Madam Palm and Her Five Fingers, Make the Bald Man Cry, Make Like a Chinese Helicopter Pilot, Milk the Snake, Oil the Bat, Oil the Truncheon, Have One Off the Wrist, Paddle the Pink Canoe, Have a Date with Palmela and Her Five Sisters, Have a Date with Palmela Handerson, Peel the Carrot, Play Five Against One, Play the Boneaphone, Play Pocket Billiards, Play Pocket Pinball, Polish the Lighthouse, Polish the Rocket, Pound the Pork, Pull the Turkey's Neck, Pull Your Pud, Ride the Baloney Pony, Ride the Great White Knuckler, Roman Helmet Rumba, Rope the Pony, Round Up the Tadpoles, Shake Hands with a Wookie, Shake Hands with the Wife's Best Friend, Shake Hands with the Unemployed, Slap the Monkey, Slap the Salami, Spank the Monkey, Spank the Plank, Strangle Kojak, Strum, Tee Off, Thrap, Throttle the Turkey, Tickle the Pickle, Toss, Tug, Turn Japanese, Twang the Wire, Varnish the Cane, Wank, Wash the Cosh, Wax the Dolphin, Whitewash the Hall, Wring the Rattlesnake, Yank Off, Yank the Plank.

THE APPLIANCE OF SCIENCE
Correct technical terminology for some of the more obscure sexual traits:

Aculeophallic—Having a pointed or conical penis

Balanotage—Playful manipulation of the head of the penis

Basculocolpia—The provocative swaying of the breasts

Botulinonia—Female masturbation utilizing a sausage that is often heated and lubricated

Callimammapygian—Having beautiful buttocks and breasts

Chezolagnia—Sexual gratification through making a bowel movement

Dasofallation—Sexual intercourse in a forest or wooded area

Ellipseur—A man who omits foreplay and has sexual intercourse in haste

Eproctophilia—Sexual arousal through flatulation

Galateism—A tendency to fall in love with female statues

Gomphipothic—Sexually aroused by seeing beautiful teeth

Iatronudia—A woman who feigns illness so she can disrobe in front of a doctor

Kokigami—The Japanese art of wrapping a penis in a paper costume

Lavacultophilia—A fondness for watching women in bathing suits

Machlobasia—Sexual stimulation in obese women obtained through friction between the thighs when walking

Malaxophobia—A woman's fear of having her breasts kneaded by a man

Mammaquatia—The bobbing of a woman's breasts during exercise

Nosophilia—Sexual arousal through the belief that a partner is terminally ill

Ozoamblyrosis—Loss of desire through a partner's body odor

Parthenophobia—A morbid fear of virgins

Peotillomania—The habit of pulling at one's penis

Pygotripsis—A sexual practice in which two or more people rub their buttocks together

Rantallion—A man whose scrotum hangs lower than his penis

Rheononia—Female masturbation using a stream of water

Temuvalent—Able to have intercourse only while under the influence of alcohol

Turpicunnia—Having an ugly vulva

Uxoravalent—A man only able to have sex with a woman who is not his wife

HOMOSEXUALS—Amy-John (lesbian), Auntie, Back Door Conquistador, Baggage Boy, Batty Boy, Bean Flicker (lesbian), Bent, Bent as a Nine Bob Note, Bertie, Brother (lesbian), Brown Hatter, Brown Pipe Engineer, Bufty, Bugger, Bull-dyke (lesbian), Bum Bandit, Bum Chum, Carpet Muncher (lesbian), Cat, Chicken, Chickenhawk, Chimney Sweep, Chocolate Shark Angler, Chocolate Speedway Rider, Chutney Ferret, Clam Jouster (lesbian), Clam Smacker (lesbian), Cocoa Sombrero, Diesel Dyke (lesbian),

Dinner Masher, Doughnut Puncher, Doormat Basher (lesbian), Dyke (lesbian), Exhaust Pipe Engineer, Fag, Feather Spitter, Fudge Packer, Gusset Nuzzler (lesbian), Hershey Highwayman, Jacksie Rabbit, Jammer, Jobby Jouster, Kakpipe Cosmonaut, Kicks with the Left Foot, Knob Jockey, Lavender, Left Footer, Lesbo (lesbian), Lettuce Licker (lesbian), Lezza (lesbian), Lunchbox Lancer, Marmite Driller, Mary, Mattress Muncher, Mud Valve Mechanic, Muddy Funster, Navigator of the Windward Pass, On the Other Bus, Pillow Biter, Pilot of the Chocolate Runway, Pipe Cleaner, Poo Packer, Poo Pipe Pirate, Poof, Poofter, Poove, Quean, Queen, Quince, Rear Admiral, Rear Gunner, Ring Bandit, Ring Master, Roger Ramjet, Rug Muncher (lesbian), Rump Ranger, Sausage Jockey, Screamer, Shirt Lifter, Shit Stabber, Stone, Tail Gunner, Tea Pot, Tuppence Licker (lesbian), Turd Burglar, Uphill Gardener, Wind Jammer, Winnie (lesbian).

HOMOSEXUALS, THE ACT—Wheel Tapping at the Bourneville Factory, Putting from the Rough, Bowl from Pavilion End, Doing the Chocolate Cha Cha.

VAGINA—Aunt Mary, Axe Wound, Baccy Pouch, Badger, Bald Man in a Boat (clitoris), Banger Hanger, Bargain Bucket, Battered Kipper, Bear Trapper's Hat, Bearded Clam, Beaver, Beef Curtains, Beetle Bonnet, Bikini Burger, Bill Poster's Bucket, Billingsgate Box, Blurt, Bliff, Boris, Box, Brillo Pad, Bush, Butcher's Window, Buttered Bun, Button (clitoris), Button Groove, Button Hole, Captain's Pie, Cat Flaps, Cathedral, Cauliflower, Chuff, Circle, Clown's Pocket, Cockwash, Cod Cove, Constable Minge, Crack, Cunny, Cunt, Fadge, Fanny, Fanny Batter, Fanny Flange (clitoris), Fish Box, Fish Mitten, Flange, Flesh Wallet, Floppy Red Cup, Front Bottom, Fud, Fur Burger, Furry Bicycle

Stand, Furry Hoop, Fuzzbox, Gammon Flaps, Gash, Haddock Pastie, Hairy Cheque Book, Hairy Cup, Hairy Doughnut, Hairy Goblet, Hairy Lasso, Hairy Pie, Hamburger, Hanging Bacon, Ha'penny, Hole, Horse's Collar, Jenny, Kipper, Lab Kebab, Lettuce, Love Palace, Love Socket, Love Tunnel, Man Trap, Mapatasi, Minge, Mink, Minnie Moo, Mohair Knickers, Monkey's Forehead, Moss Cottage, Mott, Mound of Venus, Mouse's Ear, Muff, Norton, Palace Gates, Pantie Hamster, Passion Flaps, Pink Velvet Sausage Wallet, Piss Flaps, Placket, Plumber's Toolbag, Pole Vault, Pompom, Poon, Pouch, Pussy, Quim, Rocket Socket, Saddle Bags, Salmon Canyon, Sausage, Sausage Wallet, Come Up Next Tuesday (acronym), Serpent Socket, Slit, Slot, Snatch, Spadger, Spam Alley, Spam Castanets, Spam Fritters, Spasm Chasm, Steak Drapes, Stench Trench, Stilton Muffle, Stoat, Sugared Almond (clitoris), Tardis Fanny, Thatch Hatch, Todger Toaster, Toot Toot, Toothless Sea Lion, Tuna Town, Twat, Twunt, Upright Grin, Vadge, Velcro Triangle, Vertical Bacon Sandwich, Welly Top, Whisker Pot, Wuwu, Y-Bone Steak, Yak, Yoni.

PENIS SIZE—Bugfucker, Donkey Rigged, Hung Like a Chinese Mouse, Hung Like an Arab Stallion, Kidney Buster, Lobcock.

PENIS—Acorn, Bacon Bazooka, Bald Man, Bald-headed Hermit, Beaver Cleaver, Beaver Lever, Bed Flute, Beef Bayonet, Bell End, Big Bamboo, Blue-Veined Piccolo, Bobby's Helmet, Bone Erect, Bowel Trowel, Captain, Captain Hogseye, Cavalier (uncircumcised opposite of Roundhead), Cheesepipe, Chopper, Clam Ram, Cock, Corn Beef Cudgel, Crab Ladder, Crank, Crimson Crowbar, Custard Cannon, Cyclops, Dang, Dangler, Dingaling, Donger, Eccles Snake, Fagan, Fanny Battering Ram,

Fanny Rat, Flapjack, Fleshy Flugelhorn, Fuck Stick, Gibbon Gristle, Giggling Pin, Glue Gun, Goo Gun, Gooses Neck, Guided Muscle, Ham Howitzer, Happy Lamp, Helmet Pelmet (foreskin), High Pressure Vein Cane, Hissing Sid, Horn, Hot Pudding, ICBM (intercuntinental ballistic missile), Jang, John, John Thomas, Joystick, Junior, Kidney Wiper, Knob, Kojak's Rollneck (foreskin), Kosher Dill (circumcision), Labrador Lipstick, Lamb Cannon, Langer, Lid (glans), Lingham, Live Rabbit, Lobcock, Love Sausage, Love Torpedo, Love Truncheon, Luncheon Truncheon, Mack, Main Cable, Manhood, Meat Flute, Meat-Seeking Pissile, Mickey, Middle Leg, Milkman, Mr. Jones, Mr. Sausage, Mutton Musket, Nob, Nudger, Old Man, One-holed Flute, One-eyed Pant Python, One-eyed Trouser Snake, One-eyed Willie, One-eyed Zipper Fish, Oscar, Pecker, Percy, Pink Cigar, Pink Darth Vader, Pink Oboe, Pintle, Pirate of Men's Pants, Plonker, Pocket Rocket, Pork Sword, Porridge Gun, Prick, Pud, Pump Action Mottgun, Purple-Headed Womb Broom, Purple-Headed Yogurt Warrior, Purple Helmet, Putz, Reltney, Rhythm Stick, Rising Main, Rod, Rotoplonker, Roundhead (circumcised), Rumple Foreskin, Sausage, Schlong, Schlong Shed, Schmeckie, Scrotum Pole, Skin Boat, Skin Flute, Snake, Snorker, Spam Javelin, Spam Scepter, Sperm Worm, Spurt Reynolds, Tadger, Tail, Tallywhacker, Third Leg, Thumper, Todger, Tool, Toot Meat, Trouser Mauser, Trouser Snake, Trouser Trout, Trouser Truncheon, Tube Steak, Tummy Banana, Turkey Neck, Twanger, Veiny Bang Stick, Wab, Wang, Weenie, Whanger, Wick, Willie, Winky, Yang, Yard, Zipperfish, Zoob, Zucchini.

👣 Porn Movie Slang

Like any other industry the porn film business has developed its own jargon. Some of the following terms and abbreviations are self-explanatory; most aren't.

A2M—Anus to mouth.

B/G—Boy-girl.

BEAR—A gay term for a stocky bearded older man.

BJ—Blow job.

COWGIRL—A position where a girl straddles a man lying on his back facing him. If she's facing his feet, it's a Reverse Cowgirl. The positions can be used with anal sex, i.e., a Reverse Anal Cowgirl.

CUM DODGER—A performer who tries to avoid facial ejaculations.

CUM SHOT—The moment of ejaculation. Also known as "the Money Shot."

DAP—Double Anal Penetration.

DP—Double Penetration. Penetration of the anus and vagina in heterosexual sex, or two penises in one anus in gay sex.

DPP—Double Pussy Penetration.

GANGBANG (or GB)—Orgy usually containing more than four people.

G/G—Girl on Girl.

M/M—Man on Man.

MISH—Short for "missionary."

N-WAY—Group sex. *N* can refer to any number over two.

TP—Triple Penetration—vagina, anus, and mouth.

TRADE (Straight Trade)—A male performer in gay movies who does not indulge in oral sex with other men or act as the passive partner in anal sex.

INDEX

ABOUT THE AUTHOR

STEPHEN ARNOTT is a writer and journalist, and the author of *The Languid Goat Is Always Thin*, a collection of bizarre sayings and proverbs, and *Now Wash Your Hands!*, a cultural history of the toilet.